Bloom's Classic Critical Views

WALT
WHITMAN

Bloom's Classic Critical Views

Jane Austen
Geoffrey Chaucer
Charles Dickens
Ralph Waldo Emerson
Nathaniel Hawthorne
Herman Melville
Edgar Allan Poe
Walt Whitman

Bloom's Classic Critical Views

WALT
WHITMAN

Edited and with an introduction by
Harold Bloom
Sterling Professor of the Humanities
Yale University

BLOOM'S
LITERARY CRITICISM
An imprint of Infobase Publishing

Bloom's Classic Critical Views: Walt Whitman

Copyright © 2008 Infobase Publishing

Introduction © 2008 by Harold Bloom

Bloom's Literary Criticism
An imprint of Infobase Publishing
132 West 31st Street
New York NY 10001

Library of Congress Cataloging-in-Publication Data
Walt Whitman / [edited by] Harold Bloom.
    p. cm. — (Bloom's classic critical views)
A selection of important older literary criticism on Walt Whitman.
Includes bibliographical references and index.
ISBN-13: 978-0-7910-9555-3
ISBN-10: 0-7910-9555-X
1. Whitman, Walt, 1819–1892—Criticism and interpretation. I. Bloom, Harold.
II. Title: Bloom's classic critical view : Walt Whitman.

PS3238.W3545 2007
811'.3—dc22

                    2007017029

Series design by Erika K. Arroyo
Cover design by Takeshi Takahashi

Printed in the United States of America

Bang EJB 10 9 8 7 6 5 4 3 2 1

This book is printed on acid-free paper.

All links and Web addresses were checked and verified to be correct at the time of publication. Because of the dynamic nature of the Web, some addresses and links may have changed since publication and may no longer be valid.

Contents

Series Introduction

Bloom's Classic Critical Views is a new series presenting a selection of the most important older literary criticism on the greatest authors commonly read in high school and college classes today. Unlike the Bloom's Modern Critical Views series, which for more than twenty years has provided the best contemporary criticism on great authors, Bloom's Classic Critical Views attempts to present the authors in the context of their time and to provide criticism that has proved over the years to be the most valuable to readers and writers. Selections range from contemporary reviews in popular magazines, which demonstrate how a work was received in its own era, to profound essays by some of the strongest critics in the British and American tradition, including Henry James, G.K. Chesterton, Matthew Arnold, and many more.

Some of the critical essays and extracts presented here have appeared previously in other titles edited by Harold Bloom, such as the New Moulton's Library of Literary Criticism. Other selections appear here for the first time in any book by this publisher. All were selected under Harold Bloom's guidance.

In addition, each volume in this series contains a series of essays by a contemporary expert, who comments on the most important critical selections, putting them in context and suggesting how they might be used by a student writer to influence his or her own writing. This series is intended above all for students, to help them think more deeply and write more powerfully about great writers and their works.

Introduction by Harold Bloom

For many years now I have been expounding my contention that Walt Whitman remains the most eminent author nurtured in the Western Hemisphere, in the four hundred years since European languages first invaded the shores of the Americas. When my opinion has provoked skepticism I have asked: who else, in what Goethe first called the Evening Land (Spengler later popularized the phrase), whether writing in English, French, Spanish, or Portuguese, manifested the originality, wit and wisdom (Emerson's praise), and the worldwide ever-expanding literary influence upon diverse cultures that Whitman possesses? No single figure in Latin America, or in the French West Indies and Quebec, is a plausible rival. In American English, even the best do not quite approximate his aesthetic power and his tendency to circulate now in Asia, Africa, Old Europe, or the New World itself. Walt Whitman's cosmos is as present in Russia and India, Japan and Nigeria, as it is in Mexico and Brazil. He is to America what Shakespeare is to Britain, a wild spirit that moves everywhere, destroyer of old worlds and creator of new ones.

To discuss Shakespeare and Whitman together ought to seem less surprising than it does, since in his strongest poems the American bard is haunted by Shakespeare, and by Shelley, whose "Ode to the West Wind" provides the wild spirit, destroyer and preserver I have just cited. That revolutionary ode had much to do with what Wallace Stevens called "the fiction of the leaves" in the American Bible, *Leaves of Grass*. This nuanced metaphor of a title became a lifetime's labor, and more even than *Moby-Dick*, *Adventures of Huckleberry Finn*, and Emily Dickinson's poems, Whitman's personal epic remains the masterpiece of our imaginative literature. What are leaves of grass? The leaves stand for individual lives and deaths in Homer, and then go on through Virgil and Dante to Spenser, Milton, and Shelley. Whitman's genius fuses Homeric leaves with the Bible's "all flesh is grass." Consider why the title could not be *Grass of Leaves*, where the "of" would be incoherent. In *Leaves of Grass*, "leaves of flesh," the "of" is as Biblical as in "Son of Man," while all the fragility of human flesh is summoned to an accounting that is neither moral, in any traditional way, nor religious, in regard to normative Christianity.

Whitman's parents were Quakers, but of a dissident group that was guided by the circuit-rider Elias Hicks. In rebellion against Philadelphia's taming of the fiery George Fox, seventeenth-century founder of Quakerism, Hicks preached against societal oppression, slavery, and a mercantile America.

Whitman was influenced by the eloquent Hicks, but even more by the Concord sage, Ralph Waldo Emerson, with his vision of self-reliance. The Emersonian self, against Emerson's own desire to be a seer of unity, was split into an active component and a passive ally of the soul, itself as unknowable as external nature. Whitman, even more complexly, set forth a triple division: my soul, my self, and the real me or me myself. These three diverse entities are not psychic agencies, as they would be in Sigmund Freud, but three persons who cannot be reconciled as by a trinity. Walt Whitman, "one of the roughs, an American," is the *persona* or outward mask, the "myself" in *Song of Myself.* His soul is a nature even more unknowable than Emerson's; for Whitman it comprises an uneasy aggregation of night, death, the mother, and the sea. Rich as that mythic composite may be, the authentic and fascinating enigma in Whitman is me myself, the real me.

The American bard's creative self-presentation has still to be explored. We have acknowledged very slowly the subtle complexities of Whitman's poetry. As with Shakespeare, beneath the richness is a profoundly elliptical element. Again, as in Shakespeare, what matters most is the author's labyrinthine influence upon himself. To understand the perplexities of *Drum-Taps* (1865) we need to work through the three greatest and very different editions of *Leaves of Grass* (1855, 1856, 1860).

As I go on aging, quietly conscious that death must sometime come, I care more and more for the sacred Whitman, the John Milton of our Evening Land. I cannot quite call him our Shakespeare, because he has only one living character, himself, but that self is large indeed: it contains multitudes, multitudes in the Valley of Decision. We cannot get our minds around Walt Whitman, perhaps because we see so slowly that he is a flamboyant actor in the Theater of Mind. I once believed that Whitman, like Tennyson and Stevens, was an actor in the Theater of nuance, but I feel as I closely approach seventy-seven that "nuance," as I use it, is only another evasion of how great poets subtly think: Whitman, Tennyson, Stevens. These all are Lucretians (though Tennyson fights resisting this affinity, as in his magnificent dramatic monologue, "Lucretius").

The monologues of Whitman, Tennyson, and Stevens are Epicurean self-epiphanies, which we resist because the Eliot-Pound-New Critical gang (1915-1945) was so brutal and arbitrary in exalting shallow-enough wit over the cognitive labor Epicureans demand. Even Wallace Stevens, who fought T.S. Eliot's High Church deprecation of Romantic personality, qualified nearly all his affirmations in what he grimly acknowledged was the Age of Eliot. Two thirds of a century later, I dispute my grumpy old acquaintance, the late erudite Hugh Kenner, who told me I was merely a historical anomaly, one who perversely refused to see that content and form had to be two words for the one substance. A Spinozan, not a Cartesian, I push Kenner (formidable fellow) aside and proclaim that what he called the Pound Era truly was the Age of Wallace Stevens. Pound, acknowledging that Whitman broke the new wood, called for a one-sided pact between them, but the subtle Walt would have opted instead for the deeper Covenant with Stevens, the Sage of Hartford. Both understood that: "No man would see the end." I, who dined once, rather uneasily, with Stevens, relying in my anxiety upon the presence of his splendidly pugnacious daughter Holly, would have been too shy to break bread with the greater person, our Father Walt Whitman, though a more humane bard did never in America exist. Like my surmised Shakespeare, Whitman was good company: the sublime Stevens was not, nor is always the insecure Old Bloom, whose supposed aggressive-defensive manner in youth has mutated into a benign exhaustion.

The *persona* of Walt Whitman might be called the best company in all literary history: no poet demands that the reader approach the bard more closely, particularly in "Crossing Brooklyn Ferry," the superb poem he first published in the 1856 Second Edition of *Leaves of Grass*, under the title, "Sun-Down Poem." Walt sees us here "face to face" even as he observes the setting sun, and his Hicksite Quaker immersion in the Bible is reflected (but with a Whitmanian twist) in that "face to face." We confront Walt even as Jacob wrestled with a nameless one among the Elohim, in order to win the new Name, Israel. Walt, himself a god/angel of death and life, will not let us go (or we him) until we become the American Adam, or "These States." William Carlos Williams and Hart Crane, rivals for Walt's blessing, echo his stance and rhetoric in their marvelous, belated Whitmanian epics, *Paterson* and *The Bridge*.

All major American poetry since Whitman is Whitmanian, in spite of itself in Pound, Eliot, and Wallace Stevens, and their followers. I can think only of Frost, who was ruggedly out of Emerson, just as E.A. Robinson was, as a crucial exception. May Swenson is Whitmanian; her friend, Elizabeth Bishop, found precursors in Emily Dickinson and Marianne Moore. Later poets—Merwin, Ashbery, Ammons—have also composed in the wake of Whitman. Abroad there is no contest: French Poe, the jingle man, counts for little in a cosmological matrix in comparison with Whitman. Iberian and New World Latin American Whitman is an army: Pessoa, Lorca, Cernuda, Machado, Neruda, Vallejo, Paz, Borges, Lezama Lima are among the most prominent. In England, Gerard Manley Hopkins resisted Whitman, but secretly identified with him, while D.H. Lawrence's later poetry is entirely Whitmanian, though Lawrence's ambivalence toward the breaker of the new road for the New World never abandoned him. A host of Russian poets (Mayakovsky among them), Italians (Dino Campana), Dutch, Israelis, Scandinavians, were also disciples of the sublime Walt. One could go so far as to call Walt Whitman the Real Presence in the world's poetry since 1855. He will augment in the universe's consciousness so long as it does not warm itself or war itself to total death.

BIOGRAPHY

Walt Whitman
(1819–1892)

Walt Whitman was born in West Hills, Long Island, New York, on May 31, 1819. He attended public school in Brooklyn from 1825 to 1830, then worked as an office boy (1830–31), a printer (1835–6), a schoolteacher (1836–41), and a contributor to and editor of various periodicals and magazines, including the *Long Islander* (1836–37), the *Aurora* (1842), the *Tatler* (1842), the *Statesman* (1843), the *New York Democrat* (1844), the New York *Mirror* (1844), and the Brooklyn *Daily Eagle* (1846–48). In 1848 Whitman left (or was possibly fired from) the *Eagle*. He then went to New Orleans, where he edited the *Crescent,* before returning to Brooklyn later that year. After editing the Brooklyn *Freeman* (1848–49), Whitman probably worked as a carpenter and a bookseller between 1850 and 1854.

In 1855, at the age of thirty-six, Whitman published the first edition of his most famous book, *Leaves of Grass.* This edition consisted of twelve poems, including "Song of Myself" (then titled "Walt Whitman, an American"). Whitman sent the volume to Ralph Waldo Emerson, who responded with great enthusiasm, calling it "the most extraordinary piece of wit and wisdom that America has yet contributed." A second edition, adding twenty-one poems, appeared in 1856, and a third, adding 122, appeared in 1860. Six further editions appeared over Whitman's lifetime, the result of a continuous process of revision and expansion.

In 1857 Whitman began editing the Brooklyn *Times.* After leaving the newspaper's staff in 1859, he worked during the Civil War as a clerk in the office of the army paymaster in Washington, D.C., and as a volunteer in military hospitals (1864–64). In 1865 he worked briefly as a clerk at the Department of the Interior before being fired when Secretary James Harlan read *Leaves of Grass* and condemned it as being pornographic. Also in 1865 Whitman published a collection of Civil War poems, *Drum-Taps,* followed in 1866 by the *Sequel to Drum-Taps,* containing his elegy about Lincoln, "When Lilacs Last in the Dooryard Bloom'd." Whitman, who had been largely disregarded in the United States, began to develop around this time a reputation in

England, where his poetry was championed by some of the leading British writers of the day.

In 1873 Whitman suffered a paralyzing stroke and moved from Washington, D.C., to Camden, New Jersey, to live with his brother George. "Prayer for Columbus," the most despairing of Whitman's late poems, appeared in 1874, and was followed in 1875 by the prose work *Memoranda during the War*. In 1875 Whitman recovered partially from his paralysis, but his remaining years were nonetheless marked by a decline in creative powers. In 1888, the year he published *November Boughs,* Whitman suffered another stroke. He contracted pneumonia in December 1891 and died on March 26, 1892.

PERSONAL

These entries are personal remembrances of Whitman's friends, admirers, and defenders, who publicly supported his poetry and argued for its central prominence in the American literary canon. Like much nineteenth-century writing about Whitman, these pieces link his personal character to his poetry. Several of these pieces, whether in praise or in criticism of the poet, show the influence of the pseudo-science of phrenology in their focus on Whitman's physical appearance, finding a basis for his exuberant style in his passionate gentleness and rough, physical vitality. Whitman's friend Bronson Alcott, the transcendentalist writer and father of author Louisa May Alcott, is the first to compare Whitman to Pan, a Greek satyr and god of nature, music, and sexual vitality, and to Bacchus, the Roman god of wine, revelry, and creativity. These allusions, which emphasize both Whitman's organic creativity and his spiritedness, recur in the selection from *The Good Gray Poet*, William Douglas O'Connor's influential early biography of Whitman, and are further elevated by Robert Buchanan in his reverential comparison of Whitman to Socrates and, ultimately, to Jesus Christ.

Early criticism of Whitman's poetry had frequently featured ad hominem attacks on his lack of formal education and his sexual energies. The entries from O'Connor, Buchanan, and Ernest Rhys represent an attempt to sway public opinion within the accepted framework of biographical criticism. Students interested in biographical arguments about Whitman will find that a complex, often contradictory portrait of the poet emerges from these readings, despite the fact that Whitman himself trumpeted this image in "Song of Myself" when he asked "Do I contradict myself? / Very well then I contradict myself, / (I am large, I contain multitudes.)" For students writing about the range of public attitudes toward Whitman's sexuality, this representation of the various responses to the poet's sexual energy supplies a wide and accurate portrait. As diverse as these reactions prove to be, Whitman's kindness and gentleness are almost universally confirmed, and students exploring messianic overtones in Whitman's poetry, and especially in reviews by Whitman's early proponents, will find much support for their arguments in this section.

Yet for all their focus on Whitman's personal character, the entries also address his place in the literary canon. Buchanan ranks Whitman above his contemporary, the British poet laureate Alfred, Lord Tennyson, and expresses disgust that such writers as Ralph Waldo Emerson and James Russell Lowell are embraced by the Boston literary establishment, but that Whitman is not. Ernest Rhys, the poet and publisher who made Whitman's work widely available in England, not only toasts the poet's health in old age, but also looks forward to new poems that might recapture Whitman's energy and vitality "as when in youth it shone." Finally, elegies for Whitman by the public intellectuals Edmund Clarence Stedman and Hamlin Garland look ahead to Whitman's place in the American literary canon, indicating his importance through repeated images of Whitman's integration into the landscape after his death.

Drawn from a range of sources, these personal remembrances and responses to Whitman clearly indicate the poet's popularity during his lifetime. They also reveal the mechanisms of reputation building, for Whitman's admirers worked to secure his place in the literary canon both during and after his lifetime, celebrating the originality of his poetic innovations and countering his critics' attacks by portraying Whitman as a figure of worldwide significance. Students writing about the establishment of literary reputations and legacies will find in these pieces examples of the varying arguments for and against Whitman being afforded master status. Perhaps more importantly, there is also rich evidence in the excerpts supporting the argument that literary reputations are established in numerous venues outside the halls of the academy and the pages of a literary journal. These selections are drawn from such writings as the diary, the biography, the public poem, and the *festschrift*, a volume of writings by different authors presented as a tribute or memorial. Collectively these entries suggest that the creation of literary greatness is not solely controlled by scholars, reviewers, and publishers, and while Whitman may have failed to be a poet of the common man, his work was nevertheless commonly celebrated by numerous readers and admirers.

A. Bronson Alcott (1856)

Walt the Satyr, the Bacchus, the very God Pan, and here as we found, or as I did, to my admiring surprise, bodily, boldly, standing before us—the complement your Modern Pantheon to be sure. We met with him for two hours, and much to our delight.

—A. Bronson Alcott, *Diary,* November 10, 1856

Moncure D. Conway "Walt Whitman" (1866)

We passed the remainder of the day roaming, or "loafing," on Staten Island, where we had shade, and many miles of a beautiful beach. Whilst we bathed, I was impressed by a certain grandeur about the man, and remembered the picture of Bacchus on the wall of his room. I then perceived that the sun had put a red mask on his face and neck, and that his body was a ruddy blonde, pure and noble, his form being at the same time remarkable for fine curves and for that grace of movement which is the flower of shapely and well-knit bones. His head was oviform in every way; his hair, which was strongly mixed with grey, was cut close to his head, and, with his beard, was in strange contrast to the almost infantine fulness and serenity of his face. This serenity, however, came from the quiet light blue eyes, and above these there were three or four deep horizontal furrows, which life had ploughed. The first glow of any kind that I saw about him, was when he entered the water, which he fairly hugged with a lover's enthusiasm. But when he was talking about that which deeply interested him, his voice, always gentle and clear, became slow, and his eyelids had a tendency to decline over his eyes. It was impossible not to feel at every moment the *reality* of every word and movement of the man, and also the surprising delicacy of one who was even freer with his pen than modest Montaigne.

After making an appointment to meet Walt again during the week, when we would saunter through the streets of New York, I went off to find myself almost sleepless with thinking of this new acquaintance. He had so magnetised me, so charged me, as it were, with somewhat indefinable, that for the time the only wise course of life seemed to be to put on a blue shirt and a blouse, and loafe about Manahatta and Paumanok—"loafe, and invite my soul," to use my new friend's phrase. I found time hanging heavily on my hands, and the sights of the brilliant city tame, whilst waiting for the next meeting, and wondered if he would seem such a grand fellow when I saw him again.

—Moncure D. Conway, "Walt Whitman,"
Fortnightly Review, October 15, 1866, pp. 544–45

William Douglas O'Connor
"The Good Gray Poet: Supplement" (1866)

Here is Walt Whitman—a man who has lived a brave, simple, clean, grand, manly life, irradiated with all good works and offices to his country and his fellow-men—intellectual service to the doctrines of liberty and democracy, personal service to slaves, prisoners, the erring, the sick, the outcast, the poor, the wounded and dying soldiers of the land. He has written a book, welcomed, as you know, by noble scholars on both sides of the Atlantic; and this, for ten years, has made every squirt and scoundrel on the press fancy he had a right to insult him. Witness the recent editorial in the Chicago *Republican*. Witness the newspapers and literary journals since 1856, spotted with squibs, pasquinades, sneers, lampoons, ferocious abuse, libels. The lying jabber of the boys, drunkards and libidinous persons privileged to control many of the public prints, has passed as evidence of his character; the ridiculous opinions of callow brains, the refraction of filthy hearts, have been received as true interpretations of his volume. All this is notorious. You know it, I suppose, as well as I. And finally after the years of defamation, calumny, private affronts, public contumely, my pamphlet refers to—after the social isolation, the poverty, the adversity which an evil reputation thus manufactured for a man and following him into every detail of his life, must involve—Mr. James Harlan, Secretary of the Interior, lifting the charge of autorial obscenity into the most signal consequence, puts on the top-stone of outrage by expelling him from office with this brand upon his name. The press spreads the injury. It was telegraphed from Washington to the Eastern and Western papers. It was made the subject of insulting paragraphs in some journals and of extended and actional abuse in others. Now all this, too, you seem to consider of little or no importance. You think ten years of injurious calumny crowned with this conspicuous outrage, offers no "fit occasion for such an apotheosis of the victim."

> —William Douglas O'Connor, "The Good Gray Poet:
> Supplement" (1866), *In Re Walt Whitman*, eds.
> Horace L. Traubel, Richard Maurice Bucke,
> Thomas B. Harned, 1893, p. 154

Robert Buchanan (1887)

When I shook hands with him there, at the door of his little house in Camden, I scarcely realised the great privilege that had been given to me—that of seeing face to face the wisest and noblest, the most truly great, of all modern literary men. I hope yet, if I am spared, to look upon him again, for well I know that the earth holds no such another nature. Nor do I write this with the wild hero-worship of a boy, but as the calm, deliberate judgment of a man who is far beyond all literary predilections or passions. In Walt Whitman I see more than a mere maker of poems, I see a personality worthy to rank even above that of Socrates, akin even, though lower and far distant, to that of Him who is considered, and rightly, the first of men. I know that if that Other were here, his reception in New England might be very much the same. I know, too, that in some day not so remote, humanity will wonder that men could dwell side by side with this colossus, and not realise his proportions. We have other poets, but we have no other divine poet. We have a beautiful singer in Tennyson, and some day it will be among Tennyson's highest honours that he was once named kindly and appreciatively by Whitman. When I think of that gray head, gently bowing before the contempt of the literary class in America, when I think that Boston crowns Emerson and turns aside from the spirit potent enough to create a hundred Emersons and leave strength sufficient for the making of the whole Bostonian cosmogony, from Lowell upwards, I for a moment lose patience with a mighty nation; but only for a moment: the voice of my gentle master sounds in my ear, and I am reminded that if he is great and good, it is because he represents the greatness and goodness of a free and noble people. He would not be Walt Whitman, if he did not love his contemporaries more, not less, for the ingratitude and misconception of the Scribes and Pharisees who have outlawed him. Praise, and fame, and money are of course indifferent to him. He has spoken his message, he has lived his life, and is content. But it is we that honour and love him who are not content, while the gospel of man-millinery is preached in every magazine and every newspaper, and every literary moneychanger and poetaster has a stone to throw at the patient old prophet of modern Democracy.

—Robert Buchanan, *A Look round Literature*, 1887, pp. 345–46

Ernest Rhys "To Walt Whitman on His Seventieth Birthday" (1889)

Here health we pledge you in one draught of song,
Caught in this rhymer's cup from earth's delight,
Where English fields are green the whole year long,
The wine of might,
That the new-come Spring distils, most sweet and strong,

In the viewless air's alembic, wrought too fine for sight.
Good health! we pledge, that care may lightly sleep,
And pain of age be gone for this one day,
As of this loving cup you take, and, drinking deep,
Grow glad at heart straightway
To feel once more the kindly heat of the sun
Creative in you, as when in youth it shone,
And pulsing brainward with the rhythmic wealth
Of all the summer whose high minstrelsy
Shall soon crown field and tree,
And call back age to youth again, and pain to perfect health.

> —Ernest Rhys, "To Walt Whitman on
> His Seventieth Birthday" (1889),
> A *London Rose and Other Rhymes*, 1894, p. 84

ANONYMOUS "WHITMAN'S OBITUARY" (1892)

This anonymous obituary, originally published in the *New York Times*, names Whitman one of the greatest American authors, rivaled only by Edgar Allan Poe, the widely influential author of short stories, poetry, novels, and literary theory. Acknowledging Whitman's failure to attain the widespread audience he desired, and listing among his flaws egotism, occasional humorlessness, and dandyism, the obituary nevertheless celebrates the greatness of Whitman's poetry for its boundless optimism, universal sympathy for humankind, profound contemplation of death, and celebration of the innate goodness in existence.

For modern readers, the elegant prose of Whitman's obituary may seem surprisingly literary, but such obituaries were not uncommon in Whitman's day. While this particular obituary's rich biographical detail and consideration of Whitman's literary merits may seem more appropriate as introductory material for an entry on Whitman in an anthology of literature, its depth signifies the extent to which literary criticism in the nineteenth century was more public and less a matter of specialized academic discourse. Students seeking an overview of the many topics that preoccupied early Whitman scholarship would do well to begin with his obituary, since it objectively renders the many points of praise for Whitman's poetry, as well as the controversies surrounding it. Students writing about Whitman's Quakerism, his background in journalism, or his service as a field nurse during the Civil War will find many useful links between Whitman's biography and his major poetic themes, as well as several insightful points about the links between the history of America's growth as a nation and the grandeur, "ordinary" language, and celebration of physical life in Whitman's poetry.

The old poet who for so many years has made the public his confidant during the slow stages of his departure from the world is now at rest.

To the last he expressed himself in verse after that fashion which he elaborated about the middle of the century, and which far more than the two or three indecencies he printed, set against him the prigs and the narrow-minded among literary folk. As in religion so in literature, one must genuflect and cross one's self in orthodox fashion or submit to anathema.

In his slender volume of verse and prose issued this year by David McKay in Philadelphia, Walt Whitman bade his strange, unromantic and yet imposing Muse farewell:

Good-bye, my Fancy.
Farewell, dear mate, dear love.
I'm going away I know not where.
Or to what fortune, or whether I may ever see you again.
So good-bye, my Fancy.
Now for my last—let me look back a moment.
The slower, fainter ticking of the clock is in me.
Exit, nightfall and soon the heart-thud stopping.

This is from what he called the second annex to *Leaves of Grass*, for the old poet was by nature more prone than any to linger over what he felt to be his masterpiece and add to it touch after touch. With the artist this tendency is fatal, because the touch falls direct on the canvas or marble, but with the poet, especially a poet so little careful of rhyme and rhythm as Whitman, it makes less trouble; one can always go back to the original edition to find the work free from afterthoughts. With Whitman, indeed, inspiration did not come with a rush; he brooded on his matter, perhaps because of a defective early education, which made him a laborious composer, but the very efforts which he made to overcome his disadvantage of training brought him in the end to a pitch of originality attained by few poets of the century.

In the passing away of a writer whom his admirers loved to call the Good Gray Poet, the City of New York has lost the most remarkable literary character since Washington Irving. If his merits are not conceded so generally as are those of Irving, it may be said that his was much the more singular character and career, and that while Irving followed close on English precedents in prose literature, Whitman struck out a path for himself in verse. As to originality, Poe is his only rival. Both formed other writers. Poe left his mark on Frenchmen like Baudelaire and Scotchmen like Robert Louis Stevenson. Whitman had the honor of causing Alfred Lord Tennyson to change his style late in life, as appears from the jubilee Ode published in honor of Queen Victoria in 1887. Among those of little note whom he influenced was the unfortunate Ada Isaacs Menken, whose slender volume of verse is full of Whitmanisms.

Whitman was a New York poet in more ways than one. His ancestry was half Dutch, half English; his birthplace Long Island; his home for many years alternately Brooklyn or New York, and his heart at all times was centered on our great, vibrating hive of a city. But New York never cared for Walt Whitman or bought his books or read them. Probably very few New-Yorkers have *seen* the poem which speaks of

Manhattan streets with their powerful throbs, with the beating
    drums, as now
The endless, noise chorus, the rustle and clank of muskets, (even the
    sight of the wounded,)
Manhattan crowds, with their turbulent musical chorus, with
    varied chorus and right of the sparkling eye.
Manhattan faces and eyes forever for me.

. . . The enormous size of the Union and the crude, turbulent life, the Commonwealth growing like magic along the tremendous waterways of North America fired his imagination. He appeared in his new phase—as champion of democracy and disinterested lover of all mankind—in the year 1855, when a slim, small quarto called *Leaves of Grass*, appeared in New York, including but twelve poems. . . .

Personal friends of Whitman who knew him in Washington during the war, where he held clerkships in the Department of the Interior and the Attorney General's office, speak of him as a good comrade, who seemed a trifle anxious to make himself conspicuous by a peculiar dress—broad hat, flannel shirt exposing the breast, and semi-military cloak. These peculiarities may be set down to his lack of a sense of the ridiculous, to his profound seriousness as regards himself—to his egotism, in short—rather than a purpose to attract attention.

But there was also in his mind the same impulse to throw aside clothes as well as conventions which appeared in the old gymnosophists, in Fourier, in the artist poet William Blake. Whitman sang his own body and liked to speak of the nude; he had a fixed idea found in all ages and most races that the hairy breast is the breast of a powerful man and that the power in a man, or the brute in him, deserves more admiration than is quite compatible with Christian dogmas. It must be remembered that when he sang thus the literary ideals of the United States ran toward pallor, stooping shoulders, and a minute learning in the classical tongues. In these days of athletics his deification of the body would have caused much less scandal.

The dismay which such utterances cast among cultivated men brought up under the eye of the clergy, among college professors and bardlets gazing over at the British Islands, among the fastidious and romantic who fed on Tennyson and Wordsworth and swooned at the sound of an Americanism, may well be left to the imagination. Whitman is still reviled by these and their like.

> Has any supposed it lucky to be born!
> I hasten to inform him or her it is just as lucky to die, and I know it.

These brave sentences were penned by Whitman years ago, and now he has experienced the other end of that chain of circumstances which we call life, that chain which he tried to understand in its entirety, every link of it, and to express in the prose poems called *Leaves of Grass*, *Two Rivulets*, and 'Passage to India.' It need not be inferred that a man of so great vitality as his ever wished to die while any portion of that magnificent health his parents gave him remained in his veins. Those sentences reflect the titanic optimism of the man and form part of the consoling spirit that breath through all he wrote. . . .

Nor did Whitman confine himself to a theoretical egotism in his writings, but liked the incense of public recognition so well that his dress and behavior on the street often appeared to be calculated to insure conspicuousness, but, as we have seen, this petty vanity was apparent rather than actual. In his intercourse with men and women he impressed his own personality at all times, often rousing great affection, and in many cases lifelong friendships resulted long before he reached that mellow patriarchal stage with which the present generation is familiar.

His odd dress—wide open flannel shirt, wide trousers, broad-brimmed soft hat, and thick stick—prejudiced against him many persons who thought that he was merely a vain fellow who sought notoriety at any cost. Many, also, who took the trouble to read his verse were repelled by the apparent lawlessness of versification and the tremendous heaping up of epithets, repetitions, and eccentric grammar. And of those who condoned or enjoyed these oddities a goodly part fell away when they came to read the passages in which Whitman contends like an inspired physiologist for the beauty and dignity, nay, the poetry, of functions and organs not mentioned save in medical works.

Whitman's great strength and his great weakness was generalization. He strikes it in the first line of *Leaves of Grass*. . . .

His attitude toward religion when it can be detected is distinctly Quakerish, that is to say, opposed to ecclesiastical control and in favor of great individual liberty with a corresponding equality between the sexes.

The inchoate aspirations after freedom, the rude, unmannerly, boisterous behavior of youth, the tremendous reaching out after some nebulous but gigantic ideal of the future which characterized the town populace of these States up to the time that the civil war made blood to flow and brought Americans to their bearings are reflected, wonderfully reflected, in the greater part of *Leaves of Grass*. But that book also contains the dose of the epoch in the war fever of 1861, and here again Whitman responded to the national movement with the section called *Drum-Taps* in which will be found lyrics of surpassing dignity, beauty, and thrilling grandeur, bearing that stamp of simplicity which is beyond all praise.

Whitman's bigness of heart is not merely claimed in a hundred poems, but shown in many moving passages, such as that describing the body of a fallen woman in the Morgue. The love of man for man, as well as man for woman, forms a striking element in his chaotic creed; but, indeed, with Whitman, love reaches out beyond humanity and embraces the cosmos with the same passionate affection with which he regards a blade of grass. Probably the citizens who chase dollars in New York are the human beings for whom he could cherish the greatest contempt, yet he says,

> The little plentiful manikins, skipping around in collars and
>   tail'd coats,
> I am aware who they are—(they are positively not worms and fleas)
> I acknowledge the duplicates of myself—the weakest and shallowest
>   is deathless with me.

In this passage he reached a near humor as he ever did, but according to his own view of things exhibits therein the catholicity of his benevolence toward all.

Critics may say that in absence of humor Whitman showed weakness, but such generalizations are not good for much. He took himself with immense seriousness. But had he not done so—would we have had thoughts so profound, a picture of the great bulk of Americans so interesting, verses expressed in such a novel and often effective form? Assuredly not. We would have missed the stimulus which lurks quite as much in the extraordinary and, to some minds, extravagantly dull method of his expression as in the ideas themselves, which are difficult enough to seize.

Ralph Waldo Emerson, for example, was in many ways the exact opposite of Whitman, yet, on closer analysis, there are larger likenesses than dissimilarities between the two. Both were optimists of the most exaggerated kind. Whitman took his favorable view of life, mankind, the future from the signs of vigor, advance, wealth, and populousness about him. Emerson had, perhaps, a harder task to be optimistic beneath the whining tone of Cambridge and the glacial air of Boston, and rightly saved his soul by keeping to his Concord home. But Emerson also gained a hearing, quite as narrow and scholarly as Whitman's, by the way, by an odd versification and no little obscurity of expression. Both were misunderstood and little read, finding appreciation quicker in Canada and in England than in their own land, but both earned the title first applied to Emerson, that of Great American. And Emerson was one of the first to appraise Whitman at his true value.

Since the rebellion Walt Whitman has occupied a strange position in letters and caused a little war of pens more than once across the Atlantic. He contracted hospital malaria at Washington which in 1873 brought on a paralytic attack, from which he was long in recovering. But as early as 1864 the portions of his poems which were thought by many indecent got him into trouble. Secretary Harlan removed him from his clerkship while he was at work on one of his noblest efforts, 'President Lincoln's Funeral Hymn,' a most exquisite piece, beginning 'When lilacs last in the dooryard bloomed.' . . .

It is impossible to forecast what Whitman's place in American literature is going to be. For one thing he represents, as no college graduate and scholarly man has hitherto, the great bulk of the Nation educated in common schools. Yet hitherto he has been the scholar's delight, and the people will have none of him, unless it be a jewel from *Drum-Taps* or a rhapsody entirely free from physiological theories like that beginning, 'Out of the cradle endlessly rocking,' a threnody on a forsaken mocking bird, which ranks with the greatest productions of genius in English.

At any rate, posterity is not going to judge him as harshly as some of the virtuous of to-day have done, for how can the men of the future fail to be won over by a man who believes so rapturously in the essential goodness of all created things—even of that pit, the soul of man! In one of the notes which run as the subsidiary stream in small type at the foot of the pages of *Two Rivulets*, the poet, apparently staggered at the attempt to understand himself or his real object, hazards this opinion (it is in the preface): 'Probably, indeed, the whole of these varied songs, and all my writings, both volumes, only ring changes in some sort on the ejaculation, How vast, how eligible, how joyful, how real, is a Human Being, himself or herself!'

—"Whitman's Obituary,"
New York Times, March 27, 1892

EDMUND CLARENCE STEDMAN (1892)

Good-bye, Walt!
Good-bye, from all you loved of earth—
Rock, tree, dumb creature, man and woman—
  To you, their comrade human.
    The last assault
Ends now; and now in some great world has birth
A minstrel, whose strong soul finds broader wings,
  More brave imaginings.
Stars crown the hilltop where your dust shall lie,
  Even as we say good-bye,
    Good-bye, old Walt!

—Edmund Clarence Stedman, "W.W.," 1892

HAMLIN GARLAND "WALT WHITMAN" (1893)

Serene, vast head, with silver cloud of hair,
Lined on the purple dusk of death
A stern medallion, velvet set—
Old Norseman throned, not chained upon thy chair:
Thy grasp of hand, thy hearty breath
Of welcome thrills me yet
  As when I faced thee there.
Loving my plain as thou thy sea,
Facing the east as thou the west,
I bring a handful of grass to thee,
The prairie grasses I know the best—

Type of the wealth and width of the plain,
Strong of the strength of the wind and sleet,
Fragrant with sunlight and cool with rain—
I bring it, and lay it low at thy feet,
    Here by the eastern sea.

—Hamlin Garland, "Walt Whitman," *In Re Walt Whitman,*
eds. Horace L. Traubel, Richard Maurice Bucke,
Thomas B. Harned, 1893, p. 328

GENERAL

The following selection of letters, reviews, remembrances, and scholarly articles reveals the conflict over Whitman's status as a major poet. In the earlier pieces, opinions on Whitman are polarized between unwavering admiration and profound disgust at his personal character and rejection of poetic tradition. Beginning with Sidney Lanier's essay on Whitman, however, the appraisals become more balanced, with the critics acknowledging the emotional impact and inspiration of Whitman's verse, despite its extravagance, and supporters reassessing earlier praise of Whitman's democratic impulse.

Several core issues with regard to Whitman can be gleaned from these readings. The nature of his character, which his overtly subjective writings call attention to, is analyzed closely, with debates raging over the morality of his sexually explicit images and themes. Some condemn Whitman's verse as morally repulsive, while others claim that appreciation of *Leaves of Grass* is a touchstone for one's personal character. Likewise, the aesthetic value of Whitman's poetry is questioned, with critics condemning it as bombastic prose lacking the decorum, grammatical control, and formal rigor of traditional verse, while supporters argue for its being read both as a radically innovative style of poetry reflective of the changing world and as a new, more authentic form of autobiography. Whitman's ideas about democracy are disputed, with supporters and critics alike noting the failure of Whitman's goal of being a poet read by the population at large and not simply by society's intellectual elite. Several entries analyze the different ways Whitman's work was received in the United States and Great Britain, noting the generally positive reception by the British and suggesting that Whitman's struggle to gain American support is related to his praise of America's pioneering past, a legacy deemed unsavory by the ruling elite who preferred to emulate the customs and culture of Old World Europe.

In addition to these various topics, perhaps the most recurrent issue outlined in these readings is Whitman's canonicity, or his status in relation to other writers in American, English, and world literature. Some view Whitman as an uncouth, inarticulate writer of no artistic talent whatsoever, and they are challenged by others who argue that his work is the highest, fullest expression of human experience ever written. Later reviewers claim that the particular vehemence of Whitman's detractors, and the hyperbolic praise of his supporters, tend to obscure any reasoned debate about Whitman's importance. Following Whitman's death, however, a consensus emerged that his poetry, whether it is deemed great art or not, is of such cultural and historical importance that it cannot be ignored.

A student using the readings in this section might try to identify the artistic criteria that Whitman's supporters and critics use to define and judge his poetry. In the different article reviews of Whitman, for instance, readers might examine the lines and passages the reviewers quoted and analyzed, explaining how the selections warrant the reviewer's assessment and also explaining how the selection of different passages to discuss might have altered or contradicted their judgment. When reflecting on the different ways that creative writers respond to Whitman, readers might contrast passages from other writers with passages from Whitman's poetry and ask what features of Whitman's poetry the texts respond to. For instance, one might compare Whitman's poetry with the work of the complex formal poet Gerard Manley Hopkins, identifying passages in *Leaves of Grass* that might have prompted Hopkins to identify with Whitman's spirit, if not his aesthetics. Because Whitman's canonicity is in such dispute in these pieces, one might also compare Whitman's work with examples of poetry written by the different writers referred to, such poets as Poe, Bryant, Whittier, Longfellow, Wordsworth, and Tennyson, comparing those pieces in turn to the poetry printed in American newspapers during and after the Civil War. Finally, readers might examine how the poems from Whitman's *Drum-Taps* compare with two other notable examples of Civil War poetry, Julia Ward Howe's "Battle Hymn of the Republic" and the poems from Herman Melville's book *Battle-Pieces*.

For students interested in the relation between literature and popular forms of writing such as book reviews, these excerpts offer an interesting opportunity to investigate the availability and influence of periodicals such as *The Nation*, as well as the nature of book marketing in the nineteenth century. Did reviews of Whitman's poetry, whether positive or negative, affect its sales? If so, how? From the different negative reviews of Whitman's poetry, one might construct a portrait of literary tastes in the mid-nineteenth century, or use them to clarify the ways in which Whitman might be called a literary revolutionary.

MATTHEW ARNOLD (1866)

Arnold, an English poet and critic, is perhaps best known today for his poem "Dover Beach." In the following excerpt, he condemns what he sees as Whitman's excessive originality and claims that the only way America can achieve "a great original literature" is by respecting European poetic traditions. Students writing about Whitman's status as an American author, or about the nature of American art, will find Arnold's argument on behalf of tradition an important contrast to Whitman's own emphasis on radical revolution against traditional literary standards.

As to the general question of Mr Walt Whitman's poetical achievement, you will think that it savours of our decrepit old Europe when I add that while you think it is his highest merit that he is so unlike anyone else, to me this seems to be his demerit; no one can afford in literature to trade merely on his own bottom and to take no account of what the other ages and nations have acquired: a great original literature America will never get in this way, and her intellect must inevitably consent to come, in a considerable measure, into the European movement. That she may do this and yet be an independent intellectual power, not merely as you say an intellectual colony of Europe, I cannot doubt; and it is on her doing this, and not on her displaying an eccentric and violent originality that wise Americans should in my opinion set their desires.

—Matthew Arnold,
Letter to W.D. O'Connor, (September 16, 1866)

FERDINAND FREILIGRATH "WALT WHITMAN" (1868)

Freiligrath was Whitman's first German translator. He published translations of ten of Whitman's poems in 1868, having been initially drawn to the poet by what was then a popular German interest in the American Civil War. While Freiligrath's translations actually rendered Whitman's verse more conventional in German, his introduction emphasizes Whitman's importance as a highly original poet and almost unique being, whose free verse resounds with biblical cadence and power. Freiligrath notes Whitman's cosmic inclusiveness, in which Whitman's ego, which is itself a poem, contains and is contained by all beings, countries, and

worlds. At last elevating Whitman above even the revolutionary greatness of the German composer Richard Wagner, Freiligrath looks to the
future when the art of poetry will be overthrown and transformed by
Whitman's verse. This essay makes an important case for the literary
influence of the Bible, particularly the psalms, on Whitman's poetry, and
also shows how critics were interested in Whitman's relation to opera.

—⁓— —⁓— —⁓—

WALT WHITMAN! Who is Walt Whitman?

The answer is, a poet! A new American poet! His admirers say, the first, the
only poet America has as yet produced. The only American poet of specific
character. No follower in the beaten track of the European muse, but fresh
from the prairie and the new settlements, fresh from the coast and the great
watercourses, fresh from the thronging humanity of seaports and cities, fresh
from the battle-fields of the South, and from the earthy smells in hair and
beard and clothing of the soil from which he sprang. A being not yet come to
fulness of existence, a person standing firmly and consciously upon his own
American feet, and utterer of a gross of great things, though often odd. And
his admirers go still further: Walt Whitman is to them the only poet at all, in
whom the age, this struggling, eagerly seeking age in travail with thought and
longing, has found its expression. . . .

Are these verses? The lines are arranged like verses, to be sure, but verses
they are not. No metre, no rhyme, no stanzas. Rhythmical prose, ductile
verses. At first sight rugged, inflexible, formless; but yet for a more delicate
ear, not devoid of euphony. The language homely, hearty, straightforward,
naming everything by its true name, shrinking from nothing, sometimes
obscure. The tone rhapsodical, like that of a seer, often unequal, the sublime
mingled with the trivial even to the point of insipidity. He reminds its
sometimes, with all the differences that exist besides, of our own Hamann.
Or of Carlyle's oracular wisdom. Or of the *Paroles d'un Croyant*. Through all
there sounds out the Bible—its language, not its creed.

And what does the poet propound to us in this form? First of all Himself,
his *I*. Walt Whitman. This *I* however is a part of America, a part of the earth,
a part of mankind, a part of the All. As such he is conscious of himself and
revolves, knitting the greatest to the least, ever going out from America, and
coming back to America ever again (only to a free people does the future
belong!) before our view, a vast and magnificent world-panorama. Through
this individual Walt Whitman and his Americanism marches, we may say, a

cosmical procession, such as may be suitable for reflective spirits, who, face to face with eternity, have passed solitary days on the sea-shore, solitary nights under the starry sky of the prairie. He finds himself in all things and all things in himself. He, the one man, Walt Whitman, is mankind and the world. And the world and mankind are to him one great poem. What he sees and hears, and what he comes in contact with, whatever approaches him, even the meanest, the most trifling, the most everyday matter—all is to him symbolical of a higher, of a spiritual fact. Or rather, matter and spirit, the real and the ideal are to him one and the same. Thus, produced by himself, he takes his stand; thus he strides along, singing as he goes; thus he opens from his soul, a proud free man, and *only* a man, world-wide, social and political vistas.

A wonderful appearance. We confess that it moves us, disturbs us, will not loose its hold upon us. At the same time, however, we would remark that we are not yet ready with our judgment of it, that we are still biased by our first impression. Meanwhile we, probably the first in Germany to do so, will take at least a provisional view of the scope and tendency of this new energy. It is fitting that our poets and thinkers should have a closer look at this strange new comrade, who threatens to overturn our entire *Ars Poetica* and all our theories and canons on the subject of aesthetics. Indeed, when we have listened to all that is within these earnest pages, when we have grown familiar with the deep, resounding roar of those, as it were, surges of the sea in their unbroken sequence of rhapsodical verses breaking upon us, then will our ordinary verse-making, our system of forcing thought into all sorts of received forms, our playing with ring and sound, our syllable-counting and measure of quantity, our sonnet-writing and construction of strophes and stanzas, seem to us almost childish. Are we really come to the point, when life, even in poetry, calls imperatively for new forms of expression? Has the age so much and such serious matter to say, that the old vessels no longer suffice for the new contents? Are we standing before a poetry of the ages to come, just as some years ago a music of the ages to come was announced to us? And is Walt Whitman a greater than Richard Wagner?

—Ferdinand Freiligrath, "Walt Whitman,"
Allgemeine Zeitung, Augsburg, April 24, 1868,
Trans. *The New Eclectic Magazine*, July 11, 1868, pp. 325–29

WILLIAM MICHAEL ROSSETTI
(1869)

That glorious man Whitman will one day be known as one of the greatest sons of Earth, a few steps below Shakspeare on the throne of immortality. What a tearing-away of the obscuring veil of use & wont from the visage of man & of life! . . .

The sort of thing that people object to in Whitman's writings is not so easily surmised until one sees them. It mt. be expressed thus—that he puts into print physical matters with the same bluntness & directness almost as that with wh. they present themselves to the eye & mind, or are half-worded in the thought. From one point of view this is even blameless: but from another, the modern reader's point of view, it is quite intolerable.

—William Michael Rossetti,
Letter to Anne Gilchrist (June 23, 1869)

ANNE GILCHRIST (1869)

I think it was very manly and kind of you to put the whole of Walt Whitman's poems into my hands; and that I have no other friend who would have judged them and me so wisely and generously.

I had not dreamed that words could cease to be words, and become electric streams like these. I do assure you that, strong as I am, I feel sometimes as if I had not bodily strength to read many of these poems. In the series headed *Calamus,* for instance, in some of the *Songs of Parting,* the "Voice out of the Sea," the poem beginning "Tears, Tears," etc., there is such a weight of emotion, such a tension of the heart, that mine refuses to beat under it—stands quite still—and I am obliged to lay the book down for a while. Or again, in the piece called *Walt Whitman,* and one or two others of that type, I am as one hurried through stormy seas, over high mountains, dazed with sunlight, stunned with a crowd and tumult of faces and voices, till I am breathless, bewildered, half dead. Then come parts and whole poems in which there is such calm wisdom and strength of thought, such a cheerful breadth of sunshine, that the soul bathes in them renewed and strengthened. Living impulses flow out of these that make me exult in life, yet look longingly towards "the superb vistas of Death." Those who admire this poem, and don't care for that, and talk of formlessness, absence of meter, etc., are quite as far from any genuine recognition of Walt Whitman as his bitter detractors.

—Anne Gilchrist, Letter to William Michael Rossetti
(July 11, 1869), *In Re Walt Whitman,* eds. Horace L. Traubel,
Richard Maurice Bucke, Thomas B. Harned, 1893, pp. 42–43

PETER BAYNE
"WALT WHITMAN'S POEMS" (1875)

If I ever saw anything in print that deserved to be characterized as atrociously bad, it is the poetry of Walt Whitman; and the three critics of repute, Dr. Dowden, Mr. W. Rossetti, and Mr. Buchanan, who have praised his performances, appear to me to be playing off on the public a well-intentioned, probably good-humoured, but really cruel hoax. . . . The *Leaves of Grass,* under which designation Whitman includes all his poems, are unlike anything else that has passed among men as poetry. They are neither in rhyme nor in any measure known as blank verse; and they are emitted in spurts or gushes of unequal length, which can only by courtesy be called lines. Neither in form nor in substance are they poetry; they are inflated, wordy, foolish prose; and it is only because he and his eulogists call them poems, and because I do not care to dispute about words, that I give them the name. Whitman's admirers maintain that their originality is their superlative merit. I undertake to show that it is a mere knack, a "trick of singularity," which sound critics ought to expose and denounce, not to commend.

The secret of Whitman's surprising newness—the principle of his conjuring trick—is on the surface. It can be indicated by the single word, extravagance. In all cases he virtually, or consciously, puts the question, What is the most extravagant thing which it is here in my power to say? What is there so paradoxical, so hyperbolical, so nonsensical, so indecent, so insane, that no man ever said it before, that no other man would say it now, and that therefore it may be reckoned on to create a sensation? . . .

Whitman's writings abound with reproductions of the thoughts of other men, spoiled by obtuseness or exaggeration. He can in no case give the finely correct application of a principle, or indicate the reserves and exceptions whose appreciation distinguishes the thinker from the dogmatist: intense black and glaring white are his only colours. The mysterious shadings of good into evil and evil into good, the strange minglings of pain with pleasure and of pleasure with pain, in the web of human affairs, have furnished a theme for musing to the deepest minds of our species. But problems that were felt to be insoluble by Shakespeare and Goethe have no difficulty for this bard of the West. Extravagant optimism and extravagant pessimism, both wrong and shallow, conduct him to "the entire denial of evil" (the words are Professor Dowden's), to the assertion that "there is no imperfection in the present and can be none in the future," and to the vociferous announcement that success and failure are pretty much the same. . . .

If here and there we have tints of healthful beauty, and tones of right and manly feeling, they but suffice to prove that he can write sanely and sufferably when he pleases, that his monstrosities and solecisms are sheer affectation, that he is not mad, but only counterfeits madness. He is in no sense a superlatively able man, and it was beyond his powers to make for himself a legitimate poetical reputation. No man of high capacity could be so tumid and tautological as he—could talk, for instance, of the "fluid wet" of the sea; or speak of the aroma of his armpits, or make the crass and vile mistake of bringing into light what nature veils, and confounding liberty with dissolute anarchy. The poet of democracy he is not; but his books may serve to buoy, for the democracy of America, those shallows and sunken rocks on which, if it is cast, it must inevitably, amid the hootings of mankind, be wrecked. Always, unless he chooses to contradict himself for the sake of paradox, his political doctrine is the consecration of mutinous independence and rabid egotism and impudent conceit. In his ideal city "the men and women think lightly of the laws." His advice is to resist much and to obey little. This is the political philosophy of Bedlam, unchained in these ages chiefly through the influence of Rousseau, which has blasted the hopes of freedom wherever it has had the chance, and which must be chained up again with ineffable contempt if the self-government of nations is to mean anything else than the death and putrescence of civilization. Incapable of true poetical originality, Whitman had the cleverness to invent a literary trick, and the shrewdness to stick to it. As a Yankee phenomenon, to be good-humouredly laughed at, and to receive that moderate pecuniary remuneration which nature allows to vivacious quacks, he would have been in his place; but when influential critics introduce him to the English public as a great poet, the thing becomes too serious for a joke. While reading Whitman, in the recollection of what had been said of him by those gentlemen, I realized with bitter painfulness how deadly is the peril that our literature may pass into conditions of horrible disease, the raging flame of fever taking the place of natural heat, the ravings of delirium superseding the enthusiasm of poetical imagination, the distortions of tetanic spasm caricaturing the movements, dance-like and music-measured, of harmonious strength. Therefore I suspended more congenial work to pen this little counterblast to literary extravagance and affectation.

—Peter Bayne, "Walt Whitman's Poems,"
Contemporary Review, December 1875, pp. 49–51, 68–69

ARTHUR CLIVE "WALT WHITMAN, THE POET OF JOY" (1875)

Whitman says that they who most loudly praise him are those who understand him least. I, perhaps, will not come under the censure, though I do under the description; for I confess that I do not understand this man. The logical sense of the words, the appositeness and accuracy of the images, one can indeed apprehend and enjoy; but there is an undertone of meaning in Whitman which can never be fully comprehended. This, doubtless, is true of all first-rate poetry; but it must be applied in a special sense to the writings of a man who is not only a poet but a mystic—a man who thoroughly enjoys this world, yet looks confidently to one diviner still beyond; who professes a passionate attachment to his friends, yet says that he has other friends, not to be seen with the eye, closer and nearer and dearer to him than these. The hardening, vulgarising influences of life have not hardened and vulgarised the spiritual sensibilities of this poet, who looks at this world with the wondering freshness of a child, and to the world beyond with the gaze of a seer. He has what Wordsworth lost, and in his old age comes trailing clouds of glory—shadows cast backward from a sphere which we have left, thrown forward from a sphere to which we are approaching.

He is the noblest literary product of modern times, and his influence is invigorating and refining beyond expression.

—Arthur Clive, "Walt Whitman, the Poet of Joy,"
Gentleman's Magazine, December 1875, p. 716

GEORGE ELIOT (1876)

Best known for her novel *Middlemarch*, here the British novelist George Eliot expresses regret for using an epigraph from Whitman's poetry for her novel *Daniel Deronda*. Though fond of the quoted lines, she claims no special admiration for Whitman's poetry, an uncommonly moderate

members of society, despite the fact that his work is embraced precisely by the latter group, while the work of a more traditional poet such as John Greenleaf Whittier is perceived as commonly accessible for readers of all backgrounds. For Stedman, only the educated elite could produce a poet such as Whitman, whose return to nature and physical experience would invigorate individuals occupied with issues of culture, society, and politics, but would be rejected as all too familiar by the laboring classes Whitman admires. Lastly, Stedman criticizes the monotony of Whitman's revolutionary writing, its rejection of all formal poetry amounting to a new type of formalism. Whitman's absolute belief in the rightness of his own work parallels his belief in the rightness of his own ego, which can absorb and be absorbed by all others. For Stedman, such an assured universalism invites resistance, and since Whitman's aesthetics make no allowance for variation, he ultimately pushes away many sympathetic readers in his drive for a universal individualism.

III

Here we may as well consider a trait of Mr. Whitman's early work that most of all has brought it under censure. I refer to the blunt and open manner in which the consummate processes of nature, the acts of procreation and reproduction, with all that appertain to them, are made the theme or illustration of various poems, notably of those with the title *Children of Adam*. Landor says of a poet that, "on the remark of a learned man that irregularity is no indication of genius, he began to lose ground rapidly, when on a sudden he cried out in the Haymarket, 'There is no God.' It was then rumored more generally and more gravely that he had something in him. 'Say what you will,' once whispered a friend of mine, 'there are things in him strong as poison, and original as sin.'" But those who looked upon Whitman's sexuality as a shrewd advertisement, justly might be advised to let him reap the full benefit of it, since, if he had no more sincere basis, it would receive the earlier judgment— and ere long be "outlawed of art." This has not been its fate, and therefore it must have had something of conviction to sustain it. Nevertheless, it made the public distrustful of this poet, and did much to confine his volumes to the libraries of the select few. Prurient modesty often is a sign that people are conscious of personal defects; but Whitman's physical excursions are of a kind which even Thoreau, refreshed as he was by the new poet, found it hard to keep pace with. The fault was not that he discussed matters which others timidly evade, but that he did not do it in a clean way,—that he was too anatomical and malodorous withal; furthermore, that in this department he showed excessive interest, and applied its imagery to other departments, as if with a special purpose to lug it in. His pictures sometimes were so realistic, his speech so free, as to excite the hue and cry of indecent exposure; the display of things natural, indeed, but which we think it unnatural to exhibit on the highway, or in the sitting-room, or anywhere except their wonted places of consignment.

On the poet's side it is urged that the ground of this exposure was, that thus only could his reform be consistent; that it was necessary to celebrate the body with special unction, since, with respect to the physical basis of life, our social weakness and hypocrisy are most extreme. Not only should the generative functions be proclaimed, but, also,—to show that "there is in nature nothing mean or base,"—the side of our life which is hidden, because it is of the earth, earthy, should be plainly recognized in these poems; and thus, out of rankness and coarseness, a new virility be bred, an impotent and squeamish race at last be made whole.

Entering upon this field of dispute, what I have to say—in declaring that Whitman mistakes the aim of the radical artist or poet—is perhaps different from the criticism to which he has been subjected. Let us test him solely by his own rules. Doing this, we presuppose his honesty of purpose, otherwise his objectionable phrases and imagery would be outlawed, not only of art but of criticism. Assume, then, first, that they were composed as a fearless avowal of the instincts and conditions which pertain to him in common with the race which he typifies; secondly, that he deems such a presentation essential to his revolt against the artifice of current life and sentiment, and makes it in loyal *reliance upon the excellence, the truth of nature.* To judge him in conformity with these ideas lessens our estimate of his genius. Genius is greatly consistent when most audacious. Its instinct will not violate nature's logic, even by chance, and it is something like obtuseness that does so upon a theory.

In Mr. Whitman's sight, that alone is to be condemned which is against nature, yet, in his mode of allegiance, he violates her canons. For, if there is nothing in her which is mean or base, there is much that is ugly and disagreeable. If not so in itself (and on the question of absolute beauty I accept his own ruling, "that whatever tastes sweet to the most perfect person, that is finally right"), if not ugly in itself, it seems so to the conscious spirit of our intelligence. Even Mother Earth takes note of this, and resolves, or disguises and beautifies, what is repulsive upon her surface. It is well said that an artist shows inferiority by placing the true, the beautiful, or the good above its associates. Nature is strong and rank, but not externally so. She, too, has her sweet and sacred sophistries, and the delight of Art is to heighten her beguilement, and, far from making her ranker than she is, to portray what she might be in ideal combinations. Nature, I say, covers her slime, her muck, her ruins, with garments that to us are beautiful. She conceals the skeleton, the frame-work, the intestinal thick of life, and makes fair the outside of things. Her servitors swiftly hide or transform the fermenting, the excrementitious, and the higher animals possess her instinct. Whitman fails to perceive that she respects certain decencies, that what we call decency is grounded in her law. An artist should not elect to paint the part of her to which Churchill rashly avowed that Hogarth's pencil was devoted. There is a book—*"L'Affaire Clemenceau"*—in which a Frenchman's regard for the lamp of beauty, and his indifference to that of goodness, are curiously illustrated. But Dumas points out, in the rebuke given by a sculptor to a pupil who mistakenly elevates the arm of his first model, a beautiful girl, that the Underside of things should be avoided in art,—since Nature, not meaning it to be shown, often deprives it of beauty. Finally, Mr. Whitman sins against his mistress in questioning the instinct we derive from her, one which of all is most elevating to poetry, and which is the basis of sensations that lead childhood on, that fill youth with rapture, impress with longing all human kind, and make up, impalpable as they are, half the preciousness of life. He draws away the final veil. It is not squeamishness that leaves something to the imagination, that hints at guerdons still unknown. The law of suggestion, of half-concealment, determines the choicest effects, and is the surest road to truth. Grecian as Mr. Whitman may be, the Greeks better understood this matter, as scores of illustrations, like that of the attitude of the Hermaphroditus in the Louvre, show. A poet violates nature's charm of feeling in robbing love, and even intrigue, of their esoteric quality. No human appetites need be pruriently ignored, but coarsely analyzed they fall below humanity. He even takes away the sweetness and pleasantness of stolen waters and secret bread. *Furto cuncta magis bella.* Recalling the term "over-soul," the reader insensibly accuses our poet of an over-bodiness. The mock-modesty and effeminacy of our falser tendencies in art should be chastised, but he misses the true corrective. Delicacy is not impotence, nor rankness the sure mark of virility. The model workman is both fine and strong. Where Mr. Whitman sees nothing but the law of procreation, poetry dwells upon the union of souls, devotion unto death, joys greater for their privacy, things of more worth because whispered between the twilights. It is absolutely true that the design of sexuality is the propagation of species. But the delight of lovers who now inherit the earth is no less a natural right, and those children often are the finest that were begot without thought of offspring. There are other lights in which a dear one may be regarded than as the future mother of men, and these—with their present hour of joy—are unjustly subordinated in the *Leaves of Grass*. Marked as the failure of this pseudo-naturalism has been hitherto, even thus will it continue,—so long as savages have instincts of modesty,—so long as we draw and dream of the forms and faces, not the internal substance and mechanism, of those we hold most dear,—so long as the ivy trails over the ruin, the southern jessamine covers the blasted pine, the moss hides the festering swamp,—so long as our spirits seek the spirit of all things; and thus long shall art and poesy, while calling every truth of science to their aid, rely on something else than the processes of science for the attainment of their exquisite results.

From the tenor of Mr. Whitman's later works, I sometimes have thought him half-inclined to see in what respect his effort toward a perfect naturalism was misdirected. In any case, there would be no inconsistency in a further modification of his early pieces,—in the rejection of certain passages and words, which, by the law of strangeness, are more conspicuous than ten times their amount of common phraseology, and grow upon the reader until they seem to pervade the whole volume. The examples of Lucretius, Rabelais, and other masters, who wrote in other ages and conditions, and for their own purposes, have little analogy. It well may be that our poet has more claim to a wide reading in England than here, since his English editor, without asking consent, omitted entirely every poem "which could with tolerable fairness be deemed offensive." Without going so far, and with no falseness to himself, Mr. Whitman might re-edit his home-editions in such wise that they would not be counted wholly among those books which are meat for strong men, but would have a chance among those greater books that are the treasures of the simple and the learned, the young and the old.

IV

The entire body of his work has a sign-metrical by which it is recognized—a peculiar and uncompromising style, conveyed in a still more peculiar unrhymed verse, irregular, yet capable of impressive rhythmical and lyrical effects.

The faults of his method, glaring enough in ruder passages, are quite his own; its merits often are original, but in his chosen form there is little original and new. It is an old fashion, always selected for dithyrambic oracular outpourings,—that of the Hebrew lyrists and prophets, and their inspired English translators,—of the Gaelic minstrels,—of various Oriental and

Shemitic peoples,—of many barbarous dark-skinned tribes,—and in recent times put to use by Blake, in the *Prophetic Visions,* and by other and weaker men. There are symptoms in Whitman's earlier poems, and definite proof in the later, that his studies have included Blake,—between whose traits and his own there is a superficial, not a genuine, likeness. Not as an invention, then, but as a striking and persistent renaissance, the form that has become his trademark, and his extreme claims for it, should have fair consideration. An honest effort to enlarge the poet's equipment, too long unaided, by something rich and strange, deserves praise, even though a failure; for there are failures worthier than triumphs. Our chanter can bear with dignity the provincial laughter of those to whom all is distasteful that is uncommon, and regard it as no unfavorable omen. From us the very strangeness of his chant shall gain for it a welcome, and the chance to benefit us as it may. Thereby we may escape the error pointed out by Mr. Benjamin, who says that people in approaching a work, instead of learning from it, try to estimate it from their preconceived notions. Hence, original artists at first endure neglect, because they express their own discoveries in nature of what others have not yet seen,—a truth well to bear in mind whenever a singer arrives with a new method.

Probably the method under review has had a candid hearing in more quarters than the author himself is aware of. If some men of independent thought and feeling have failed to accept his claims and his estimate of the claims of others, it possibly has not been through exclusiveness or malice, but upon their own impression of what has value in song.

Mr. Whitman never has swerved from his primal indictment of the wonted forms, rhymed and unrhymed, dependent upon accentual, balanced and stanzaic effects of sound and shape,—and until recently has expressed his disdain not only of our poets who care for them, but of form itself. So far as this cry was raised against the technique of poetry, I not merely think it absurd, but that when he first made it he had not clearly thought out his own problem. Technique, *of some kind,* is an essential, though it is equally true that it cannot atone for poverty of thought and imagination. I hope to show that he never was more mistaken than when he supposed he was throwing off form and technique. But first it may be said that no "form" ever has sprung to life, and been handed from poet to poet, that was not engendered by instinct and natural law, and each will be accepted in a sound generalization. Whitman avers that the time has come to break down the barriers between prose and verse, and that only thus can the American bard utter anything commensurate with the liberty and splendor of his themes. Now, the mark of a poet is that he is at ease everywhere,—that nothing can hamper his gifts, his exultant freedom. He is a master of expression. There are certain points—note this—where expression takes on rhythm, and certain other points where it ceases to be rhythmical,—places where prose becomes poetical, and where verse grows prosaic; and throughout Whitman's productions these points are more frequent and unmistakable than in the work of any other writer of our time. However bald or formal a poet's own method, it is useless for him to decry forms that recognize the pulses of time and accent, and the linked sweetness of harmonic sound. Some may be tinkling, others majestic, but each is suited to its purpose, and has a spell to charm alike the philosopher and the child that knows not why. The human sense acknowledges them; they are the earliest utterance of divers peoples, and in their later excellence still hold their sway. Goethe discussed all this with Eckermann, and rightly said there were "great and mysterious agencies" in the various poetic forms. He even added that if a sort of poetic prose should be introduced, it would only show that the distinction between prose and poetry had been lost sight of completely. Rhyme, the most conventional feature of ballad verse, has its due place, and will keep it; it is an artifice, but a natural artifice, and pleases accordingly. Milton gave reasons for discarding it when he perfected an unrhymed measure for the stateliest English poem; but what an instrument rhyme was in his hands that made the sonnets and minor poems! How it has sustained the whole carnival of our heroic and lyric song, from the sweet pipings of Lodge and Chapman and Shakspere, to the undertones of Swinburne and Poe. There are endless combinations yet in the gamut. The report is that Mr. Whitman's prejudice is specially strong against our noblest unrhymed form, "blank-verse." Its variety and freedom, within a range of accents, breaks, caesural effects,—its rolling organ-harmonies,—he appreciates not at all. Rhythmical as his own verse often can be, our future poets scarcely will discard blank-verse in its behalf—not if they shall recall *The Tempest*, "Hail, Holy Light," "Tintern Abbey," *Hyperion*, the *Hellenics*, *Ulysses*, and *Thanatopsis*. Mr. Parke Godwin, in a recent private letter, terms it "the grandest and most flexible of English measures," and adds, with quick enthusiasm: "Oh, what a glory there is in it, when we think of what Shakspere, Milton, Wordsworth and Landor made of it, to say nothing of Tennyson and Bryant!" I doubt not that new handlings of this measure will produce new results, unsurpassed in any tongue. It is quite as fit as Mr. Whitman's own, if he knows the use of it, for "the expression of American democracy and manhood." Seeing how dull and prolix he often becomes, it may be that even for him his measure has been too facile, and that the curb of a more regular unrhymed form would have spared us many tedious curvetings and grewsome downfalls.

Strenuous as he may be in his belief that the old methods will be useless to poets of the future, I am sure that he has learned the value of technique through his long practice. He well knows that whatever claims to be the poetry of the future speedily will be forgotten in the past, unless consonant with the laws of expression in the language to which it belongs; that verse composed upon a theory, if too artificial in its contempt of art, may be taken up for a while, but, as a false fashion, anon will pass away. Not that his verse is of this class; but it justly has been declared that, in writing with a purpose to introduce a new mode or revolutionize thought, and not because an irresistible impulse seizes him, a poet is so much the less a poet. Our question, then, involves the spontaneity of his work, and the results attained by him.

His present theory, like most theories which have reason, seems to be derived from experience: he has learned to discern the good and bad in his work, and has arrived at a rationale of it. He sees that he has been feeling after the irregular, various harmonies of nature, the anthem of the winds, the roll of the surges, the countless laughter of the ocean waves. He tries to catch this "under-melody and rhythm." Here is an artistic motive, distinguishing his chainless dithyrambs from ordinary verse, somewhat as the new German music is distinguished from folk-melody, and from the products of an early, especially the Italian, school. Here is not only reason, but a theoretical advance to a grade of art demanding extreme resources, because it affords the widest range of combination and effect.

But this comprehension of his own aim is an afterthought, the result of long groping. The genesis of the early *Leaves* was in motives less artistic and penetrating. Finding that he could not think and work to advantage in the current mode, he concluded that the mode itself was at fault; especially, that the poet of a young, gigantic nation, the prophet of a new era, should have a new vehicle of song. Without looking farther, he spewed out the old forms, and avowed his contempt for American poets who use them. His off-hand course does not bring us to the conclusion of the whole matter. So far as the crudeness of the *juventus mundi* is assumed by him, it must be temporal and passing, like the work of some painters, who, for the sake of startling effects, use ephemeral pigments. A poet does not, perforce, restore the lost foundations of his art by copying the manner natural to an aboriginal time and people. He is merely exchanging masters, and certainly is not founding a new school. Only as he discovers the inherent tendencies of song does he belong to the future. Still, it is plain that Whitman found a style suited to his purposes, and was fortunate both as a poet and a diplomatist. He was sure to attract notice, and to seem original, by so pronounced a method. Quoth the monk to Gargantua, "A mass, a matin, or vesper, well rung, is half said." It was suited to him as a poet, because he has that somewhat wandering sense of form, and of melody, which often makes one's conceptions seem the more glorious to himself, as if invested with a halo or blended with concurrent sound, and prevents him from lessening or enlarging them by the decisive master-hand, or at once perfecting them by sure control.

A man who finds that his gloves cripple him does right in drawing them off. At first, Whitman certainly meant to escape all technique. But genius, in spite of itself, makes works that stand the test of scientific laws. And thus he now sees that he was groping toward a broader technique. Unrhymed verse, the easiest to write, is the hardest to excel in, and no measure for a bardling. And Mr. Whitman never more nearly displayed the feeling of a true artist than when he expressed a doubt as to his present handling of his own verse, but hoped that, in breaking loose from ultramarine forms, he had sounded, at least, the key for a new paean. I have referred to his gradual advances in the finish of his song. Whether he has revived a form which others will carry to a still higher excellence, is doubtful. Blank-verse, limitless in its capacities, forces a poet to stand without disguise, and reveals all his defects. Whitman's verse, it is true, does not subject him to so severe a test. He can so twist and turn himself, and run and jump, that we are puzzled to inspect him at all, or make out his contour. Yet the few who have ventured to follow him have produced little that has not seemed like parody, or unpleasantly grotesque. It may be that his mode is suited to himself alone, and not to the future poets of These States,—that the next original genius will have to sing "as Martin Luther sang," and the glorious army of poetic worthies. I suspect that the old forms, in endless combinations, will return as long as new poets arise with the old abiding sense of time and sound.

The greatest poet is many-sided, and will hold himself slavishly to no one thing for the sake of difference. He is a poet, too, in spite of measure and material, while, as to manner, the style is the man. Genius does not need a special language; it newly uses whatever tongue it finds. Thought, fire, passion, will overtop everything,—will show, like the limbs of Teverino, through the clothes of a prince or a beggar. A cheap and common instrument, odious in foolish hands, becomes the slave of music under the touch of a master. I attach less importance, therefore, to Mr. Whitman's experiment in verse than he and his critics have, and inquire of his mannerism simply how far it represents the man. To show how little there is in itself, we only have to think of Tupper; to see how rich it may be, when the utterance of genius, listen to Whitman's teacher, William Blake. It does not prove much, but still is interesting, to note that the pieces whose quality never fails with any class of hearers—of which "My Captain" is an example—are those in which our poet has approached most nearly, and in a lyrical, melodious manner, to the ordinary forms.

He is far more original in his style proper than in his metrical inventions. His diction, on its good behavior, is copious and strong, full of surprises, utilizing the brave, homely words of the people, and assigning new duties to common verbs and nouns. He has a use of his own for Spanish and French catch-words, picked up, it may be, on his trip to Louisiana or in Mexican war times. Among all this is much slang that now has lived its life, and is not understood by a new generation with a slang of its own. This does not offend so much as the mouthing verbiage, the "ostent evanescent" phrases, wherein he seems profoundest to himself, and really is at his worst. The titles of his books and poems are varied and sonorous. Those of the latter often are taken from the opening lines, and are key-notes. What can be fresher than *Leaves of Grass* and *Calamus?* What richer than "The Mystic Trumpeter," "O Star of France!" "Proud Music of the Storm," or simpler than *Drum-Taps,* "The Wound-Dresser," "The Ox-Tamer"? or more characteristic than "Give me the Splendid Silent Sun," "Mannahatta," "As a Strong Bird on Pinions Free," "Joy, Shipmate, Joy"? Some are obscure and grandiose—"Eidolons," "Chanting the Square Deific," but usually his titles arrest the eye and haunt the ear; it is an artist that invents them, and the best pieces have the finest names. He has the art of "saying things"; his epithets, also, are racier than those of other poets; there *is* something of the Greek in Whitman, and his lovers call him Homeric, but to me he shall be our old American Hesiod, teaching us works and days.

V

His surest hold, then, is as an American poet, gifted with language, feeling, imagination, and inspired by a determined purpose. Some estimate, as I have said, may be made of his excellence and shortcomings, without waiting for that national absorption which he himself declares to be the test.

As an assimilating poet of nature he has positive genius, and seems to me to present his strongest claims. Who else, in fact, has so true a hand or eye for the details, the sweep and color, of American landscape? Like others, he confronts those superb physical aspects of the New World which have controlled our poetry and painting, and deferred the growth of a figure-school, but in this conflict with nature he is not overcome; if not the master, he is the joyous brother-in-arms. He has heard the message of the pushing, wind-swept sea, along Paumanok's shore; he knows the yellow, waning moon and the rising stars,—the sunset, with its cloud-bar of gold above the horizon,—the birds that sing by night or day, bush and brier, and every shining or swooning flower, the peaks, the prairie, the mighty, conscious river, the dear common grass that children fetch with full hands. Little escapes him, not even "the mossy scabs of the worm fence, and heap'd stones, mullen and poke-weed"; but his details are massed, blended,—the wind saturates and the light of the American skies transfigures them. Not that to me, recalling the penetrative glance of Emerson, the wood and way-side craft that Lowell carried lightly as a sprig of fir, and recalling other things of others, does Whitman seem our "only" poet of nature; but that here he is on his own ground, and with no man his leader.

Furthermore, his intimacy with nature is always subjective,—she furnishes the background for his self-portraiture and his images of men. None so apt as he to observe the panorama of life, to see the human figure,—the hay-maker, wagoner, boatman, soldier, woman and babe and maiden, and brown, lusty boy,—to hear not only "the bravuras of birds, bustle of growing wheat, gossip of flames, clack of sticks cooking my meals," but also "the sound I love, the sound of the human voice." His town and country scenes, in peace or in war, are idyllic. Above the *genre,* for utter want of sympathy, he can only name and designate—he does not depict. A single sketch, done in some original way, often makes a poem; such is that reminiscence (in rhyme) of the old Southern negress, "Ethiopia Saluting the Colors," and such the touching conceit of Old Ireland—no fair and green-robed Hibernia of the harp, but an ancient, sorrowful mother, white-haired, lean and tattered, seated on the ground, mourning for her children. He tells her that they are not dead, but risen again, with rosy and new blood, in another country. This is admirable, I say, and the true way to escape tradition; this is imaginative,—and there is imagination, too, in his apostrophe to "The Man-of-War-Bird" (carried beyond discretion by this highest mood, he finds it hard to avoid blank-verse):

> Thou who hast slept all night upon the storm,
> Waking renewed on thy prodigious pinions! . . .
>
> Thou, born to match the gale (thou art all wings)!
> To cope with heaven and earth and sea and hurricane;

Thou ship of air that never furl'st thy sails,
Days, even weeks, untried and onward, through spaces—realms gyrating.
At dark that look'st on Senegal, at morn, America;
That sport'st amid the lightning-flash and thundercloud!
In these—in thy experiences—hadst thou my soul,
What joys! What joys were thine!

Imagination is the essential thing; without it poetry is as sounding brass or a tinkling cymbal. Whitman shows it in his sudden and novel imagery, and in the subjective rapture of verse like this, but quite as often his vision is crowded and inconsistent. The editor of a New York magazine writes to me: "In so far as imagination is thinking through types (eidullia), Whitman has no equal," adding that he does not use the term as if applied to Coleridge, but as limited to the use of types, and that "in this sense it is really more applicable to a master of science than to a poet. In the poet the type is lodged in his own heart, and when the occasion comes he is mastered by it, and he must sing. In Whitman the type is not so much in his heart as in his thought. While he is moved by thought, often grand and elementary, he does not give the intellectual satisfaction warranted by the thought, but a moving panorama of objects. He not only puts aside his 'singing robes,' but his 'thinking-cap,' and resorts to the stereopticon." How acute, how true! There is, however, a peculiar quality in these long catalogues of types,—such as those in the "Song of the Broad-Axe" and "Salut au Monde," or, more poetically treated, in "Longings for Home." The poet appeals to our synthetic vision. Look through a window; you see not only the framed landscape, but each tree and stone and living thing. His page must be seized with the eye, as a journalist reads a column at a glance, until successive "types" and pages blend in the mind like the diverse colors of a swift-turning wheel. Whitman's most inartistic fault is that he overdoes this method, as if usually unable to compose in any other way.

The tenderness of a strong and robust nature is a winning feature of his song. There is no love-making, no yearning for some idol of the heart. In the lack of so refining a contrast to his realism, we have gentle thoughts of children, images of grand old men, and of women clothed with sanctity and years. This tenderness, a kind of natural piety, marks also his poems relating to the oppressed, the suffering, the wounded and dying soldiers. It is the soul of the pathetic, melodious threne for Lincoln, and of the epilogue—"My Captain!" These pieces remind us that he has gained some command of his own music, and in the matter of tone has displayed strength from the first. In revising his early poems he has improved their effect as a whole. It must be owned that his wheat often is more welcome for the chaff in which it is scattered; there is none of the persistent luxury which compels much of Swinburne's unstinted wealth to go unreckoned. Finally, let us note that Whitman, long ago, was not unread in the few great books of the world, nor inapt to digest their wisdom. He was among the first to perceive the grandeur of the scientific truths which are to give impulse to a new and loftier poetic imagination. Those are significant passages in the poem *Walt Whitman,* written by one who had read the xxxviiith chapter of Job, and beginning, "Long I was hugg'd close—long and long."

The *Leaves of Grass,* in thought and method, avowedly are a protest against a hackney breed of singers, singing the same old song. More poets than one are born in each generation, yet Whitman has derided his compeers, scouted the sincerity of their passion, and has borne on his mouth Heine's sneer at the eunuchs singing of love. In two things he fairly did take the initiative, and might, like a wise advocate, rest his case upon them. He essayed, without reserve or sophistry, the full presentment of the natural man. He devoted his song to the future of his own country, accepting and outvying the loudest peak-and-prairie brag, and pledging These States to work out a perfect democracy and the salvation of the world. Striking words and venturesome deeds, for which he must have full credit. But in our studies of the ideal and its votaries, the failings of the latter cannot be lightly passed over. There is an inconsistency, despite the gloss, between his fearful arraignment, going beyond Carlyle's, of the outgrowth of our democracy, thus far, and his promise for the future. In his prose, he sees neither physical nor moral health among us: all is disease, impotency, fraud, decline. In his verse, the average American is lauded as no type ever was before. These matters renew questions which, to say the least, are still open. Are the lines of caste less sharply divided every year, or are the high growing higher, and the low lower, under our democracy? Is not the social law of more import than the form of government, and has not the quality of race much to do with both? Does Americanism in speech and literature depend upon the form and letter, or upon the spirit? Can the spirit of literature do much more than express the national spirit as far as it has gone, and has it not, in fact, varied with the atmosphere? Is a nation changed by literature, or the latter by the former, in times when journalism so swiftly represents the thought and fashion of each day? As to distinctions in form and spirit between the Old-World literature and our own, I have always looked for this to enlarge with time. But with the recent increase of travel and communication, each side of the Atlantic now more than ever seems to affect the other. Our "native flavor" still is distinct in proportion to the youth of a section, and inversely to the development. It is an intellectual narrowness that fails to meditate upon these things.

Thus we come to a defect in Mr. Whitman's theories, reasoning and general attitude. He professes universality, absolute sympathy, breadth in morals, thought, workmanship,—exemption from prejudice and formalism. Under all the high poetic excellences which I carefully have pointed out, I half suspect that his faults lie in the region where, to use his own word, he is most complacent: in brief, that a certain *narrowness* holds him within well-defined bounds. In many ways he does not conform to his creed. Others have faith in the future of America, with her arts and letters, yet hesitate to lay down rules for her adoption. These must come of themselves, or not at all. Again, in this poet's specification of the objects of his sympathy, the members of every class, the lofty and the lowly, are duly named; yet there always is an implication that the employer is inferior to the employed,—that the man of training, the civilizee, is less manly than the rough, the pioneer. He suspects those who, by chance or ability, rise above the crowd. What attention he does pay them is felt to be in the nature of patronage, and insufferable. Other things being equal, a scholar is as good as an ignoramus, a rich man as a poor man, a civilizee as a boor. Great champions of democracy—poets like Byron, Shelley, Landor, Swinburne, Hugo—often have come from the ranks of long descent. It would be easy to cite verses from Whitman that apparently refute this statement of his feeling, but the spirit of his whole work confirms it. Meanwhile, though various editions of his poems have found a sale, he is little read by our common people, who know him so well, and of whose democracy he is the self-avowed herald. In numberless homes of working-men—and all Americans are workers—the books of other poets are treasured. Some mental grip and culture are required, of course, to get hold of the poetry of the future. But Whittier, in this land, is a truer type of the people's poet,—the word "people" here meaning a vast body of freemen, having a common-school education, homes, an honest living, and a general comprehension far above that of the masses in Europe. These folks have an instinct that Whittier, for example, has seized his day with as much alertness and self-devotion as this other bard of Quaker lineage, and has sung songs "fit for the New World" as he found it. Whitman is more truly the voice and product of the culture of which he bids us beware. At least, he utters the cry of culture for escape from over-culture, from the weariness, the finical precision, of its own satiety. His warmest admirers are of several classes: those who have carried the art of verse to super-refined limits, and seeing nothing farther in that direction, break up the mold for a change; those radical enthusiasts who, like myself, are interested in whatever hopes to bring us more speedily to the golden year; lastly, those who, radically inclined, do not think closely, and make no distinction between his strength and weakness. Thus he is, in a sense, the poet of the over-refined and the doctrinaires. Such men, too, as Thoreau and Burroughs have a welcome that scarcely would have been given them in an earlier time. From the discord and artifice of our social life we go with them to the woods, learn to name the birds, note the beauty of form and flower, and love these healthy comrades who know each spring that bubbles beneath the lichened crag and trailing hemlock. Theocritus learns his notes upon the mountain, but sings in courts of Alexandria and Syracuse. Whitman, through propagandists who care for his teachings from metaphysical and personal causes, and compose their own ideals of the man, may yet reach the people, in spite of the fact that lasting works usually have pleased all classes in their own time.

Reflecting upon his metrical theory, we also find narrowness instead of breadth. I have shown that the bent of a liberal artist may lead him to adopt a special form, but not to reject all others; he will see the uses of each, demanding only that it shall be good in its kind. Swinburne, with his cordial liking for Whitman, is too acute to overlook his formalism. Some of his eulogists, those whom I greatly respect, fail in their special analysis. One of them rightly says that Shakspere's sonnets are artificial, and that three lines which he selects from *Measure for Measure* are of a higher grade of verse. But these are the reverse of "unmeasured" lines,—they are in Shakspere's free and artistic, yet most measured, vein. Here comes in the distinction between art and artifice; the blank-verse is conceived in the broad spirit of the former, the finish and pedantry of the sonnet make it an artificial form. A master enjoys the task of making its artifice artistic, but does not employ it exclusively. Whitman's irregular, manneristic chant is *at the other extreme of artificiality,* and equally monotonous. A poet can use it with feeling and majesty; but to use it invariably, to laud it as the one mode of future expression, to decry all others, is formalism of a pronounced kind. I have intimated that Whitman has carefully studied and improved it. Even Mr. Burroughs does him injustice in admitting that he is not a poet and artist in the current acceptation of those terms, and another writer simply is just in declaring that when he undertakes to give us poetry he can do it. True, the long prose sentences thrown within his ruder pieces resemble nothing so much as the comic recitativos in the buffo-songs of the concert-cellars. This is not art, nor wisdom, but sensationalism. There is narrowness in his failure to recast and modify these and other depressing portions of various poems, and it is sheer Philistinism for one to coddle all the weaknesses of his experimental period, because they have been a product of himself.

One effect of the constant reading of his poetry is that, like the use of certain refections, it mars our taste for the proper enjoyment of other kinds. Not, of course, because it is wholly superior, since the subtlest landscape by Corot or Rousseau might be utterly put to nought by a melodramatic neighbor, full of positive color and extravagance. Nor is it always, either, to our bard's advantage that he should be read with other poets. Consider Wordsworth's exquisite lyric upon the education which Nature gives the child whom to herself she takes, and of whom she declares:

The stars of midnight shall be dear
To her; and she shall lean her ear
In many a secret place,
Where rivulets dance their wayward round,
And beauty born of murmuring sound
Shall pass into her face.

It happens that Whitman has a poem on the same theme, describing the process of growth by sympathy and absorption, which thus begins and ends:

There was a child went forth every day;
And the first object he look'd upon, that object he became;
And that object became part of him for the day, or a certain part of the
day, or for many years, or stretching
cycles of years. . . .

The horizon's edge, the flying sea-crow, the fragrance of salt-marsh and
shore-mud;
These became part of that child who went forth every day, and who now
goes,
and will always go forth every day.

Plainly there are some comparative advantages in Wordsworth's treatment of this idea. It would be just as easy to reverse this showing by quoting other passages from each poet: the purpose of my digression is to declare that by means of comparative criticism any poet may be judged unfairly, and without regard to his general claims.

So far as Mr. Whitman's formalism is natural to him, no matter how eccentric, we must bear with it; whenever it partakes of affectation, it is not to be desired. The charge of attitudinizing, so often brought against his writings and personal career, may be the result of a popular impression that the border-line is indistinct between his self-assertion as a type of Man, and the ordinary self-esteem and self-advancement displayed by men of common mold. Pretensions have this advantage, that they challenge analysis, and make a vast noise even as we are forced to examine them. In the early preface to the *Leaves* there is a passage modeled, in my opinion, upon the style of Emerson, concerning simplicity,—with which I heartily agree, having constantly insisted upon the test of simplicity in my discussion of the English poets. Yet this quality is the last to be discerned in many portions of the *Leaves of Grass*. In its stead we often find boldness, and the "pride that apes humility,"—until the reader is tempted to quote from the "Poet of Feudalism" those words of Cornwall upon the roughness which brought good Kent to the stocks. Our bard's self-assertion, when the expression of his real manhood, is bracing, is an element of poetic strength. When it even seems to be "posing," it is a weakness, or a shrewdness, and 'tis a weakness in a poet to be unduly shrewd. Of course a distinction must be carefully made between the fine extravagance of genius, the joy in its own conceptions, and self-conscious vanity or affectation,—between, also, occasional weaknesses of the great, of men like Browning, and like the greatest of living masters, Hugo, and the afflatus of small men, who only thus far succeed in copying them. And it would be unjust to reckon Whitman among the latter class.

Doubtless his intolerant strictures upon the poets of his own land and time have made them hesitate to venture upon the first advances in brotherhood, or to intrude on him with their recognition of his birthright. As late as his latest edition, his opinion of their uselessness has been expressed in withering terms. It may be that this is merely consistent, an absolute corollary of his new propositions. There is no consistency, however, in a complaint of the silence in which they have submitted to his judgments. They listen to epithets which Heine spared Platen and his clique, and surely Heine would have disdained to permit a cry to go up in his behalf concerning a want of recognition and encouragement from the luckless victims of his irony. There is ground enough for his scorn of the time-serving, unsubstantial quality of much of our literature. But I should not be writing this series of papers, did I not well know that there are other poets than himself who hear the roll of the ages, who look before and after, above and below. The culture which he deprecates may have done them an ill turn in lessening their worldly tact. I am aware that Mr. Whitman's poems are the drama of his own life and passions. His subjectivity is so great that he not only absorbs all others into himself, but insists upon being absorbed by whomsoever he addresses. In his conception of the world's equality, the singer himself appears as the one Messianic personage, the answerer and sustainer, the universal solvent,—in all these respects holding even "Him that was crucified" to be not one whit his superior. It is his kiss, his consolation, that all must receive,—whoever you are, these are given especially to you. But men are egotists, and not all tolerant of one man's selfhood; they do not always deem the affinities elective. Whitman's personality is too strong and individual to be universal, and even to him it is not given to be all things to all men.

—Edmund Clarence Stedman, "Walt Whitman,"
Scribner's Monthly, November 1880, pp. 4–63

FITZGERALD MOLLOY
"LEADERS OF MODERN THOUGHT" (1882)

Walt Whitman was the outcome of a great era and a great country—they worthy of him in all things, he worthy of them; and as a poet and a prophet he sings of all that he sees in the present, and of the future, peering beyond the surface of things, and crying aloud of the changes to come in the fulness of time.

—Fitzgerald Molloy, "Leaders of Modern Thought,
no. XXVII, Walt Whitman," <i>Modern Thought,</i>
September 1882

GERARD MANLEY HOPKINS (1882)

Hopkins, a Jesuit priest and inventive formal poet known for such works as "The Windhover" and "Spring and Fall," confesses his admiration for Whitman's poetry and his dislike of his character, which Hopkins regrets resembles his own. Given that both poets were likely homosexual, this admission foreshadows Whitman's later prominence as a gay poet, while also revealing nineteenth-century social pressures against homosexuality. Hopkins further praises Whitman's use of the alexandrine, a metrical line with seven stressed feet, an astute observation about the formal properties underlying Whitman's free verse, though Hopkins denies Whitman's influence on his own use of the line, an indirect admission of Whitman's emerging influence as a world writer. This excerpt could prove useful in an examination of Whitman's sexuality or a discussion of how other authors responded to it. In addition, Hopkins's discussion of Whitman's rhythms offers a specific example of how other authors responded to or were influenced by Whitman's style.

I may as well say what I should not otherwise have said, that I always knew in my heart Walt Whitman's mind to be more like my own than any other man's living. As he is a very great scoundrel this is not a pleasant confession. And this also makes me the more desirous to read him and the more determined that I will not. . . . His 'savage' style has advantages, and he has chosen it; he says so. But you cannot eat your cake and keep it: he eats his offhand, I keep mine. It makes a very great difference. Neither do I deny all resemblance. In particular I noticed in 'Spirit that formed this scene' a preference for the alexandrine. I have the same preference: I came to it by degrees, I did not take it from him.

—Gerard Manley Hopkins,
Letter to Robert Bridges (October 18, 1882)

G.C. Macaulay "Walt Whitman" (1882)

Macaulay, an English translator of the classics, here praises Whitman's almost unequalled passion and deep expressions of grief, while also faulting him for bombast, bloated syntax, egotism, and a lack of reticence about subjects ordinarily deemed indecent. Yet for Macaulay, such flaws are the minor side effects of Whitman's desire to create a distinctly American literature and champion the individual human self (not just his own). Critical yet sympathetic, Macaulay's review indirectly compares Whitman to another poet, Alfred, Lord Tennyson, known for deep but tonally restrained expressions of grief. The excerpt could thus prove a useful starting point for a comparison of the poets' use of elegy in their work.

He is perhaps of all writers the most repellent to the reader who glances at him superficially. In the first place he is indecent, and that too not accidentally but on principle. Whatever may be thought of his morality, and that I hold to be essentially sound and healthy, it cannot be denied that in one section of his work, and occasionally throughout the poems and prose, he outrages every ordinary rule of decency. There is nothing impure in this kind of exposure; it has indeed the direct antithesis to prurient suggestion, and the intention of it is unquestionably honest, but from an artistic point of view it is the gravest of faults, it is essentially and irredeemably ugly and repulsive. We are most of us agreed that there is and ought to be a region of reticence, and into this region the writer has rushed himself and drags us unwillingly after him. He stands convicted of ἀπειροκαλία, if of nothing worse. Akin to this first instance of defect in artistic perception is a second—his use, namely, of words which are either not English or essentially vulgar; and to this must be added a not unfrequent neglect of syntax, which, together with looseness in the application of some words, makes him at times vague or unintelligible. Occasionally there occur words or expressions which, though not ordinarily found in literature, have a native force which justifies them; but generally it is the case that for the French word or for the vulgarism savouring either of the gutter on the one hand or of the Yankee penny-a-liner on the other might be substituted a good English word equally expressive. But here also we too probably have before us a fault of wilfulness, for we know that he will not allow the language of English literature to be large enough for the poets of America, but expects accessions to it from Tennessee and California. If, however, he has in his choice of words sought that simplicity which (to quote his own words) is 'the art of art, the glory of expression, and the sunshine of the light of letters,' he has certainly not seldom failed to attain it, and it was hardly to be attained by pouring out indiscriminately into his pages the words which ran naturally off his pen. The 'art of sinking' is illustrated in his juxtaposition of the most incongruous things, and this especially in his well-known catalogues, which, though sometimes picturesque and interesting, are generally only absurd and dull. The fact that they are introduced on principle is not to be admitted as an excuse for their inartistic and formless character, any more than a similar excuse is to be allowed for offences against decency. From many of these faults a sense of humour would have protected him; and this also might have preserved him from some of that violently feeble exaggeration with which he speaks especially of his own countrymen and their institutions, and from the parade with which he sometimes announces truisms, as if they had been just now for the first time discovered by himself. His defence on the general charge is finely given in a poem now published for the first time, written in Platte Cañon, Colorado.

Spirit that formed this scene,
These tumbled rock-piles grim and red,
These reckless heaven-ambitious peaks,
These gorges, turbulent-clear streams, this naked freshness,
These formless wild arrays. . .

Was't charged against my chants they had forgotten art? . . .
But thou that revelest here, spirit that formed this scene,
They have remembered thee.

But the grandeur of nature is not always to be attained by heaping together uncouth masses. We complain not so much that the work lacks polish, as that the writer has not been preserved by his own native genius from ugly excrescences.

These artistic defects and his general disregard of form make many of his works repulsive, and do not allow us to accept any one as faultless. But they are mostly such as expurgation could remove, and therefore are not vital. The characteristic which cannot be got rid of, and yet repels, is his intense egotism and self-assertion. His longest, and in some respects most important, work—a poem of twelve or fourteen hundred lines, with which the original *Leaves of Grass* opened—has or had his own name as the title and his own personality as the subject; and this self-assertion of the individual is perhaps the prevailing characteristic of Whitman's work, that which makes it in fact representative in some degree of the spirit of the age; and the egotism, after all, is not so much personal as typical. The poet is a Kosmos, and contains within himself all unity and all diversity. What he claims for himself he thereby claims for others on the same terms. 'Underneath all, to me is myself, to you yourself. We feel when the poet proclaims himself' 'an acme of things accomplished,' for whose birth all the forces of the universe have been a preparation, he is speaking less for himself individually than for humanity, the humanity of his own day and of future days. The egotism becomes more offensive when it is obviously personal and indicates himself as the Michael Angelo of literature; and that, it must be admitted, is not unseldom, though here too he claims to be speaking less for himself than for the future race of democratic poets. To these charges it may be added that, notwithstanding his boasted freedom from the trammels of conventionality, he is in his more ordinary work a mannerist of the most vulgar kind. 'Oh! to realise space!' 'Have you reckoned a thousand acres much?' 'Has any one supposed it lucky to be born? I hasten to inform him or her that it is just as lucky to die.' 'I have said that the soul is not more than the body, and I have said that the body is not more than the soul.' 'I swear I think there is nothing but immortality, that the exquisite scheme is for it, and the nebulous float is for it, and the cohering is for it!' If these are not all exact quotations, every one will recognise them as genuine types. No style lends itself more readily to parody and burlesque. But when he is at his best the mannerism is in a great measure shaken off. . . .

If we were asked for justification of the high estimate of this poet, which has been implied, if not expressed, in what has been hitherto said, the answer would be perhaps first, that he has a power of passionate expression, of strong and simple utterance of the deepest tones of grief, which is almost or altogether without its counterpart in the world. Not often has he exerted his power, but often enough to let us understand that he possesses it, and to stamp him as a poet inferior to few, if any, of our time in strength of native genius, however he may fall behind many in artistic perception.

—G.C. Macaulay, "Walt Whitman," *Nineteenth Century,*
December 1882, pp. 905–09

ROBERT LOUIS STEVENSON
"WALT WHITMAN" (1882)

The writer Robert Louis Stevenson was best known in his lifetime for the novels *Treasure Island* (1883) and *The Strange Case of Dr. Jekyll and Mr. Hyde* (1886), but early in his career, Stevenson was a productive essayist and reviewer. Here, he accounts for differences in the appreciation of Whitman's poetry, but nevertheless asserts Whitman's importance in American and world literature. Frequently referring to Whitman as a poetic theorist, Stevenson finds that Whitman's verse consists more of theories about poetry and American society than it does traditional poems, yet he claims that this subject matter is of undeniable importance, whereas Whitman's style or manner of expression remains open to praise or criticism. Like a prophet, Stevenson claims, Whitman wakes readers to the marvels of creation, bidding them return to the experience of life itself.

Stevenson disarms one of the usual points of contention in the discussion of Whitman by distinguishing between manner, or poetic style, and subject matter. Whitman may be judged as a writer according to a reader's own tastes, he claims, and to deny the poet's literary merit is no great sin. But what Whitman chooses to write about is unavoidably important. Stevenson posits that Whitman is a "symptom" of his historical era, especially in the way the origins of America are reflected in the mass of images and ideas Whitman draws from all walks of life and includes in his poems. Yet Whitman is no mere raconteur of the American experience. Rather, his work is driven by theories about American society and about poetry itself, notions that do not necessarily result in great poetry but do make important literature. Whitman advocates a "democratic ideal of humanity" that transcends class, education, and even national identity, while also calling for and attempting to write poems that reinvigorate the human experience of creation.

For Stevenson, Whitman's greatest insight seems to accord with Stevenson's own theory of language. For Stevenson, language is a means of communicating experience, but it can never surpass the complexity and wonder of experience itself. Thus, if the poet is to intensify lived reality for the reader, then poems with the force of reality are called for. For Stevenson, Whitman's greatness comes from writing about the one subject whose reality poetry truly can convey: the poet's own thoughts. Yet these thoughts must themselves reflect the reader's own thoughts if they are to have any effect, for poetry has the power to reveal, but not persuade. A witness to America's rebellious individualism and its competing drive to unify and cohere, Whitman portrays "the average population of America . . . as it is," with all the force of prophecy.

Stevenson's assessment of Whitman has proved persuasive and long lasting. Given the assertion that Whitman "was a theorizer about society before he was a poet," readers might ask to what extent Whitman would have agreed with the different theories Stevenson attributes to him: that the great poet electrifies society by revealing its own thoughts to itself; that Whitman's poems are more often theories about society and about poetry writing than they are poems; that the one subject a poet can portray with the force of reality is the poet's own mind; and that language communicates but never equals real experience. What works of Whitman's most support these claims? Which, if any, contradict them? Do Stevenson's arguments do justice to Whitman's other interests in history, nature, and human sexuality? Lastly, readers might pay particular attention to Stevenson's final claim about Whitman—that he accepted the inconsistencies of society and urged it forward through praise—in light of the idea of manifest destiny. To what extent does Whitman's poetry support American expansionism? Should his poetry be treated with the same scrutiny and criticism that is today accorded manifest destiny?

———————

Of late years the name of Walt Whitman has been a good deal bandied about in books and magazines. It has become familiar both in good and ill repute. His works have been largely bespattered with praise by his admirers, and cruelly mauled and mangled by irreverent enemies. Now, whether his poetry is good or bad as poetry, is a matter that may admit of a difference of opinion without alienating those who differ. We could not keep the peace with a man who should put forward claims to taste and yet depreciate the choruses in *Samson Agonistes;* but, I think, we may shake hands with one who sees no more in Walt Whitman's volume, from a literary point of view, than a farrago of incompetent essays in a wrong direction. That may not be at all our own opinion. We may think that, when a work contains many unforgettable phrases, it cannot be altogether devoid of literary merit. We may even see passages of a high poetry here and there among its eccentric contents. But when all is said, Walt Whitman is neither a Milton nor a Shakespeare; to appreciate his works is not a condition necessary to salvation; and I would not disinherit a son upon the question, nor even think much the worse of a critic, for I should always have an idea what he meant.

What Whitman has to say is another affair from how he says it. It is not possible to acquit any one of defective intelligence, or else stiff prejudice, who is not interested by Whitman's matter and the spirit it represents. Not as a poet, but as what we must call (for lack of a more exact expression) a prophet, he occupies a curious and prominent position. Whether he may greatly influence the future or not, he is a notable symptom of the present. As a sign of the times, it would be hard to find his parallel. I should hazard a large wager, for instance, that he was not unacquainted with the works of Herbert Spencer; and yet where, in all the history books, shall we lay our hands on two more incongruous contemporaries? Mr. Spencer so decorous—I had almost said, so dandy—in dissent; and Whitman, like a large shaggy dog, just unchained, scouring the beaches of the world and baying at the moon. And when was an echo more curiously like a satire, than when Mr. Spencer found his Synthetic Philosophy reverberated from the other shores of the Atlantic in the "barbaric yawp" of Whitman?

Whitman, it cannot be too soon explained, writes up to a system. He was a theorizer about society before he was a poet. He first perceived something wanting, and then sat down squarely to supply the want. The reader, running over his works, will find that he takes nearly as much pleasure in critically expounding his theory of poetry as in making poems. This is as far as it can be from the case of the spontaneous village minstrel dear to elegy, who has no theory whatever, although sometimes he may have fully as much poetry as Whitman. The whole of Whitman's work is deliberate and preconceived. A man born into a society comparatively new, full of conflicting elements and interests, could not fail, if he had any thoughts at all, to reflect upon the tendencies around him. He saw much good and evil on all sides, not yet settled down into some more or less unjust compromise as in older nations, but still in the act of settlement. And he could not but wonder what it would turn out; whether the compromise would be very just or very much the reverse, and give great or little scope for healthy human energies. From idle wonder to active speculation is but a step; and he seems to have been early struck with the inefficacy of literature and its extreme unsuit-ability to the conditions. What he calls "Feudal Literature" could have little living action on the tumult of American democracy; what he calls the "Literature of Wo," meaning the whole tribe of Werther and Byron, could have no action for good in any time or place. Both propositions, if art had none but a direct moral influence, would be true enough; and as this seems to be Whitman's view, they were true enough for him. He conceived the idea of a Literature which was to inhere in the life of the present; which was to be, first, human, and next, American; which was to be brave and cheerful as per contract; to give culture in a popular and poetical presentment; and, in so doing, catch and stereotype some democratic ideal of humanity which should be equally natural to all grades of wealth and education, and suited, in one of his favorite phrases, to "the average man." To the formation of some such literature as this his poems are to be regarded as so many contributions, one sometimes explaining, sometimes superseding, the other: and the whole together not so much a finished work as a body of suggestive hints. He does not profess to have built the castle, but he pretends he has traced the lines of the foundation. He has not made the poetry, but he flatters himself he has done something toward making the poets.

His notion of the poetic function is ambitious, and coincides roughly with what Schopenhauer has laid down as the province of the metaphysician. The poet is to gather together for men, and set in order, the materials of their existence. He is "The Answerer;" he is to find some way of speaking about life that shall satisfy, if only for the moment, man's enduring astonishment at his own position. And besides having an answer ready, it is he who shall provoke the question. He must shake people out of their indifference, and force them to make some election in this world, instead of sliding dully forward in a dream. Life is a business we are all apt to mismanage; either living recklessly from day to day, or suffering ourselves to be gulled out of our moments by the inanities of custom. We should despise a man who gave as little activity and forethought to the conduct of any other business. But in this, which is the one thing of all others, since it contains them all, we cannot see the forest for the trees. One brief impression obliterates another. There is something stupefying in the recurrence of unimportant things. And it is only on rare provocations that we can rise to take an outlook beyond daily concerns, and comprehend the narrow limits and great possibilities of our existence. It is the duty of the poet to induce such moments of clear sight. He is the declared enemy of all living by reflex action, of all that is done betwixt sleep and waking, of all the pleasureless pleasurings and imaginary duties in which we coin away our hearts and fritter invaluable years. He has to electrify his readers into an instant unflagging activity, founded on a wide and eager observation of the world, and make them direct their ways by a superior prudence, which has little or nothing in common with the maxims of the copy-book. That many of us lead such lives as they would heartily disown after two hours' serious reflection on the subject is, I am afraid, a true, and, I am sure, a very galling thought. The Enchanted Ground of dead-alive respectability is next, upon the map, to the Beulah of considerate virtue. But there they all slumber and take their rest in the middle of God's beautiful and wonderful universe; the drowsy heads have nodded together in the same position since first their fathers fell asleep; and not even the sound of the last trumpet can wake them to a single active thought. The poet has a hard task before him to stir up such fellows to a sense of their own and other people's principles in life.

And it happens that literature is, in some ways, but an indifferent means to such an end. Language is but a poor bull's-eye lantern wherewith to show off the vast cathedral of the world; and yet a particular thing once said in words is so definite and memorable, that it makes us forget the absence of the many which remain unexpressed; like a bright window in a distant view, which dazzles and confuses our sight of its surroundings. There are not words enough in all Shakespeare to express the merest fraction of a man's experience in an hour. The speed of the eyesight and the hearing, and the continual industry of the mind, produce, in ten minutes, what it would require a laborious volume to shadow forth by comparisons and roundabout approaches. If verbal logic were sufficient, life would be as plain sailing as a piece of Euclid. But, as a matter of fact, we make a travesty of the simplest process of thought when we put it into words; for the words are all colored and forsworn, apply inaccurately, and bring with them, from former uses, ideas of praise and blame that have nothing to do with the question in hand. So we must always see to it nearly, that we judge by the realities of life and not by the partial terms that represent them in man's speech; and at times of choice, we must leave words upon one side, and act upon those brute convictions, unexpressed and perhaps inexpressible, which cannot be flourished in an argument, but which are truly the sum and fruit of our experience. Words are for communication, not for judgment. This is what every thoughtful man knows for himself, for only fools and silly schoolmasters push definitions over far into the domain of conduct; and the majority of women, not learned in these scholastic refinements, live all-of-a-piece and unconsciously, as a tree grows, without caring to put a name upon their acts or motives. Hence, a new difficulty for Whitman's scrupulous and argumentative poet; he must do more than waken up the sleepers to his words; he must persuade them to look over the book and at life with their own eyes.

This side of truth is very present to Whitman; it is this that he means when he tells us that "To glance with an eye confounds the learning of all times." But he is not unready. He is never weary of descanting on the undebatable conviction that is forced upon our minds by the presence of other men, of animals, or of inanimate things. To glance with an eye, were it only at a chair or a park railing, is by far a more persuasive process, and brings us to a far more exact conclusion, than to read the works of all the logicians extant. If both, by a large allowance, may be said to end in certainty, the certainty in the one case transcends the other to an incalculable degree. If people see a lion, they run away; if they only apprehend a deduction, they keep wandering around in an experimental humor. Now, how is the poet to convince like nature, and not like books? Is there no actual piece of nature that he can show the man to his face, as he might show him a tree if they were walking together? Yes, there is one: the man's own thoughts. In fact, if the poet is to speak efficaciously, he must say what is already in his hearer's mind. That, alone, the hearer will believe; that, alone, he will be able to apply intelligently to the facts of life. Any conviction, even if it be a whole system or a whole religion, must pass into the condition of commonplace, or postulate, before it becomes fully operative. Strange excursions and high-flying theories may interest, but they cannot rule behavior. Our faith is not the highest truth that we perceive, but the highest that we have been able to assimilate into the very texture and method of our thinking. It is not, therefore, by flashing before a man's eyes the weapons of dialectic; it is not by induction, deduction, or construction; it is not by forcing him on from one stage of reasoning to another, that the man will be effectually renewed. He cannot be made to believe anything; but he can be made to see that he has always believed it. And this is the practical canon. It is when the reader cries, "Oh, I know!" and is, perhaps, half irritated to see how nearly the author has forestalled his own thoughts, that he is on the way to what is called in theology a Saving Faith.

Here we have the key to Whitman's attitude. To give a certain unity of ideal to the average population of America—to gather their activities about some conception of humanity that shall be central and normal, if only for the moment—the poet must portray that population as it is. Like human law, human poetry is simply declaratory. If any ideal is possible, it must be already in the thoughts of the people; and, by the same reason, in the thoughts of the poet, who is one of them. And hence Whitman's own formula: "The poet is individual—he is complete in himself: the others are as good as he; only he sees it, and they do not." To show them how good they are, the poet must study his fellow-countrymen and himself somewhat like a traveller on the hunt for his book of travels. There is a sense, of course, in which all true books are books of travel; and all genuine poets must run their risk of being charged with the traveller's exaggeration; for to whom are such books more surprising than to those whose own life is faithfully and smartly pictured? But this danger is all upon one side; and you may judiciously flatter the portrait without any likelihood of the sitter's disowning it for a faithful likeness. And so Whitman has reasoned: that by drawing at first hand from himself and his neighbors, accepting without shame the inconsistencies and brutalities that go to make up man, and yet treating the whole in a high, magnanimous spirit, he would make sure of belief, and at the same time encourage people forward by the means of praise.

—Robert Louis Stevenson, "Walt Whitman,"
Familiar Studies of Men and Books, 1882, pp. 104–12

SIDNEY LANIER (1883)

Opposing Whitman's lack of reserve and his particular theories of democracy, poet and literary theorist Sidney Lanier nevertheless praises the "bigness and naivety" of Whitman's poetry in the following excerpt. A poetic experimentalist, Lanier suggests that in at least one instance, "O Captain, My Captain," Whitman's poetry becomes most tender and moving when it abandons radical free verse for traditional verse form, an opinion Whitman himself rejected. Yet Lanier's analysis proves astute when he compares Whitman to another poet who praised the lives of common men, the British Romantic poet William Wordsworth. Both poets, Lanier writes, address lowly themes in common language, but ironically are appreciated only by elite, intellectual readers. Lanier's discussion invites thematic comparisons of Whitman and Wordsworth, and also comparative assessments of Whitman's free verse and his less frequent formal writings.

Here let me first carefully disclaim and condemn all that flippant and sneering tone which dominates so many discussions of Whitman. While I differ from him utterly as to every principle of artistic procedure; while he seems to me the most stupendously mistaken man in all history as to what constitutes true democracy, and the true advance of art and man; while I am immeasurably shocked at the sweeping invasions of those reserves which depend on the very personality I have so much insisted upon, and which the whole consensus of the ages has considered more and more sacred with every year of growth in delicacy; yet, after all these prodigious allowances, I owe some keen delights to a certain combination of bigness and naivety which make some of Whitman's passages so strong and taking, and indeed, on the one occasion when Whitman has abandoned his theory of formlessness and written in form he has made "My Captain, O My Captain" surely one of the most tender and beautiful poems in any language. . . .

In examining [Whitman's doctrine], a circumstance occurs to me at the outset which throws a strange but effective light upon the whole argument. It seems curious to reflect that the two poets who have most avowedly written for the people, who have claimed most distinctively to represent and embody the thought of the people, and to be bone of the people's bone and flesh of the people's flesh, are precisely the two who have most signally failed of all popular acceptance and who have most exclusively found audience at the other extreme of culture. These are Wordsworth and Whitman. We all know how strenuously and faithfully Wordsworth believed that in using the simplest words and treating the lowliest themes, he was bringing poetry back near to the popular heart; yet Wordsworth's greatest admirer is Mr. Matthew Arnold, the apostle of culture, the farthest remove from anything that could be called popular: and in point of fact it is probable that many a peasant who would feel his blood stir in hearing "A man's a man for a' that," would grin and guffaw if you should read him Wordsworth's "Lambs" and *Peter Bells*.

And a precisely similar fate has met Whitman. Professing to be a mudsill and glorying in it, chanting democracy and shirt-sleeves and equal rights, declaring that he is nothing if not one of the people, nevertheless the people, the democracy, will yet have nothing to do with him, and it is safe to say that his sole audience has lain among such representatives of the highest culture as Emerson and the English *illuminated*.

The truth is, that if closely examined, Whitman, instead of being a true democrat, is simply the most incorrigible of aristocrats masquing in a peasant's costume, and his poetry, instead of being the natural outcome of a fresh young democracy, is a product which would be impossible except in a highly civilized society.

—Sidney Lanier, *The English Novel*, 1883, pp. 45–47

GEORGE SELWYN
"WALT WHITMAN AT CAMDEN" (1885)

Let me round off with an opinion or two, the result of my thirteen years' acquaintance. . . . Both Walt Whitman's book and personal character need to be studied a long time and in the mass, and are not to be gauged by custom. I never knew a man who—for all he takes an absorbing interest in politics, literature, and what is called 'the world'—seems to be so poised on himself alone. Dr. Drinkard, the Washington physician who attended him in his paralysis, wrote to the Philadelphia doctor into whose hands the case passed, saying among other things: 'In his bodily organism, and in his constitution, tastes and habits, Whitman is the most *natural* man I have ever met.' The primary foundation of the poet's character, at the same time, is certainly spiritual. Helen Price, who knew him for fifteen years, pronounces him [in Dr. Bucke's book] the most essentially religious person she ever knew. On this foundation has been built up, layer by layer, the rich, diversified, concrete experience of his life, from its earliest years. Then his aim and ideal have not been the technical literary ones. His strong individuality, wilfulness, audacity, with his scorn of convention and rote, have unquestionably carried him far outside the regular metes and bounds. No wonder there are some who refuse to consider his *Leaves* as 'literature.' It is perhaps only because he was brought up a printer, and worked during his early years as newspaper and magazine writer, that he has put his expression in typographical form, and made a regular book of it, with lines, leaves and binding.

—George Selwyn, "Walt Whitman at Camden,"
Critic, February 28, 1885, p. 98

CHARLES F. RICHARDSON (1887)

In absolute ability he is about equal to Taylor, Stoddard, Stedman, or Aldrich; but by minimizing the spiritual and the artistic, and magnifying the physical and the crudely spontaneous, he has attracted an attention among critics in America, England, and the Continental nations greater, for the moment, than that bestowed upon any contemporary singer of his nation, and fairly rivalling the international adulation of his exact opposite, Poe. To him the ideal is little and the immediately actual is much; love is merely a taurine or passerine passion; and to-day is a thing more important than all the past. His courage is unquestionable; his vigor is abounding; and therefore, by the very paradox of his extravagant demands, he has impressed some and interested more, and has induced a limited but affectionate and exceedingly vociferous coterie to attempt, for his sake, to revise the entire canon of the world's art. Many famous authors have bestowed upon him high praise—sometimes revoked or ignored in the calmer years of advancing life; and though unread by the masses whose spokesman and prophet he claims to be, and without special influence or increasing potency, he has been for a generation one of the most conspicuous of his country's authors.

—Charles F. Richardson, *American Literature,*
1607–1885, 1887, Vol. 2, p. 269

ALGERNON CHARLES SWINBURNE "WHITMANIA" (1887)

In this scathingly satirical essay, which repudiates Swinburne's earlier praise of Whitman, the British poet and critic condemns the newest generation of Whitman admirers—whom he accuses of "Whitmania"—for daring to rank Whitman among such great poets as Shakespeare, Milton, Dante, Homer, and Aeschylus. Swinburne finds this effort to place Whitman in the canon of world literature more troublesome than the absolute praise offered by Whitman's earliest admirers, who either believed Whitman a prophet rather than a poet, or felt that Whitman's poetry was the only true poetry ever to have been written, and therefore disqualified all other writers from comparison. In the later portion of the essay, Swinburne identifies Whitman's goodness, noble attitude toward death, attention to nature, and rhetorical sweep as the strengths of his poetry, yet argues that none of these adequately substitutes for the precision of matter and manner expected of "the science of verse."

In his study *William Blake* (1868), Swinburne had compared Whitman favorably to the Romantic poet/artist William Blake for the freshness of his writing. Over time, though, he came to criticize Whitman's formal looseness, suggesting it ultimately impeded the subject matter. Swinburne's essay echoes earlier criticisms of Whitman's verse: that it is metrically (and therefore artistically) deficient, that its moments of heroic beauty are overshadowed by a prevailing vague optimism, and that it substitutes oratorical bravado for rigorous thought. But Swinburne's analysis of the social phenomenon of "Whitmania" raises important questions about the figure of the poet in nineteenth-century popular culture and the influence of popular culture on the literary canon, or set of literary works generally regarded as having the most enduring value. Swinburne likens Whitman to the English Romantic poet Lord Byron, a notorious but nevertheless fascinating public figure whose work Swinburne disparages and whose continued repute perplexes him. The issue of artistic celebrity then leads to a discussion of aesthetics, Swinburne asserting that the manner of a poem (including its meter, tone, and decorousness) outweighs its subject matter. Thus, while Swinburne does not reject Whitman's decision to write about the human body in all its physicality, he finds Whitman's treatment of the body to be an "unhealthily demonstrative and obtrusive animalism."

This excerpt might urge readers to compare a poem of Swinburne's to one of Whitman's to clarify their formal differences, or readers might compare examples of both writers' poetic treatment of sexual and bodily experience to ascertain their different notions of decorum. Students might also compare the grounds for Swinburne's repudiation of Whitman with Emerson's, particularly the latter's advice that Whitman excise the "Children of Adam" section from his 1860 edition of *Leaves of Grass*. Finally, if considering the issue of artistic celebrity, readers might explore the extent to which Swinburne, himself a somewhat notorious figure, sustained rather than reduced Whitman's public acclaim through this repudiation.

The remarkable American rhapsodist who has inoculated a certain number of English readers and writers with the singular form of ethical and aesthetic rabies for which his name supplies the proper medical term of definition is usually regarded by others than Whitmaniacs as simply a blatant quack—a vehement and emphatic dunce, of incomparable vanity and volubility, inconceivable pretentions, and incompetence. That such is by no means altogether my own view I need scarcely take the trouble to protest. Walt Whitman has written some pages to which I have before now given praise enough to exonerate me, I should presume, from any charge of prejudice or prepossession against a writer whose claims to occasional notice and occasional respect no man can be less desirous to dispute than I am. Nor should I have thought it necessary to comment on the symptoms of a disorder which happily is not likely to become epidemic in an island or on a continent not utterly barren of poetry, had the sufferers not given such painfully singular signs of inability to realize a condition only too obvious to the compassionate bystander. While the preachers or the proselytes of the gospel according to Whitman were content to admit that he was either no poet at all, or the only poet who had ever been born into this world—that those who accepted him were bound to reject all others as nullities—they had at least the merit of irrefragable logic; they could claim at least the credit of indisputable consistency. But when other gods or godlings are accepted as participants in the divine nature; when his temple is transformed into a pantheon, and a place assigned his godhead a little beneath Shakespeare, a little above Dante, or cheek by jowl with Homer; when Isaiah and Æschylus, for anything we know, may be admitted to a greater or lesser share in his incommunicable and indivisible supremacy— then, indeed, it is high time to enter a strenuous and (if it be possible) a serious protest. The first apostles alone were the depositaries of the pure and perfect evangel: these later and comparatively heterodox disciples have adulterated and debased the genuine metal of absolute, coherent, unalloyed and unqualifed nonsense.

To the better qualities discernible in the voluminous and incoherent effusions of Walt Whitman it should not be difficult for any reader not unduly exasperated by the rabid idiocy of the Whitmaniacs to do full and ample justice: for these qualities are no less simple and obvious than laudable and valuable. A just enthusiasm, a genuine passion of patriotic and imaginative sympathy, a sincere though limited and distorted love of nature, an eager and earnest faith in freedom and in loyalty—in the loyalty that can only be born of liberty; a really manful and a nobly rational tone of mind with regard to the crowning questions of duty and of death; these excellent qualities of emotion and reflection find here and there a not inadequate expression in a style of rhetoric not always flatulent or inharmonious. Originality of matter or of manner, of structure or of thought, it would be equally difficult for any reader not endowed with a quite exceptional gift of ignorance or of hebetude to discover in any part of Mr. Whitman's political or ethical or physical or proverbial philosophy. But he has said wise and noble things upon such simple and eternal subjects as life and death, pity and enmity, friendship and fighting; and even the intensely conventional nature of its elaborate and artificial simplicity should not be allowed, by a magnanimous and candid reader, too absolutely to eclipse the genuine energy and the occasional beauty of his feverish and convulsive style of writing.

All this may be cordially conceded by the lovers of good work in any kind, however imperfect, incomposite, and infirm; and more than this the present writer at any rate most assuredly never intended to convey by any tribute of sympathy or admiration which may have earned for him the wholly unmerited honour of an imaginary enlistment in the noble army of Whitmaniacs. He has therefore no palinode to chant, no recantation to intone; for if it seems and is unreasonable to attribute a capacity of thought to one who has never given any sign of thinking, a faculty of song to one who has never shown ability to sing, it must be remembered, on the other hand, that such qualities of energetic emotion and sonorous expression as distinguish the happier moments and the more sincere inspirations of such writers as Whitman or as Byron have always, in common parlance, been allowed to pass muster and do duty for the faculty of thinking or the capacity of singing. Such a use of common terms is doubtless inaccurate and inexact, if judged by the "just but severe law" of logical definition or of mathematical precision: but such abuse or misuse of plain words is generally understood as conveying no more than a conventional import such as may be expressed by the terms with which we subscribe an ordinary letter, or by the formula through which we decline an untimely visit. Assuredly I never have meant to imply what most assuredly I never have said—that I regarded Mr. Whitman as a poet or a thinker in the proper sense; the sense in which the one term is applicable to Coleridge or to Shelley, the other to Bacon or to Mill. Whoever may have abdicated his natural right, as a being not born without a sense of music or a sense of reason, to protest against the judgment which discerns in *Childe Harold* or in *Drum-Taps* a masterpiece of imagination and expression, of intelligence or of song, I never have abdicated mine. The highest literary quality discoverable in either book is rhetoric: and very excellent rhetoric in either case it sometimes is; what it is at other times I see no present necessity to say. But Whitmaniacs and Byronites have yet to learn that if rhetoric were poetry John Bright would be a poet at least equal to John Milton, Demosthenes to Sophocles, and Cicero to Catullus. Poetry may be something more—I certainly am not concerned to deny it—than an art or a science; but not because it is not, stricly speaking, a science or an art. There is a science of verse as surely as there is a science of mathematics: there is an art of expression by metre as certainly as there is an art of representation by painting. To some poets the understanding of this science, the mastery of this art, would seem to come by a natural instinct which needs nothing but practice for its development, its application, and its perfection: others by patient and conscientious study of their own abilities attain a no less unmistakable and a scarcely less admirable success. But the man of genius and the dullard who cannot write good verse are equally out of the running. "Did you ask dulcet rhymes from me?" inquires Mr. Whitman of some extraordinary if not imaginary interlocutor; and proceeds, with some not ineffective energy of expression, to explain that "I lull nobody—and you will never understand me." No, my dear good sir—or camerado, if that be the more courteous and conventional address (a modest reader might deferentially reply): not in the wildest visions of a distempered slumber could I ever have dreamed of doing anything of the kind. Nor do we ask them even from such other and inferior scribes or bards as the humble Homer, the modest Milton, or the obsolete and narrow-minded Shakespeare— poets of sickly feudality, of hidebound classicism, of effete and barbarous incompetence. But metre, rhythm, cadence not merely appreciable but definable and reducible to rule and measurement, though we do not expect from you, we demand from all who claim, we discern in the works of all who have achieved, any place among poets of any class whatsoever. The question whether your work is in any sense poetry has no more to do with dulcet rhymes than with the differential calculus. The question is whether you have any more right to call yourself a poet, or to be called a poet by any man who knows verse from prose, or black from white, or speech from silence, or his right hand from his left, than to call yourself or to be called, on the strength of your published writings, a mathematician, a logician, a painter, a political economist, a sculptor, a dynamiter, an old parliamentary hand, a civil engineer, a dealer in marine stores, an amphimacer, a triptych, a rhomboid, or a rectangular parallelogram. "Vois-tu bien, tu es baron comme ma pantoufle!" said old Gillenormand—the creature of one who was indeed a creator or a poet: and the humblest of critics who knows any one thing from any one other thing has a right to say to the man who offers as poetry what the exuberant incontinence of a Whitman presents for our acceptance—"Tu es poete comme mon—soulier."

But the student has other and better evidence than any merely negative indication of impotence in the case of the American as in the case of the British despiser and disclaimer of so pitiful a profession or ambition as that of a versifier. Mr. Carlyle and Mr. Whitman have both been good enough to try their hands at lyric verse: and the ear which has once absorbed their dulcet rhymes will never need to be reminded of the reason for their contemptuous abhorrence of a diversion so contemptible as the art of Coleridge and Shelley.

Out of eternity
  This new day is born:
Into eternity
  This day shall return.

Such were the flute-notes of Diogenes Devilsdung: comparable by those who would verify the value of his estimate with any stanza of Shelley's "To a Skylark." And here is a sample of the dulcet rhymes which a most tragic occasion succeeded in evoking from the orotund oratist of Manhattan.

The port is near, the bells I hear, the people all
exulting,
While follow eyes the steady keel, the vessel grim
and daring; . . .

For you bouquets and ribbon'd wreaths—for you the
shores a-crowding; (sic)
For you they call, the surging mass, their eager faces
turning.

Ἰοὺ ἰοὺ ὢ ὢ κακά. Upon the whole, I prefer Burns—or Hogg—to Carlyle, and Dibdin—or Catnach—to Whitman.

A pedantic writer of poems distilled from other poems (which, as the immortal author of the imperishable *Leaves of Grass* is well aware, must "pass away")—a Wordsworth, for example, or a Tennyson—would hardly have made "eyes" follow the verb they must be supposed to govern. Nor would a poor creature whose ear was yet unattuned to the cadence of "chants democratic" have permitted his Pegasus so remarkable a capriole as to result in the rhythmic reverberation of such rhymes as these. When a boy who remains unable after many efforts to cross the Asses' Bridge expresses his opinion that Euclid was a beastly old fool, his obviously impartial verdict is generally received by his elders with exactly the same amount of respectful attention as is accorded by any competent reader to the equally valuable and judicial deliverances of Messrs. Whitman, Emerson, and Carlyle on the subject of poetry—that is, of lyrical or creative literature. The first critic of our time—perhaps the largest-minded and surest-sighted of any age—has pointed out, in an essay on poetry which should not be too long left buried in the columns of the *Encyclopaedia Britannica,* the exhaustive accuracy of the Greek terms which define every claimant to the laurel as either a singer or a maker. There is no third term, as there is no third class. If then it appears that Mr. Walt Whitman has about as much gift of song as his precursors and apparent models in rhythmic structure and style, Mr. James

Macpherson and Mr. Martin Tupper, his capacity for creation is the only thing that remains for us to consider. And on that score we find him, beyond all question, rather like the later than like the earlier of his masters. Macpherson could at least evoke shadows: Mr. Tupper and Mr. Whitman can only accumulate words. As to his originality in the matter of free speaking, it need only be observed that no remarkable mental gift is requisite to qualify man or woman for membership of a sect mentioned by Dr. Johnson—the Adamites, who believed in the virtue of public nudity. If those worthies claimed the right to bid their children run about the streets stark naked, the magistrate, observed Johnson, "would have a right to flog them into their doublets;" a right no plainer than the right of common sense and sound criticism to flog the Whitmaniacs into their strait-waistcoats; or, were there any female members of such a sect, into their strait-petticoats. If nothing that concerns the physical organism of men or of women is common or unclean or improper for literary manipulation, it may be maintained, by others than the disciples of a contemporary French novelist who has amply proved the sincerity of his own opinion to that effect, that it is not beyond the province of literature to describe with realistic exuberance of detail the functions of digestion or indigestion in all its processes—the objects and the results of an aperient or an emetic medicine. Into "the troughs of Zolaism," as Lord Tennyson calls them (a phrase which bears rather unduly hard on the quadrupedal pig), I am happy to believe that Mr. Whitman has never dipped a passing nose: he is a writer of something occasionally like English, and a man of something occasionally like genius. But in his treatment of topics usually regarded as no less unfit for public exposition and literary illustration than those which have obtained notoriety for the would-be bastard of Balzac—the Davenant of the (French) prose Shakespeare, he has contrived to make "the way of a man with a maid" (Proverbs xxx. 19) almost as loathsomely ludicrous and almost as ludicrously loathsome— I speak merely of the aesthetic or literary aspect of his effusions—as the Swiftian or Zolaesque enthusiasm of bestiality which insists on handling what "goeth into the belly, and is cast out into the draught" (St. Mark xv. 17). The Zolas and the Whitmen, to whom nothing, absolutely and literally nothing, is unclean or common, have an obvious and incalculable advantage over the unconverted who have never enjoyed the privilege of a vision like St. Peter's, and received the benefit of a supernatural prohibition to call anything common or unclean. They cannot possibly be exposed, and they cannot possibly be put to shame: for that best of all imaginable reasons which makes it proverbially difficult to "take the breeks off a Highlander."

It would really seem as though, in literary and other matters, the very plainness and certitude of a principle made it doubly necessary for those who maintain it to enforce and reinforce it over and over again; as though, the more obvious it were, the more it needed indication and demonstration, assertion and reassertion. There is no more important, no more radical and fundamental truth of criticism than this: that, in poetry perhaps above all other arts, the method of treatment, the manner of touch, the tone of expression, is the first and last thing to be considered. There is no subject which may not be treated with success (I do not say there are no subjects which on other than artistic grounds it may not be as well to avoid, it may not be better to pass by) if the poet, by instinct or by training, knows exactly how to handle it aright, to present it without danger of just or rational offence. For evidence of this truth we need look no further than the pastorals of Virgil and Theocritus. But under the dirty clumsy paws of a harper whose plectrum is a muck-rake any tune will become a chaos of discords, though the motive of the tune should be the first principle of nature—the passion of man for woman or the passion of woman for man. And the unhealthily demonstrative and obtrusive animalism of the Whitmaniad is as unnatural, as incompatible with the wholesome instincts of human passion, as even the filthy and inhuman asceticism of SS. Macarius and Simeon Stylites. If anything can justify the serious and deliberate display of merely physical emotion in literature or in art, it must be one of two things: intense depth of feeling expressed with inspired perfection of simplicity, with divine sublimity of fascination, as by Sappho; or transcendant supremacy of actual and irresistible beauty in such revelation of naked nature as was possible to Titian. But Mr. Whitman's Eve is a drunken apple-woman, indecently sprawling in the slush and garbage of the gutter amid the rotten refuse of her overturned fruit-stall: but Mr. Whitman's Venus is a Hottentot wench under the influence of cantharides and adulterated rum. Cotytto herself would repudiate the ministration of such priestesses as these.

But what then, if anything, is it that a rational creature who has studied and understood the work of any poet, great or small, from Homer down to Moschus, from Lucretius down to Martial, from Dante down to Metastasio, from Villon down to Voltaire, from Shakespeare down to Byron, can find to applaud, to approve, or to condone in the work of Mr. Whitman? To this very reasonable and inevitable question the answer is not far to seek. I have myself repeatedly pointed out—it may be (I have often been told so) with too unqualified sympathy and too uncritical enthusiasm—the qualities which give a certain touch of greatness to his work, the sources of inspiration which infuse into its chaotic jargon some passing or seeming notes of cosmic beauty, and diversify with something of occasional harmony the strident and barren discord of its jarring and erring atoms. His sympathies, I repeat, are usually generous, his views of life are occasionally just, and his views of death are invariably noble. In other words, he generally means well, having a good stock on hand of honest emotion; he sometimes sees well, having a natural sensibility to such aspects of nature as appeal to an eye rather quick than penetrating; he seldom writes well, being cabined, cribbed, confined, bound in, to the limits of a thoroughly unnatural, imitative, histrionic and affected style. But there is a thrilling and fiery force in his finest bursts of gusty rhetoric which makes us wonder whether with a little more sense and a good deal more cultivation he might not have made a noticeable orator. As a poet, no amount of improvement that self-knowledge and self-culture might have brought to bear upon such exceptionally raw material could ever have raised him higher than a station to which his homely and manly patriotism would be the best claim that could be preferred for him; a seat beside such writers as Ebenezer Elliot—or possibly a little higher, on such an elevation as might be occupied by a poet whom careful training had reared and matured into a rather inferior kind of Southey. But to fit himself for such promotion he would have in the first place to resign all claim to the laurels of Gotham, with which the critical sages of that famous borough have bedecked his unbashful brows; he would have to recognise that he is no more, in the proper sense of the word, a poet, than Communalists or Dissolutionists are, in any sense of the word, Republicans; that he has exactly as much claim to a place beside Dante as any Vermersch or Vermorel or other verminous and murderous muckworm of the Parisian Commune to a place beside Mazzini: in other words, that the informing principle of his work is not so much the negation as the contradiction of the creative principle of poetry. And this it is not to be expected that such a man should bring himself to believe, as long as he hears himself proclaimed the inheritor of a seat assigned a hundred years ago by the fantastic adulation of more or less distinguished literary eccentrics to a person of the name of Jephson—whose triumphs as a tragic poet made his admirers tremble for Shakespeare.

—Algernon Charles Swinburne, "Whitmania,"
Fortnightly Review, August 1887, pp. 170–76

OLIVER ELTON (1890)

Could there be a greater, and apparently more dismal, paradox than the sight of the seer of democracy sitting serene under the total neglect of the democracy? If anything could bely the faith of the *Democratic Vistas,* if anything could make one think the loud energetic civilisation of America nothing but a gigantic imposture, it is the spectacle of the only great living American poet dependent in his old age upon the sympathy—and at one moment almost upon the maintenance—of foreign friends. And yet he keeps his faith in the faithless people unshaken, for it is not at the mercy of personal neglect or personal discomfort; and, if he is right in his robust belief, surely the solution of the paradox lies in the meaning of that much-abused word the "people." The "people" in whom his confidence burns so unquenchably are not the rich people, not the millions of wire-pullers and place-hunters, not the spurious *elite* of culture, but the mass of the people, who know little of Whitman and his books, or of any books, who labour obscurely, manfully, and restlessly, who represent the vast sum-total of energy comparable to the energies of nature herself—the mass of the people whose force and fertility are independent of all possible vicissitudes in institutions.

Mr. Ellis's account of this great poet is probably the best that has been supplied by anyone except the poet himself. There is but one departure from sobriety—a sufficiently startling one—in almost his first words. "Whitman," he says, "has been placed while yet alive by the side of the world's greatest teachers, beside Jesus and Socrates." Who said this is not stated; but it would be small honour to be canonised by a person who could perpetrate such a comparison. This is the sole extravagance in the whole essay; but it is not the only thing that will arouse resentment in the orthodox breast. The large number of persons who are blinded to Whitman's genius by the incidental nakedness of his writing would do well to ponder Mr. Ellis's most apposite contrast in this particular of Whitman with Swift. Swift regarded men and women not only as beasts, but as lower than other beasts, on account of the grotesque hypocrisy which leads them to muffle up their beasthood under decorous names; and this mask his dire indignation and misapplied sincerity impelled him ruthlessly to strip off. There is all the legacy of mediaeval body-hatred in the portrait of the Yahoo; and Swift is a Christian *manque*. Whitman is a pagan, and takes his nudity as sanely as he does everything else. Neither writer is likely to hurt any healthy and grown person; it is the thin and eager minds, the erotic mystics, who really have the "seminal principle in their brains," not these burly and virile spirits. Where many of Whitman's poems fall short is, in one word, in *Art*. That is a sufficiently fatal shortcoming, and one which avenges itself speedily by the extinction of the peccant work. Whitman's capacity for inspiration, for prophecy, and for hope is very far ahead of his literary sense; he wrestles with difficulties of expression and construction, and constantly succumbs before them. Now and then he conquers; and an immortal flower of verse is born like

Warble me now for joy of lilac-time,

or like "Captain! my Captain!" Some, therefore, of the poetry, or rhythmic prose, which contains certain of Whitman's farthest-reaching thought, is artistically faulty; and Mr. Ellis, as befits his somewhat doctrinal purpose, puts aside the question of Whitman's poetic accomplishment, and is engrossed rather with inquiring what creed he can extract from him.

—Oliver Elton, *Academy,* April 5, 1890, p. 231

Robert G. Ingersoll
"Liberty in Literature" (1890)

Yes, Walt Whitman has appeared. He has his place upon the stage. The drama is not ended. His voice is still heard. He is the Poet of Democracy—of all people. He is the poet of the body and soul. He has sounded the note of Individuality. He has given the pass-word primeval. He is the Poet of Humanity—of Intellectual Hospitality. He has voiced the aspirations of America—and, above all, he is the poet of Love and Death.

—Robert G. Ingersoll, "Liberty in Literature" (1890),
In Re Walt Whitman, eds. Horace L. Traubel,
Richard Maurice Bucke, Thomas B. Harned, 1893, p. 281

William Clarke (1892)

When beginning his self-imposed task, Whitman appears to have been staggered by the vastness of his own conceptions. The view was so extensive, the distance was so great, the sights that could be seen, and the tendencies that were unseen, so overwhelming, that the poet was intoxicated by the vision. He lacked, too, discrimination and art. He had absorbed divine influences from past thinkers, but he had no sense of the laws of style, or, indeed, the sense that there were any laws. Hence, the sometimes—one might be induced to say, the frequent—formless lines, and the attempts to produce effects which no great artist would have employed. The poet was unable, through lack of literary culture, to clothe his novel and often glowing conceptions in any ideal poetic form. Rather he flings his ideas at us in a heap, leaving it to us to arrange them in order in our own minds. His results, therefore, fail to satisfy many not unsympathetic readers. And yet of these results Mr. Havelock Ellis has truly said that "they have at times something of the divine felicity, unforeseen and incalculable, of Nature; yet always, according to a rough but convenient distinction, it is the poetry of energy rather than the poetry of art. When Whitman speaks prose, the language of science, he is frequently incoherent, emotional, unbalanced, with no very just and precise sense of the meaning or words, or the structure of reasoned language."

But it may be fairly argued whether, when he began to write, Whitman did not gain immensely from this imperfect artistic form. He in some sense carried on the tradition of English literature in some of its most virile representatives; which, as has been well said by one of our greatest critics, is a literature of power, as contrasted with the French literature of intelligence. And, further, Whitman the more faithfully expressed the life of his own nation, the very character of his own continent. America had scarcely arrived, has hardly arrived yet, at any consciousness of her true life. She is the land of beginnings and tendencies, her very physical aspect is shaggy and unshorn. She is like a vast edifice, only half finished, with the scaffolding up, and the litter of masonry all round. An American lady is said to have asked a gardener in one of the beautiful Oxford quadrangles, how a lawn could be brought to such a condition of perfection as the emerald turf she saw before her. The reply was, "If you roll and water it regularly for about three centuries you will get such results as you see here." America, with her brief history, rush of immigrants, and dominating materialism, has not been able to reach the artistic repose, the placid beauty to which we are accustomed in Western Europe. Had Whitman lived in an atmosphere of such repose; had he been brought up on European culture, he could only at best have added to the kind of work which Longfellow and Irving did so well. In that case he could not have been the voice of this great, rough, virile America, with its "powerful uneducated persons," of whom the cultivated Bostonian authors knew no more than they did of the working-classes of Europe. The very value of Whitman, then, is that he is a genuine American bard. In the conditions of his life and work must be found the justification of his method. His writings contain the promise and potency of future greatness; and he makes no claim for them beyond that they are the first rough draft of a great American literature.

—William Clarke, *Walt Whitman*, 1892, pp. 50–52

Harriet Monroe "A Word about
Walt Whitman" (1892)

Critic, scholar, and founding editor of the major modern American literary journal *Poetry*, Harriet Monroe profoundly influenced American poetry in the twentieth century. This essay, an appreciation of Whitman written in the year of the poet's death, surveys many key issues and debates
related to Whitman's poetry during his lifetime. Monroe discusses the
ironic nature of Whitman's audience, noting that his democratically
themed poetry is admired by a small minority of American intellectual
elite and more generally by the English public, but ignored by most ordinary American readers, who favor such traditional poets as Longfellow
and Whittier. She suggests that the prejudice against Whitman stems
not only from his rejection of traditional poetic decorum, but largely
from the way his energetic free verse reflects the country's pioneering
past, a past shameful to America during the Gilded Age, when the newly
wealthy country tried to measure itself against standards and models
set by European society. Monroe argues that Whitman's poetry is not
art, for art excludes all that is trivial and fleeting in its quest for truth,
while Whitman's inclusive imagination creates work with "all the exact
faithfulness of an inventory." Yet she claims that such amplitude gives his
poetry a greatness unlike any other creation, one which future American
artists will draw on as they craft their own art. In the twentieth century,
Monroe claims, this great inclusiveness will attract later generations to
Whitman's poetry, where they will find relief in "his open-air honesty
and moral ruggedness" and glean insight into the energy and spirit that
founded America. Given her influential editorial role, Monroe's essay
invites study of the response of modern poets, particularly those Monroe
published (Ezra Pound, T.S. Eliot, and Wallace Stevens), to Whitman's
poetry, whether in essays or poems.

—⁓⁓— —⁓⁓— —⁓⁓—

The persistence of prejudice is illustrated by various phases of Walt
Whitman's reputation at home and abroad. In spite of the appreciative
sympathy of fellow-poets who feel the wide swing of his imagination and
the force of its literary expression, in spite of the tardy acknowledgments
of critics who have gradually learned to find power and melody in some
of his rugged verse, it cannot be said that the venerable bard is widely
honored in his own country. Songs which celebrate the toils and pleasures
of the masses have thus far found small audience among the common

people of the nation, being read chiefly by the cultivated few. Aristocratic rhymesters, weavers of triolets and madrigals, have reached a greater number of humble homes than this prophet of democracy, and the toilers of the land care more for jingles than for the barbaric majesty of his irregular measures. The poet of the people is neglected by the people, while the works of scholarly singers like Longfellow and Bryant find a place in every farmer's library.

Humanity does not enjoy the scientific method of reasoning from facts to theories, preferring unphilosophically to adjust the facts to its preconceived ideas. In this country we are proud of the swift conquests of civilization, and too willing to forget the free simplicity and uncouth heroism of pioneer times. We boast of our borrowed culture and keep our truly great achievements in the background. We look forward to a powerful future and too often obliterate the memory of a valiant past, allowing details to slip unrecorded into oblivion which might serve as the foundation of epics as majestic as Homer's. Reason about it as we will, Americans have an instinctive feeling that the formative period of the national character should be out of sight and out of mind as soon as possible, so that our virgin republic may at once take a place of assured wisdom among the gray and hardened dames of the old world, decked like them with the splendid trophies of twenty centuries of civilization.

Walt Whitman tries to arrest this ill-directed current of false vanity, to reveal to the nation her true glory of physical and moral prowess, to unveil a superb figure of strong and courageous youth playing a new part in the world with all of youth's tameless energy and daring. He finds her achievements beautiful and heroic, worthy to be celebrated and immortalized by art, and feels that the adornments of culture and civilization must be gradually wrought out from her own consciousness, not imitated from outworn models or adopted ready-made. Thus he strives to discard from his singing all the incidents of American life which are not indigenous to American soil, bringing himself closely in contact with the primeval elements of nature and man.

> Long I roamed the woods of the North—long I
>   watched Niagara pouring;
> I travelled the prairies over, and slept on their
>   breast—I crossed the Nevadas, I crossed the plateaus;
> I ascended the towering rocks along the Pacific, I
>   sailed out to sea;
> I sailed through the storm, I was refreshed by the
>   storm.

Then from the majesty of ocean and plain to the higher majesty of cities:—

> What, to pavements and homesteads here—what
>   were those storms of the mountains and sea?
> What, to passions I witness around me to-day, was
>   the sea risen?

The glory of cataracts and thunders, of crowds and wars, appeals to him for utterance, and with the scrupulous loyalty of a true poet he does his utmost to answer the call. Whether his answer is adequate or not, we must honor his fidelity. The spirit of modern criticism becomes too finical, too much a command that the aspirant should fling away ambition, should be content with pleasant little valleys, and avoid the unexplored heights where precipices and avalanches threaten to destroy. This spirit is a blight upon all high endeavor, and he who resists it and travels upward, even though he fall exhausted by the wayside, achieves a nobler success than a thousand petty triumphs could have brought him.

It is too soon for the world to decide how far this barbaric poet has fulfilled his mission. At present the mass of his countrymen brush aside his writings with a gesture of contempt, finding there what they most wish to forget—a faithful reflection of the rudeness, the unsettled vastness, the formlessness of an epoch out of which much of our country has hardly yet emerged. But theirs is not the final verdict; their desire to be credited with all the decorative embellishments which older states enjoy may yield when ours shall have won these ornaments and learned to regret the old unadorned strength and simplicity. Races which have passed their youth appreciate these vigorous qualities, which put them once more in touch with primitive nature, with the morning, with the wisdom of children, which is, after all, the serenest wisdom. Thus in England Walt Whitman's singing has thus far been more effectual than at home. There his work humors the prepossessions of the people, who find in him the incarnation of young democracy. To minds puzzled by the formality of other American poets, by Longfellow's academic precision, Whittier's use of time-worn measures, and Poe's love of rich orchestral effects of rhythm, Whitman's scorn of prosodical rules and of the accepted limitations of artistic decorum brings the revelation of something new in the brown old world. They greet him as a poet fresh from the wilds of which, to their persistent ignorance, both Americas are still made up. To them his songs seem as free and trackless as his native prairies, revealing once more the austerity and joyousness of primeval nature, so different from their elaborate civilization. It is possible that the next century of our own national life may find the same relief in his open-air honesty and moral ruggedness. It may turn to him to gain ideal comprehension of the forces which peopled this continent and redeemed its wastes from barrenness. His poetry is unruly and formless, but so were the times it mirrors—no harmony of fulfilment, but a chaos of forces struggling and toiling together for the evolution of a great nation. He sweeps the continent and gathers up all he finds, good, bad and indifferent, serenely conscious that to omniscience all is good, that to omnipotence all is important. The result is not art, perhaps; for art chooses and combines, gives form and life and color to nature's elements of truth. Art realizes the limitations of our finite humanity, appreciates our poverty of time for the multitudinous objects of thought, and indulgently omits all that is trivial and inessential from her epitome of truth. What does not emphasize she discards; to her fine judgment an hundred details serve but to weaken the force of one. Thus Walt Whitman may never be called an artist. What he finds he gives us with all the exact faithfulness of an inventory. In the mass of his discoveries there is much that is precious, many a treasure of rare and noble beauty; but its beauty is that of rich quartz, of uncut jewels, rather than that of the coin and the cameo. He offers us a collection of specimens from the splendid laboratory of nature. It will scarcely be strange if the future guards them in cabinets instead of circulating them far and wide among the people.

—Harriet Monroe, "A Word about Walt Whitman," *Critic*, April 16, 1892, p. 231

PAULINE W. ROOSE
"A CHILD-POET: WALT WHITMAN" (1892)

In this essay, Roose characterizes Whitman as a child-poet, whose independence from the refined constraints of civilization allows his imagination to create "miracles and transformations." Her description accords with Romantic notions of the poet as child, as divinely inspired, and as being a product of nature. While Roose focuses on Whitman's nature imagery, her highest praise is reserved for his treatment of the theme of mortality. Comparing him indirectly to the Roman emperor and Stoic philosopher Marcus Aurelius, Roose argues that Whitman "is too sure of his own identity to be afraid of ever losing it," and she praises his child-like certainty concerning the soul's immortality. Similar assurances of

immortality abound in literature and religion, but for Roose, Whitman's
most important function is to explore and explain the passage from life
to death and to purify that passage's foreboding associations.

His imagination being of a character at once wild and practical, he exhibits
the most fantastic notions in a matter-of-fact manner, as if they were nothing
out of the way. With a child's spirit of wilful self-deception he tries to beguile
himself into the belief that the birds in his favourite haunts sing and fly about
for his especial benefit, and repays such of them as have mainly contributed to
his comfort with the dedication of a part of one of his books; nor them only,
but likewise a whole array of trees and insects, amid whose motley crew the
mosquitoes are honoured by particular mention. Nor is he by any means sure
but that those queer allies of his will somehow get wind of the compliment. In
a sublimer mood he has fancied the ocean and the daylight, the mountain
and the forest, putting their spirit in judgment on our writings.

Independently of all witchcraft and fairy lore, he can create for himself
the very miracles and transformations of which the little ones are always
dreaming. The old woodland kings, in his belief, hold great thoughts,
which they drop down upon him as he passes beneath them. There was a
small boy who once prayed that God would make the trees walk. This very
conceit was almost realised by the vivid fancy of Walt Whitman, who, in
a "sort of dream-trance," as he calls it, beheld his favourite trees "step out
and promenade up, down, and around, very curiously—with a whisper
from one, leaning down as he passed me: 'We do all this on the present
occasion, exceptionally, just for you.'" That they could do it if they chose
seems indeed to be his deliberate opinion.

Children are notably devoid of humour, and in Whitman that quality is
conspicuous by its absence. Who, however, better than children—or than
Whitman—can appeal to the humour of others? There is something touching
in the unconsciousness with which he lays himself open to the sneers of
whoever may be willing to avail himself of the opportunity. His sense of fun,
of which he has his full share, never interferes with the most preposterous
statements on his own part, even while he allows no oddity of life nor
any ludicrous effect of nature to escape him. Of what has been called the
cockneyism of the nineteenth century not a trace is to be found in him, nor
of the modern smartness and indifference. He cannot content himself with
superficial views any more than childhood can be put off with the flippant
answers which grown-up persons of a certain calibre amuse themselves by

returning to its earnest questionings. Life to him is not a speculation nor a "bon-mot." He does not profess to know what it is, "except that it is grand, and that it is happiness"; also (and this above all), that it is never ending, and that death will make no very appreciable difference in it.

"I have dreamed," he says, with one of those sudden startling glimpses which he is in the habit of flashing, not only backward upon the past but onward into the future, "that we are not to be changed so much, nor the law of us changed."

Amid what to others might seem the most appalling, most annihilating discoveries in science, he moves familiarly as in his old paternal homestead, and finds in them the wholesomest nutriment for his dreams of universal joy and immortality. For it is not in his relations to earth alone that he maintains his trustful attitude. A child of the universe, he can not only look with unflinching gaze at the sun in its noon-day splendour, but he loves also to blend himself with the shadows, to creep into the very heart of midnight, that he may come upon the "budding morrow" there, and discover it to others. For of the child no less than of the philosopher it is a distinctive attribute to be everywhere at home. With his unbiassed spiritual vision he can discern, through all the perplexities of life, that "divine clue and unseen thread which holds the whole congeries of things, all history and time, and all events, however trivial, however momentous, like a leashed dog in the hand of the hunter." The "ultimate perfecton" toward which all, according to his judgment, are tending, links everything, from the lowest to the highest, together in one unbroken chain:

> All, all for immortality,
> Love like the light silently wrapping all,
> Nature's amelioration blessing all.

"Is it a dream?" he pauses in his rapt soliloquy to ask:

> Nay, but the lack of it the dream,
> And failing it life's lore and wealth a dream,
> And all the world a dream.

His thoughts, like those of the old philosophers (or *philosophs,* as, with his peculiar partiality for the suggestion of something foreign in a word, he calls them), flit from present to past and back again with sympathetic quickness. Many a passage, indeed, from Marcus Aurelius in particular, in its unadorned enumeration of things passing under his notice, its unexpected rapid turns of observation and keen appreciation of effect, might have been penned—all but the moral—by Walt Whitman. The poet of to-day, in very much the manner of the Imperial philosopher of old, is given to reflect how all those who have gone before, who have "feasted and married, and were sick and chaffered, and fought, and flattered, and plotted, and grumbled . . . are dead; and all the idle people who are doing the same thing now are doomed to die." Only Whitman cannot reconcile himself, as did the Emperor of old, to the thought of man's nothingness; that oblivion is to swallow up all him and his:

> O, I know that those men and women were not for
>   nothing, any more than we are for nothing. . . .
> I believe of all those men and women that filled the
>   unnamed lands, everyone exists this hour here
>   or elsewhere, invisible to us.

He will not believe that seventy years, "nor that seventy millions of years" (with a child's love of large impressions), is the span of human life. He is too sure of his own identity to be afraid of ever losing it. Nor in his eyes do the most fleeting, the most insignificant of things appear ephemeral and worthless. The music of humanity is by no means still and sad to him; there is no lost chord in its harmonies. Past, present, and to-come are blent in one bright, invigorating strain of trust and promise. His is the optimism of a child, as different from the shallow, unreal hopes with which some are able to content themselves as the void Nirvana is from Paradise. He clings to present possessions, and would have nothing but the merest accidents of evil done away with, if even them; for Whitman has all the defects of his quality, amongst which inconsistency is by no means least. Emerson's doctrine that what is excellent is permanent does not suffice for him. Opinions differ as to what is excellent. Things which to some may not come within that definition belong, with others, to their hopes of heaven. Now and then, with something of that vague, unspeakable reluctance peculiar almost to childhood, he will entertain the possibility of his being deceived. Amid his sense of what is real, the misgiving lest after all it should prove unreal will dart through his mind, as through that of the representative child of his poem. Nay, a dark suspicion will occasionally overtake him, "that maybe identity beyond the grave is a beautiful fable only"—as when, in the midst of some gay scene, the thought occurs to him of a ship going down at sea, of women sinking "while the passionless wet flows on"; and he ponders within himself: "Are those women indeed gone?"

> Are souls drown'd and destroy'd so?
> Is only matter triumphant?

But again and again he returns victorious answer:

Did you think life was so well provided for, and
    Death, the purport of all Life, is not well
    provided for?

I do not doubt that wrecks at sea, no matter what the
    horrors of them, no matter whose wife, child,
    husband, father, lover, has gone down, are
    provided for, to the minutest points.

How inspiriting in their juvenile positiveness, in these days of doubt and pessimism, are his hearty assurances of immortality, in which not man alone, but all nature, what we deem the inanimate as well as the animate, is included:

I swear I think now that everything without exception
    has an eternal soul!
The trees have, rooted in the ground! the weeds of
    the sea have! the animals!

And in this he goes no further than Charles Lamb, who, loving houses as Walt Whitman loves trees, hazards the wild and beautiful surmise that "as men, when they die, do not die all, so of their extinguished habitations there may be a hope—a germ to be revivified."

Whitman's belief, however, is no vague theory reserved for imaginative moods. He subjects it to the most crucial tests. In the midst of the conflicting emotions roused in him by the news of the death of Carlyle, whose personality had powerfully impressed him, "and now that he has gone hence," he asks, "can it be that Thomas Carlyle, soon to chemically dissolve in ashes and by winds, remains an identity still? In ways, perhaps, eluding all the statements, lore, and speculations of ten thousand years—eluding all possible statements to mortal sense—does he yet exist, a definite, vital being, a spirit, an individual. I have no doubt of it." When depressed, he tells us, by some specially sad event or tearing problem, he waits till he can go out under the stars at midnight to consider it, to be soothed and spiritualised, and to receive an answer to his soul. It was to this means of tranquillity he had resorted on the present occasion, and this was the answer he received concerning the author of *Sartor Resartus*.

There is something so touching in this consideration of the death of one lonely old man by another, in a different hemisphere, younger, but in the evening of his day, and appearing feebler and more helpless in every glimpse we have of him, that the momentary departure from our point of view in referring to it may be pardoned.

For all Whitman's love of life, for all the joy of existence with which he overflows, the themes he loves best, according to his own statement, are "night, sleep, death, and the stars." Death's gloomier aspects he ignores as completely as the child of Wordsworth's poem, not, however, in the spirit of thoughtless childhood, by denying its reality, but by adopting it into his life. "Chanter of pains and joys, uniter of here and hereafter," his object is to bridge the way from life to death. As different from the Emperor Adrian's melancholy foreboding as the gay anticipation of a young sailor setting out on his first voyage, the spirit of adventure strong upon him, differs from the troubled outlook of some anxious mariner, is his brief lyrical address to his soul on parting:

Joy, shipmate, joy!
    (Pleas'd to my soul at death I cry)
Our life is closed, our life begins,
The long, long anchorage we leave,
The ship is clear at last, she leaps!
She swiftly courses from the shore,
Joy, shipmate, joy!

Life may be full of suffering and contradictions, but "sane and sacred death" will make amends for all. It is the answer to every question; the fall of the young hero in battle, the unsatisfied love, the disappointed life—all sorrows, wants, and imperfections will be accounted for by this.

As if aware, by some subtle undefined instinct, of the child-element in himself, he traces back the full-flowing stream of his poetry to its first source in his awakened child's heart. In soft hushed strains, like the whispers rapt and awestruck of a child just wakened from some dream of heaven, he tells us how it was a wild bird moaning for its mate (and whose wistful ignorant lament he interprets with such exquisite insight that it seems he has taken its spirit into his own) which roused the fire, the "unknown want" within him, when a boy, with bare feet, the wind wafting his hair, he wandered down to the shore by night and listened, with childish intuitive sympathy, to the lone singer calling on his love; till, revisiting the scene,

A man, yet by these tears a little boy again,

he confronted the dark problem of earthly griefs and partings.

> O give me the clue (it lurks in the night here
>   somewhere)!
> O if I am to have so much, let me have more!

rose his yearning cry toward heaven. And from the wet sands, the calm unhurrying sea, the stars, the winds, came the answer whispering through the night, reiterated with strong reverberation:

> Death, death, death, death, death.

Once again he became the peaceful child he was before the nameless longing had been roused, though with the added assurance of one who has wrestled with an angel and prevailed; and it is henceforth in the spirit of confiding happy childhood that he goes through life:

> My own songs awaked from that hour,
> And with them the key, the word up from the waves,
> The word of the sweetest song and all songs,
> That strong and delicious word which, creeping to
>   my feet. . .
> The sea whisper'd me.

In accordance with this faith the dead to Whitman are living, "Haply the only living, only real." Item for item, body as well as soul, they have eluded burial and passed to fitting spheres. He walks often when in solitude as if accompanied by his departed, and scatters flowers to them on his way, not so much in kind remembrance as for present token of affection.

> As if a phantom caress'd me,

he bursts forth, in one of those rare abrupt little Heine-like effusions of his which suggest so much in a line or two.

> I thought I was not alone walking here by the shore;
> But the one I thought was with me. . .
> As I lean and look through the glimmering light, that one has utterly
>   disappear'd,
> And those appear that are hateful to me and mock me:

the unexpected turn of the last line being, however, singularly out of keeping with his usual utterances, for to Walt Whitman in his normal mood no one is hateful. Like the little child of the story, he loves everyone. "I am in love with you, and with all my fellows upon the earth," is from first to last the burden of his poems.

Whitman alludes somewhere to "the great charity of the earth." Of the same kind is his own. Subjected to the alchemy of his close loving sympathy, his respectful consideration, the vilest things seem to emerge purified and fit for noble uses. Nothing is too abandoned in its baseness but he will shed some shadow of healing, some light of comfort on it. To him the dirtiest puddle reflects the beauty of the skies. We have heard of a child who wept on being told that a flower she admired was nothing but a weed. To Whitman there are no weeds in the world. With the child's simple eye to nature he takes them all for plants of precious growth, bearing each one of them, buried deep, perhaps, within its calyx, the seed of perfection. And in this he is not like the child, that his trust can be destroyed by the first rude unthinking hand. With authority, as if he spoke for God, he gives his imperious verdict on behalf of what the world despises and pronounces it also to be good. He rejects nothing, he despises nothing: "Good or bad, I never question you, I love all—I do not condemn anything." For the poet, as in one of his softly rounded, tenderly suggestive phrases he asserts, "judges not as the judge judges, but as the sun falling round a helpless thing;" or else, as in this case, like the young child who has no standard but its own clinging nature to measure people by. To his pure, spiritualised vision "objects gross and the unseen soul are one." No head to him but wears its "nimbus of gold-coloured light." He takes everyone, the meanest and most worthless, by the hand, and whispers to him or her that he understands and loves what none others have understood or loved; that the true being, soul and body (he will never separate them), stands revealed in its glory and perfection to him, unhidden by the most repulsive exterior; that at the worst, though premature death should have already fallen, the means will be provided that it may "pick its way."

"Maybe I am non-literary and non-decorous," Whitman says of himself on some special occasion. Maybe he is. But literature and decorum are not the highest things. What might shock and disgust if it came from any one else only startles us with its note of strangeness from him. His coarseness is as the coarseness of the earth, which, with "disdainful innocence," takes all for clean. Or rather, to maintain our point of view, he is a "vulgar child" indeed, but after the fashion of the youngster to whose harmless improprieties Sterne, in justification of his own deliberate offences, drew its mother's attention—not after that of the sentimentalist himself. The "chaste indecency of childhood" is not so hard to forgive.

As we study him his utterances take on power and beauty. His character seems to gather cohesion and to expand; so that whereas, in our first perusal of him, when we came across some passage of exquisite beauty or on some announcement of matured wisdom, we were startled almost as if a very child amid its careless babblings had uttered words of inspiration, we end by acknowledging in him both the giant and the child, a man full-statured in magnificence.

Notes

1. Since this was written Walt Whitman has passed away.

—Pauline W. Roose, "A Child-Poet: Walt Whitman,"
Gentleman's Magazine, May 1892, pp. 473–80

RICHARD MAURICE BUCKE
"THE MAN WALT WHITMAN" (1893)

Whatever Walt Whitman's subject matter,   whether he is ostensibly speaking of himself, of some other individual, of the animals, of something impersonal, he is always speaking really of himself—of himself treated as the typical man, and so treated not so much as being better than others but as seeing more clearly the divinity that is in every human being:

> I celebrate myself, and sing myself,
> And what I assume you shall assume.

The man himself, the whole man, body and soul, including his relations to the material world about him and the practical and social life of his time, is faithfully mirrored in his book. The outward and inward experiences of a long life are vividly and truthfully briefed; nothing is omitted, the most trivial and the most vital equally finding place. The whole is done in a manner far removed from the usual direct autobiographic prose; in a manner, indeed, quite unusual, special, poetic and indirect. The result is such that future ages will know this man as perhaps no human being heretofore has been ever known either to his cotemporaries or successors. The exposition of the person involving equally that of his environment gives us incidentally a photograph of America, 1850–90. The breathing man, Walt Whitman, in his surroundings, as he lived, is so faithfully reproduced, and with such vitality, that all must admit the justice of his final dictum:

> This is no book,
> Who touches this touches a man.

The reader who should peruse *Leaves of Grass* as he would an ordinary book, for the thoughts which the words immediately express, and should rest there, would be like a child who, having learned the alphabet, should consider his education complete. The thoughts, feelings, images, emotions which lie directly behind the words constitute merely the facade of the temple, the introduction to the real object to be presented. That object, as has been said, is an embodiment of its author, Walt Whitman. This being the case, the value of the book will depend largely upon the sort of man he proves to be.

—Richard Maurice Bucke, "The Man Walt Whitman,"
In Re Walt Whitman, eds. Horace L. Traubel,
Richard Maurice Bucke, Thomas B. Harned, 1893, p. 59

BARRETT WENDELL
"AMERICAN LITERATURE" (1893)

In this same period, however, there is a single figure who seems steadily and constantly to face not what is now past, but what is now present or to come. Though his right to respect is questioned oftenest of all, we cannot fairly pass Walt Whitman without mention. He lacks, of course, to a grotesque degree, artistic form; but that very lack is characteristic. Artistic form, as we have seen, is often the final stamp that marks human expression as a thing of the past. Whitman remarkably illustrates this principle: he lacks form chiefly because he is stammeringly overpowered by his bewildering vision of what he believes to be the future. He is uncouth, inarticulate, whatever you please that is least orthodox; yet, after all, he can make you feel for the moment how even the ferry-boats plying from New York to Brooklyn are fragments of God's eternities. Those of us who love the past are far from sharing his confidence in the future. Surely, however, that is no reason for denying the miracle that he has wrought by idealizing the East River. The man who has done this is the only one who points out the stuff of which perhaps the new American literature of the future may in time be made, who foreruns perhaps a spirit that may inspire that literature, if it grow at last into an organic form of its own, with a meaning not to be sought in other worlds than this western world of ours.

—Barrett Wendell, "American Literature," *Stelligeri and Other Essays Concerning America,* 1893, pp. 142–43

WILLIAM MORTON PAYNE "WHITMANIANA" (1893)

Walt Whitman's figure is surely one of the most commanding in American literature, yet its full stature will never be realized by the cultivated public at large, so long as the fanatical devotees of the poet's memory continue to lavish their extravagant encomiums upon his faults and his virtues alike.

—William Morton Payne, "Whitmaniana," *Dial,* December 16, 1893, p. 390

WILLIAM DEAN HOWELLS "FIRST IMPRESSIONS OF LITERARY NEW YORK" (1895)

Unlike Henry James, who eventually championed Whitman's poetry after condemning it early in his career, the American novelist William Dean Howells held to the original tone he struck in his early negative reviews of Whitman, though he did at least come to appreciate Whitman's character later in life. In this essay, Howell warmly recalls several meetings with Whitman, characterizing him as a person of spiritual dignity and purity. Yet Howells cannot reconcile these personal traits with Whitman's unrefined poetry, though he admits to liking Whitman's prose for its "genial and comforting quality." Ultimately, Howells concedes Whitman's profoundly liberating effect on American literature, though he finds the poetry itself full of unrealized greatness. This essay offers a useful example of how Whitman's contemporaries struggled to separate their responses to his personal character from their responses to his work.

I remember how he leaned back in his chair, and reached out his great hand to me, as if he were going to give it me for good and all. He had a fine head, with a cloud of Jovian hair upon it, and a branching beard and mustache, and gentle eyes that looked most kindly into mine, and seemed to wish the liking which I instantly gave him, though we hardly passed a word, and our acquaintance was summed up in that glance and the grasp of his mighty fist upon my hand. I doubt if he had any notion who or what I was beyond the fact that I was a young poet of some sort, but he may possibly have remembered seeing my name printed after some very Heinesque verses in the Press. I did not meet him again for twenty years, and then I had only a moment with him when he was reading the proofs of his poems in Boston. Some years later I saw him for the last time, one day after his lecture on Lincoln, in that city, when he came down from the platform to speak with some handshaking friends who gathered about him. Then and always he gave me the sense of a sweet and true soul, and I felt in him a spiritual dignity which I will not try to reconcile with his printing in the forefront of his book a passage from a private letter of Emerson's, though I believe he would not have seen such a thing as most other men would, or thought ill of it in another. The spiritual purity which I felt in him no less than the dignity is something that I will no more try to reconcile with what denies it in his page; but such things we may well leave to the adjustment of finer balances than we have at hand. I will make sure only of the greatest benignity in the presence of the man. The apostle of the rough, the uncouth, was the gentlest person; his barbaric yawp, translated into the terms of social encounter, was an address of singular quiet, delivered in a voice of winning and endearing friendliness.

As to his work itself, I supposed that I do not think it so valuable in effect as in intention. He was a liberating force, a very "imperial anarch" in literature; but liberty is never anything but a means, and what Whitman achieved was a means and not an end, in what must be called his verse. I like his prose, if there is a difference, much better; there he is of a genial and comforting quality, very rich and cordial, such as I felt him to be when I met him in person. His verse seems to me not poetry, but the materials of poetry, like one's emotions; yet I would not misprize it, and I am glad to own that I have had moments of great pleasure in it. Some French critic quoted in the Saturday Press (I cannot think of his name) said the best thing of him when he said that he made you a partner of the enterprise, for that is precisely what he does, and that is what alienates and what endears in him, as you like or dislike the partnership. It is still something neighborly, brotherly, fatherly, and so I felt him to be when the benign old man looked on me and spoke to me.

—William Dean Howells, "First Impressions of
Literary New York," *Harper's New Monthly Magazine,*
June 1895, p. 65

MAX NORDAU (1895)

One of the deities to whom the degenerate and hysterical of both hemispheres have for some time been raising altars. Lombroso ranks him expressly among 'mad geniuses.' Mad Whitman was without doubt. But a genius? That would be difficult to prove. He was a vagabond, a reprobate rake, and his poems contain outbursts of erotomania so artlessly shameless that their parallel in literature could hardly be found with the author's name attached. For his fame he has to thank just those bestially sensual pieces which first drew to him the attention of all the pruriency of America. He is morally insane, and incapable of distinguishing between good and evil, virtue and crime. 'This is the deepest theory of susceptibility,' he says in one place, 'without preference or exclusion; the negro with the woolly head, the bandit of the highroad, the invalid, the ignorant—none are denied.' And in another place he explains he 'loves the murderer and the thief, the pious and good, with equal love.' An American driveller, W. D. O'Connor, has called him on this account 'The good gray Poet.' We know, however, that this 'goodness,' which is in reality moral obtuse-ness and morbid sentimentality, frequently accompanies degeneration, and appears even in the cruellest assassins, for example, in Ravachol. . . .

In his patriotic poems he is a sycophant of the corrupt American vote-buying, official-bribing, power-abusing, dollar-democracy, and a cringer to the most arrogant Yankee conceit. His war poems—the much renowned *Drum Taps*—are chiefly remarkable for swaggering bombast and stilted patter.

His purely lyrical pieces, with their ecstatic 'Oh!' and 'Ah!' with their soft phrases about flowers, meadows, spring and sunshine, recall the most arid, sugary and effeminate passages of our old Gessner, now happily buried and forgotten.

As a man, Walt Whitman offers a surprising resemblance to Paul Verlaine, with whom he shared all the stigmata of degeneration, the vicissitudes of his career, and, curiously enough, even the rheumatic ankylosis. As a poet, he has thrown off the closed strophe as too difficult, measure and rhyme as too oppressive, and has given vent to his emotional fugitive ideation in hysterical exclamations, to which the definition of 'prose gone mad' is infinitely better suited than it is to the pedantic, honest hexameters of Klopstock. Unconsciously, he seemed to have used the parallelism of the Psalms, and Jeremiah's eruptive style, as models of form. We had in the last century the *Paramythien* of Herder, and the insufferable 'poetical prose' of Gessner already mentioned. Our healthy taste soon led us to recognise the inartistic, retrogressive character of this lack of form, and that error in taste has found no imitator among us for a century. In Whitman, however, his hysterical admirers commend this *rechauffe* of a superannuated literary fashion as something to come; and admire, as an invention of genius, what is only an incapacity for methodical work. Nevertheless, it is interesting to point out that two persons so dissimilar as Richard Wagner and Walt Whitman have, in different spheres, under the pressure of the same motives, arrived at the same goal—the former at 'infinite melody,' which is no longer melody; the latter at verses which are no longer verses, both in consequence of their incapacity to submit their capriciously vacillating thoughts to the yoke of those rules which in 'infinite' melody, as in lyric verse, govern by measure and rhyme.

—Max Nordau, *Degeneration*, 1895, pp. 230–32

WILLA CATHER "WHITMAN" (1896)

Feminist, poet, chronicler of life on the American plains, and author of such novels as *My Ántonia, O Pioneers!*, and *Death Comes for the Archbishop*, Willa Cather criticizes, in this excerpt, the moral relativism she finds at the heart of Whitman's poetry. Cather condemns Whitman's lack of moral judgment while acknowledging her fondness for the "good fellowship and whole-heartedness in every line he wrote," a quality that almost, though not entirely, compensates for his all-too-accepting conscience. Writing a few years after the "Deathbed" edition of *Leaves of Grass*, Cather is less concerned with Whitman's status in the literary canon than with the aesthetic and ethos of his work. Like many of Whitman's other admirers, Cather praises his elemental energy, his joy in all creation, and his optimism. Yet his poetry conflicts with her artistic values, which esteem traditional poetic subjects, refinement of language, and a discernible moral code. Because Whitman venerates every aspect of the physical world without distinction, one cannot help but be swept up in his enthusiasm, but such charm is all the more troublesome for Cather, for she believes that humankind's spiritual faculties should enable them to separate the beautiful portions of the world from the base.

Cather's essay not only provides excellent material for students writing a critical assessment of Whitman's poetry, but also offers a useful counterpoint to the common praise of Whitman. Students writing about Whitman's representation of America's pioneering past might explore differences between these two authors' attitudes regarding that past, contrasting Whitman's Romantic enthusiasm with Cather's more reserved realism. For students exploring responses to Whitman's sexuality, particularly from other homosexual authors such as Cather, Gerard Manley Hopkins, and John Addington Symonds, they might ask to what extent Cather's critique was motivated by internalized social mores. Was the overt sensuality of Whitman's poetry troubling to her? Lastly, since Cather clearly subscribes to a particular set of poetic values, students writing about Whitman as an experimental poet might contrast Cather's own poetry with Whitman's, looking not only for Cather's traditional, formal aesthetics, but for passages where she seems influenced, perhaps unconsciously, by Whitman.

Speaking of monuments reminds one that there is more talk about a monument to Walt Whitman, "the good, gray poet." Just why the adjective good is always applied to Whitman it is difficult to discover, probably because people who could not understand him at all took it for granted that he meant well. If ever there was a poet who had no literary ethics at all beyond those of nature, it was he. He was neither good nor bad, any more than are the animals he continually admired and envied. He was a poet without an exclusive sense of the poetic, a man without the finer discriminations, enjoying everything with the unreasoning enthusiasm of a boy. He was the poet of the dung hill as well as of the mountains, which is admirable in theory but excruciating in verse. In the same paragraph he informs you that, "The pure contralto sings in the organ loft," and that "The malformed limbs are tied to the table, what is removed drop horribly into a pail." No branch of surgery is poetic, and that hopelessly prosaic word "pail" would kill a whole volume of sonnets. Whitman's poems are reckless rhapsodies over creation in general, sometimes sublime, sometimes ridiculous. He declares that the ocean with its "imperious waves, commanding" is beautiful, and that the fly-specks on the walls are also beautiful. Such catholic taste may go in science, but in poetry their results are sad. The poet's task is usually to select the poetic. Whitman never bothers to do that, he takes everything in the universe from fly-specks to the fixed stars. His *Leaves of Grass* is a sort of dictionary of the English language, and in it is the name of everything in creation set down with great reverence but without any particular connection.

But however ridiculous Whitman may be there is a primitive elemental force about him. He is so full of hardiness and of the joy of life. He looks at all nature in the delighted, admiring way in which the old Greeks and the primitive poets did. He exults so in the red blood in his body and the strength in his arms. He has such a passion for the warmth and dignity of all that is natural. He has no code but to be natural, a code that this complex world has so long outgrown. He is sensual, not after the manner of Swinburne and Gautier, who are always seeking for perverted and bizarre effects on the senses, but in the frank fashion of the old barbarians who ate and slept and married and smacked their lips over the mead horn. He is rigidly limited to the physical, things that quicken his pulses, please his eyes or delight his nostrils. There is an element of poetry in all this, but it is by no means the highest. If a joyous elephant should break forth into song, his lay would probably be very much like Whitman's famous *Song of Myself.* It would have just about as much delicacy and deftness and discrimination. He says: "I think I could turn and live with the animals. They are so placid and self-contained, I stand and look at them long and long. They do not sweat and whine about their condition. They do not lie awake in the dark and weep for their sins. They do not make me sick discussing their duty to God. Not one is dissatisfied nor not one is demented with the mania of many things. Not one kneels to another nor to his kind that lived thousands of years ago. Not one is respectable or unhappy, over the whole earth." And that is not irony on nature, he means just that, life meant no more to him. He accepted the world just as it is and glorified it, the seemly and unseemly, the good and the bad. He had no conception of a difference in people or in things. All men had bodies and were alike to him, one about as good as another. To live was to fulfil all natural laws and impulses. To be comfortable was to be happy. To be happy was the ultimatum. He did not realize the existence of a conscience or a responsibility. He had no more thought of good or evil than the folks in Kipling's *Jungle Book.*

And yet there is an undeniable charm about this optimistic vagabond who is made so happy by the warm sunshine and the smell of spring fields. A sort of good fellowship and whole-heartedness in every line he wrote. His veneration for things physical and material, for all that is in water or air or land, is so real that as you read him you think for the moment that you would rather like to live so if you could. For the time you half believe that a sound body and a strong arm are the greatest things in the world. Perhaps no book shows so much as *Leaves of Grass* that keen senses do not make a poet. When you read it you realize how spirited a thing poetry really is and how great a part spiritual perceptions play in apparently sensuous verse, if only to select the beautiful from the gross.

—Willa Cather, "Whitman" (1896),
The Kingdom of Art, ed. Bernice Slote, 1966, pp. 351–53

WILLIAM SLOANE KENNEDY
"WHITMAN'S WORD-MUSIC" (1896)

A devoted correspondent, friend, and follower of Whitman's, Kennedy authored or edited several biographical works about Whitman. In this extract from his personal reminiscences, Kennedy writes extensively about the musicality of Whitman's poetry. He contrasts Whitman's free verse rhythms with those of traditional metrical writers and of Whitman's imitators, the former being merely virtuosic, the latter third rate. Arguing that poetic form should arise organically from its subject, Kennedy celebrates Whitman's free verse for diligently shedding the artificial syntax of traditional poetry, thereby evoking the spontaneous rhythms and turns of phrase characteristic of authentic human speech. Leaving behind the ten-syllable count of blank verse, Whitman's lines range from sixteen to twenty-five syllables, an expansiveness Kennedy likens to the dactylic hexameter of Greek epic poetry. This similarity is not merely metrical, though; Kennedy claims that the heroic effort of speaking such long lines is reflective of and commensurate with Whitman's noble and epic ambition to give voice to the "Soul of Nature."

Any student interested in theories about the prosody of free verse, which might better be called nonregular metrical verse, will find Kennedy's discussion of value, not only because he describes certain patterns in Whitman's poetry, but also because he draws particular attention to the rhythmic effect of the printed line. Kennedy writes that while some of Whitman's verse might be reorganized into more or less regularly metrical lines, the use of long lines on the page affects their verbal recitation (an argument that anticipates the modern poet William Carlos Williams's theories about the relation between breath, pauses, and line length in free verse).

Kennedy's ideas on the nature and purpose of literary criticism are particularly useful for students formulating arguments about the thematic implications of Whitman's free verse experiments. Kennedy argues for an organic relation between form and content, claiming that the poem's form is intrinsically related to some aspect of subject matter, whether through tone, mood, theme, or the artist's vision of reality. The critic's purpose, Kennedy argues, is to identify the poet's particular aims in a poem and to judge how successful those aims have been realized; thus, while he clearly admires the democratic and spiritual ideals underlying Whitman's poetic vision, he does not judge it explicitly, but attempts to show how Whitman brings his free-verse rhythms to bear on the expression of that vision.

—⁓⁓— —⁓⁓— —⁓⁓—

After this preliminary survey I come at length to Whitman, who is one of the few writers in the world besides Swinburne able to compose symphonic word-music. It can be indubitably proved that his poetic art, *as shown in his most finished productions*, the rhythmic chants,—and especially in his later poems,—is profoundly consonant with the laws of nature and symphonic music; and that conversely and necessarily, therefore, the whole body of English poetry, with the exception of a few lyrical masterpieces, is composed (technically or metrically considered) upon a system as false to nature as it is to the higher harmonies of music.

The great gain in casting nobler and longer works in non-rhyming form is release from the degrading task of sentence-sawing and twisting, and the fixing of the attention on the message to be spoken. Nor is this offering the least encouragement to idleness or inferior work. It is precisely the most difficult thing in the world for a poet or painter to imitate nature's spontaneity. In the first place, his songs must be the pulsations of a profoundly musical nature; and second, while allowing the hand of the Unconscious to wander over the darkling strings of his soul, he must yet know how to so subtly mingle himself in the creative process as, by the higher instinct of his culture, to guide all to a supreme musical expression and shaping which shall surpass the careless work of the pseudo-naturalist in the exact measure of the deeper thought and wider intellectual range they represent. This psychical performance is the pinnacle of the soul's art-life, the farthest point reached by the fountain in its sunward leap. Here the circle of intellectual growth returns to its starting point, and the mind of man comes into electric and vital contact with the Soul of Nature, partaking by hidden inlet of her high powers and virtues.

Let it be premised that to the creations of the seer-poets technique adds very little value. The supreme art of these poets is to forget all art, to have a high moral or emotional aim, and noble passion, and let the style flow spontaneously out of these. Indeed, if the whole mind of any poet is directed chiefly to artistic form, he will never attain supreme artistic form. Plato has said, 'Art is the expression of the highest moral energy.' Poetry is not a thing of yard-sticks and tinkling brasses, but is 'the measure of the intensity of the human soul.' Where the air is densest, as on the plains, there the roll of the thunder and the splendor of the lightning are most sublime. The greater number of current poems are to the mind what cork is to water:

they have form, but no weight, and refuse to sink into the memory; they are like brooks without water. 'Genius is nothing but love,' said W. M. Hunt: 'whatever the artist paints must be from the heart's blood, if it is only two marks on a shingle.' But poetry today has become partly a matter of trick, as it was with Simmias of Rhodes, who wrote verses in the shape of an altar, an egg, a double-edged axe, etc. About the only emotion excited in our breasts by this all-prevalent brand of poetry is that which we feel in looking at the contortions of a circus gymnast. No matter about the thought, but only see how the juggler keeps those nine rhymes going in the air at once! How deftly he managed that difficult line! (and twisted the neck of his thought in doing it). The painful interest we feel in a milliner with her mouth full of pins (as in Maria Edgeworth's 'Mademoiselle Panache'), that is how the average sonneteer affects us. I repeat, the style of the poem will flow spontaneously and in original forms from noble aim and passion. And never doubt that there are as many ways of expressing poetic thought as there are original souls. 'Never was a song good or beautiful which resembled any other,' said Pierre d'Auvergne. We should always expect from a great artist a new style, one that must win its way into favor through abuse, as in the case of Turner, Victor Hugo, Shakspere [sic]. 'The melange of existence is but an eternal font of type, and may be set up to any text, however different—with room and welcome, at whatever time, for new compositors.'

It is passing strange how incapable otherwise intelligent persons are of true critical judgments. The A, B, C, of criticism is to put yourself in an author's place, judge him by what he proposed to attain. Now, Walt Whitman, from the very start, gave notice in the preface to his first volume that, in his opinion, the time had come to 'break down the barriers of form between prose and poetry' (*Specimen Days*, pp. 226 and 322); and he proceeded to illustrate his theory in poems—when, lo! a chorus of jeering voices exclaiming, 'These 'poems' are half prose: do you call such and such lines poetry?'[1] No, my bat-eyed ones, we do not: did we not distinctly premise the contrary,—that the work was to be partly in prose? Now, as to the poetical portions of *Leaves of Grass*, let us see if they meet the tests of true art. Beyond question there are certain fundamentals which will never be found lacking in pure poetry. one of these is *Music*, and another is *Form*.

There is music and music,—the simple ballad of the harper and the intricate symphony of the modern composer. Whitman, as has often been said, is the Wagner of poets. As Wagner abandoned the cadences of the old sonatas and symphonies,—occurring at the end of every four, eight, or sixteen bars,—so Whitman has abandoned the measured beat of the old rhymed see-saw poetry, after having himself thoroughly tried it, as the early poems appended to his prose volume attest. In the old operas you were always let down every few seconds by the regularly recurrent cadences: in the dramas of Wagner you never touch ground, but soar, like an eagle or a planet, in great, spiral, Geryon-flights of harmony. So with Whitman poetry has now become an instrument breathing a music in so vast a key that even the stately wheelings and solemn pomp of Milton's verse seem rather formal and mechanical. Whitman's dithyrambic chants, with their long, winding fiords of sound, require—like summer thunder or organ music—perspective of the ear, if the phrase will be allowed: they must be considered in vocal mass, and not in parts; and, when so considered, it will be found that nearly every page is held in solution by a deep-running undertone of majestic rhythm.[2] 'Harmony latent,' said Heracleitus, 'is of more value than that which is patent.' In the matter of orchestral word-music, Whitman, in his rhythmic chants, does at any rate more than any other mortal has yet accomplished. Only consider how inferior, for the expression of deep emotion, the cold, solitary, inarticulate words of ink and paper are to music:

> The swift contending fugue,—the wild escape
>> Of passions,—long-drawn wail and sudden blast,
> The low sad mutterings and entangled dreams
>> Of viols and basoons, . . .
> The trumpet-cries of anger and despair,
>> The mournful marches of the muffled drum;
> The bird-like flute-notes leaping into air,—

how will you imprison the vague-sweet and mysterious suggestions of the voices of these children of sound in lifeless, breathless words?

I do not affirm that every part of Whitman's work is musical. There are prosaic intervals in all poetry—in Tennyson's, Shakspere's, and Browning's as much as in any,—only with them the prose is masked in the *form* of poesy, without possessing its lyric soul. But what I do affirm is that the proportion of poetry to prose in *Leaves of Grass* is no less than in any other poet's work, and that the proportion of *symphonic* music—rude at times, if you choose—is immensely greater than in the compositions of any other bard. I cannot quote to illustrate, because I should have to quote whole poems. Read the Sea Chants, *Drum-Taps*, 'Italian Music in Dakota,' 'Proud Music of the Storm,' 'That Music always around Me,' 'Vigil Strange,' 'The Singer in the Prison,' 'Pioneers, O Pioneers,' and the 'Burial Hymn of

Lincoln,' and you will catch the interior music I speak of. It will be different from what you expected: it will not remind you of a church choir; but it is there, nevertheless.

'In the rhythm of certain poets,' says Emerson, 'there is no manufacture, but a vortex or musical tornado, which falling on words and the experience of a learned mind whirl these materials into the same grand order as planets or moons obey, and seasons and monsoons.' That is the kind of rhythm you will find in the best of Whitman's chants. For twenty years Whitman absorbed the strains of the best singers of the world in the New York operas, and many of his lines were written down while hearing the music, or immediately after (Bucke, p. 157), a fact that gives us the key to many a bit of wonderful melody that sparkles out of his interspaces of prose. The little poem, 'Weave in, my Hardy Life,' when analysed and divided as the ordinary poets would divide it, turns out to be made up of regular four foot iambic lines, with two three-foot iambics and one or two lines long or short by a foot—licenses which every poet takes. I add the poem entire, with the lines cut up in the ordinary unnatural way. But first let us have the three opening lines as they stand on the poet's page:

Weave in, weave in, my hardy life,
Weave yet a soldier strong and full for great campaigns to come,
Weave in red blood, weave sinews in like ropes, the senses, sight
    weave in.

The ordinary method would be as follows. (At the close of each of Whitman's lines I place a perpendicular bar):

Weave in, weave in, my hardy life, |
Weave yet a soldier strong and full
    For great campaigns to come, |
Weave in red blood, weave sinews in
Like ropes, the senses, sight weave in, |
Weave lasting sure, weave day and night
The weft, the warp, incessant weave, tire not, |
(We know not what the use O life,
    Nor know the aim, the end,
    Nor really aught we know |
But know the work, the need goes on
And shall go on, the death-envelop'd march
Of peace as well as war goes on,) |

For great campaigns of peace the same
The wiry threads to weave, | we know not why
Or what, yet weave, forever weave. |

Now, one may venture to say that, if these musical lines had been written in the above orthodox way, not a critic would have peeped. But the awful heresy of originality! The daring to be natural! Nor is this poem a solitary exception. If the reader will turn to pages 366 and 368 of *Leaves of Grass*, and read the poems 'By Broad Potomac's Shore,' 'From Far Dakota's Canons,' 'What Best I see in Thee,' and 'Spirit that formed this Scene,' he will discover that the iambic movement in these is almost perfect, containing only such variations as nature approves and as the most cultivated musical sense indorses. And these instances might be multiplied many times, especially from the more recent poems,—as 'Of that Blithe Throat of Thine,' published in *Harper's Monthly*, Jan. 1885; 'If I should need to name, O Western World' (*Philadelphia Press*, 1884); and 'Red Jacket from Aloft' (1884). 'To a Man-of-War-Bird' is a poem almost purely iambic in form: so are 'Ethiopia saluting the Colors,' 'World, take Good Notice,' 'Delicate Cluster,' 'Joy, Shipmate, Joy.' There is plenty of music in Whitman's poems, if you only have the ear to detect it, and are not fooled by the visible form, or mould, the poet has chosen.

As to form, poetry may legitimately be divided into two groups or styles,—the sculpturesque and the pictorial. Hitherto the poets have only attempted to create in the sculpturesque, or Greek, style. All Greek art is based on the principle of form, summed up in the saying of Plato, 'Beauty is proportion,' and in the dictum of a modern Greek (the poet Goethe), 'Die Kunst ist nur Gestaltung,' 'Art is form alone.' But Walt Whitman exfoliates the art of poetry into a wider air and range. He would make it less artificial, give it more of a grandeur of nature. 'Poetic style,' he says, 'when address'd to the soul, is less definite form, outline, sculpture, and becomes vista, music, half-tints, and even less than half-tints. True, it may be architecture; but again it may be the forest wild-wood, or the best effect thereof, at twilight, the waving oaks and cedars in the wind, and the impalpable odor.'

If you see nothing to like in Walt Whitman's lines, you will see nothing to please you in the long leaves of coloured lights that rock in sumptuous idleness on the waves, nothing in the purple-floating richness of the flower-de-luce, nothing in the exquisite clare-obscure, soft craterous glooms, and rolling dream-drapery emergent from the locomotive's funnel, nothing in the bobolincoln's pretty little orchestra,—gurgle, whistle, trill, and steady undertone of chime,—nothing in the great bell's resonant roar and long, tapering after-hum; for in all these forms and sounds there is the vague irregularity and asymmetry of all natural phenomena.

But to come closer to the details of our poet's art in this matter of form. As I have said, the fatal defect of the ten-syllable, or heroic, line is that it is too short. To fit your delicate fancy with blank verse, you have got to mangle its joints. But Whitman never breaks a verse on the wheel. So far as I can discover, about the average number of syllables required to express a single poetical thought is from sixteen or twenty to twenty-five.[3] I at least affirm that about one half of all simple poetical thoughts require that much articulated breath to get them uttered. Every one of Whitman's lucid Greek pages illustrates the statement. His work is nearly always blocked out into lines or periods the length of which corresponds with the natural length of the thoughts. As, for example, in these lines:

O Western orb sailing the heaven,
Now I know what you must have meant as a month since I walk'd,
As I walk'd in silence the transparent shadowy night,
As I saw you had something to tell as you bent to me night after night,
As you droop'd from the sky low down as if to my side, (while the other
    stars all look'd on,)
As we wander'd together the solemn night, (for something I know not
    what kept me from slap.)
As the night advanced, and I saw on the rim of the west how full you
    were of woe,
As I stood on the rising ground in the brow in the cool transparent
    night,
As I watch'd where you pass'd and was lost in the netherward black of
    the night,
As my soul in its trouble dissatisfied sank, as where you sad orb,
Concluded, dropt in the night, and was gone.

These flowing epic lines are the counterpart in English of Homer's hexameters, and are the only possible hexameters for us. They have the required weight and momentum, are strong enough to bear the pressure of the thought, and are the first true, unborrowed heroics ever written in a Germanic tongue. It is doubtless true, as Dr O. W. Holmes has pointed out, that the ten-syllable line owes much of its impressiveness to the sense of difficulty we have in the reading, since a longer respiration than ordinary is required for each line; but this advantage will not overbalance the other defects. Ours is an age of great and difficult thoughts. Now, a great poet always reflects the ideas and passions of his own day. And just as in a painting showing action all the lines must be agitated or undulating, in sympathy with the leading emotional purpose, and not horizontal, angular, and regular, as in a painting showing repose, so our poet's irregular and fluent twenty-syllable lines are in harmony with the agitated nature of his leading motives,—as well as with the spirit of the age,—and suit the largeness of his themes.

Notes

1. I suppose the chief bar to the action of the imagination, and stop to all greatness in this present age of ours, is its mean and shallow love of jest: so that if there be in any good and lofty work a flaw, failing, or undipped vulnerable part, where sarcasm may stick or stay, it is caught at, and pointed at, and buzzed about, and fixed upon, and stung into as a recent wound is by flies, and nothing is ever taken seriously or as it was meant, but always, if it may be, turned the wrong way, and misunderstood; and, while this is so, there is not, nor cannot be, any hope of achievement of high things. Men dare not open their hearts, if we are to broil them on a thorn-fire.—*John Ruskin.*

2. For the benefit of people who have no musical ear I will adduce the testimony of Mrs Fanny Raymond Ritter, wife of the Professor of Music at Vassar College, who speaks of the strong rhythmical pulsing musical power of *Leaves of Grass* (Bucke, p. 157), and also that of one who belongs to the native home of music—Signor Enrico Nencioni of Italy, who in an article published in the *Nuova Antologia* magazine of Rome, August, 1885, affirms with emphasis the existence of a 'grandiose e musicale struttura' in Whitman's poetry.

3. The opening lines of the Sapphic 'Hymn to the Aphrodite' show that the law is as old as Greece:

Aphrodite; daughter of Zeus, undying
Goddess, throned in glory, of love's beguilements,
Do not now with frenzy and desperation
Utterly crush me.

Compare also the opening sentences of the *Iliad* and the *Odyssey*.

—William Sloane Kennedy, "Whitman's Word-Music,"
Reminiscences of Walt Whitman, London, 1896, pp. 162–90

HENRY CHILDS MERWIN
"MEN AND LETTERS" (1897)

Walt Whitman was unable or unwilling to master the art of writing, and consequently his works, though abounding in lines and phrases of the highest excellence in form as well as in substance, are so uneven and unfinished that he cannot be called a great writer, and can hardly be expected to endure. But he was a man of great democratic ideas. He is the only author yet produced, in his country or in any other, who has perceived what democracy really means, and who has appreciated the beauty and the heroism which are found in the daily lives of the common people.

—Henry Childs Merwin, "Men and Letters,"
Atlantic, May 1897, p. 719

HALLAM TENNYSON (1897)

In this excerpt from his biography of his father, the British poet laureate Alfred, Lord Tennyson, Hallam Tennyson offers a glimpse into Tennyson's feelings for his contemporary and poetic rival. Though later in life the two men enjoyed a twenty-year friendship in correspondence, Whitman himself had earlier criticized Tennyson's traditional, formal verse as poetry for the upper class. Eventually, Whitman accepted the strong character of Tennyson's work despite its aristocratic sensibility, and Tennyson here shows an appreciation of the spiritual character of Whitman's free verse, despite its almost unbearable lack of poetic form. Hallam Tennyson's reminiscence provides useful thematic material for a comparison of the two poets.

Speaking of Walt Whitman, he (Tennyson) said to me, "Walt neglects form altogether, but there is a fine spirit breathing through his writings. Some of them are quite unreadable from nakedness of expression."

—Hallam Tennyson, *Alfred Lord Tennyson:
A Memoir*, 1897, Vol. 2, p. 424

JOHN JAY CHAPMAN "WALT WHITMAN" (1898)

In this scathingly critical and often sardonic study of Whitman, Chapman accuses the poet of numerous artistic and moral sins, from intellectual incoherence and quackery to egomania and affected patriotism.

Reviving the ad hominem attacks characteristic of early Whitman criticism, Chapman seems to praise Whitman for being absolutely and incomparably true to his own nature, but then turns this praise to mockery in describing Whitman as a lazy, vain, excessively sensuous tramp with no genuine understanding of his fellow human beings or of American democracy. When Chapman chooses to rein in his satire, he offers several astute comments about Whitman as a poetic observer whose work fails to probe beneath the surface of the natural landscape or of the city, but which nevertheless provides an accurate and obviously enthusiastic picture of those settings.

Chapman's essay is perhaps most valuable for students writing about Whitman's reception during the Gilded Age (1865–1901). Characterizing Whitman as a loafer and a charlatan, Chapman discloses the premium placed on high social and economic status, in sharp contrast to the ideals of independence and self-reliance Whitman himself seems to champion. Students writing about Whitman as a poet of the picturesque, or about the influence of landscape art and photography on Whitman's poetry, may find that Chapman's comments about Whitman as an observer offer some strong support for these arguments, in spite of the essay's overall satirical tone. Finally, Chapman's satirical treatment of Whitman may provide the starting point for an analysis of humor, or the perceived lack of it, in authors such as Whitman and Ralph Waldo Emerson generally associated with American transcendentalism.

—◁◁◁— —◁◁◁— —◁◁◁—

Walt Whitman has given utterance to the soul of the tramp. A man of genius has passed sincerely and normally through this entire experience, himself unconscious of what he was, and has left a record of it to enlighten and bewilder the literary world.

In Whitman's works the elemental parts of a man's mind and the fragments of imperfect education may be seen merging together, floating and sinking in a sea of insensate egotism and rhapsody, repellent, divine, disgusting, extraordinary.

Our inability to place the man intellectually, and find a type and reason for his intellectual state, comes from this: that the revolt he represents is not an intellectual revolt. Ideas are not at the bottom of it. It is a revolt from drudgery. It is the revolt of laziness.

There is no intellectual coherence in his talk, but merely pathological coherence. Can the insulting jumble of ignorance and effrontery, of scientific phrase and French paraphrase, of slang and inspired adjective, which he puts forward with the pretence that it represents thought, be regarded, from any possible point of view, as a philosophy, or a system, or a belief? Is it individualism of any statable kind? Do the thoughts and phrases which float about in it have a meaning which bears any relation to the meaning they bear in the language of thinkers? Certainly not. Does all the patriotic talk, the talk about the United States and its future, have any significance as patriotism? Does it poetically represent the state of feeling of any class of American citizens towards their country? Or would you find the nearest equivalent to this emotion in the breast of the educated tramp of France, or Germany, or England? The speech of Whitman is English, and his metaphors and catchwords are apparently American, but the emotional content is cosmic. He put off patriotism when he took to the road.

The attraction exercised by his writings is due to their flashes of reality. Of course the man was a poseur, a most horrid mountebank and ego-maniac. His tawdry scraps of misused idea, of literary smartness, of dog-eared and greasy reminiscence, repel us. The world of men remained for him as his audience, and he did to civilized society the continuous compliment of an insane self-consciousness in its presence.

Perhaps this egotism and posturing is the revenge of a stilled conscience, and we ought to read in it the inversion of the social instincts. Perhaps all tramps are poseurs. But there is this to be said for Whitman, that whether or not his posing was an accident of a personal nature, or an organic result of his life, he was himself an authentic creature. He did not sit in a study and throw off his saga of balderdash, but he lived a life, and it is by his authenticity, and not by his poses, that he has survived.

The descriptions of nature, the visual observation of life, are first-hand and wonderful. It was no false light that led the Oxonians to call some of his phrases Homeric. The pundits were right in their curiosity over him; they went astray only in their attempt at classification.

It is a pity that truth and beauty turn to cant on the second delivery, for it makes poetry, as a profession, impossible. The lyric poets have always spent most of their time in trying to write lyric poetry, and the very attempt disqualifies them.

A poet who discovers his mission is already half done for, and even Wordsworth, great genius though he was, succeeded in half drowning his talents in his parochial theories, in his own self-consciousness and self-conceit.

Walt Whitman thought he had a mission. He was a professional poet. He had purposes and theories about poetry which he started out to enforce and illustrate. He is as didactic as Wordsworth, and is thinking of himself the whole time. He belonged, moreover, to that class of professionals who are always particularly self-centred, autocratic, vain, and florid,—the class of quacks. There are, throughout society, men, and they are generally men of unusual natural powers, who, after gaining a little unassimilated education launch out for themselves and set up as authorities on their own account. They are, perhaps, the successors of the old astrologers, in that what they seek to establish is some personal professorship or predominance. The old occultism and mystery was resorted to as the most obvious device for increasing the personal importance of the magician; and the chief difference today between a regular physician and a quack is, that the quack pretends to know it all.

Brigham Young and Joseph Smith were men of phenomenal capacity, who actually invented a religion and created a community by the apparent establishment of supernatural and occult powers. The phrenologists, the vendors of patent medicine, the Christian Scientists, the single-taxers, and all who proclaim panaceas and nostrums make the same majestic and pontifical appeal to human nature. It is this mystical power, this religious element which floats them, sells the drugs, cures the sick, and packs the meetings.

By temperament and education Walt Whitman was fitted to be a prophet of this kind. He became a quack poet, and hampered his talents by the imposition of a monstrous parade of rattletrap theories and professions. If he had not been endowed with a perfectly marvellous capacity, a wealth of nature beyond the reach and plumb of his rodomontade, he would have been ruined from the start. As it is, he has filled his work with grimace and vulgarity. He writes a few lines of epic directness and cyclopean vigor and naturalness, and then obtrudes himself and his mission.

He has the bad taste bred in the bone of all missionaries and palmists, the sign-manual of a true quack. This bad taste is nothing more than the offensive intrusion of himself and his mission into the matter in hand. As for his real merits and his true mission, too much can hardly be said in his favor. The field of his experience was narrow, and not in the least intellectual. It was narrow because of his isolation from human life. A poet like Browning, or Heine, or Alfred de Musset deals constantly with the problems and struggles that arise in civilized life out of the close relationships, the ties, the duties and desires of the human heart. He explains life on its social side. He gives us some more or less coherent view of an infinitely complicated matter. He is a guide-book or a notebook, a highly trained and intelligent companion.

Walt Whitman has no interest in any of these things. He was fortunately so very ignorant and untrained that his mind was utterly incoherent and unintellectual. His mind seems to be submerged and to have become almost a part of his body. The utter lack of concentration which resulted from living his whole life in the open air has left him spontaneous and unaccountable. And the great value of his work is, that it represents the spontaneous and unaccountable functioning of the mind and body in health.

It is doubtful whether a man ever enjoyed life more intensely than Walt Whitman, or expressed the physical joy of mere living more completely. He is robust, all tingling with health, and the sensations of health. All that is best in his poetry is the expression of bodily well-being.

A man who leaves his office and gets into a canoe on a Canadian river, sure of ten days' release from the cares of business and housekeeping, has a thrill of joy such as Walt Whitman has here and there thrown into his poetry. One might say that to have done this is the greatest accomplishment in literature. Walt Whitman, in some of his lines, breaks the frame of poetry and gives us life in the throb.

It is the throb of the whole physical system of a man who breathes the open air and feels the sky over him. 'When lilacs last in the dooryard bloomed' is a great lyric. Here is a whole poem without a trace of self-consciousness. It is little more than a description of nature. The allusions to Lincoln and to the funeral are but a word or two—merest suggestions of the tragedy. But grief, overwhelming grief, is in every line of it, the grief which has been transmuted into this sensitiveness to the landscape, to the song of the thrush, to the lilac's bloom, and the sunset.

Here is truth to life of the kind to be found in King Lear or Guy Mannering, in Aeschylus or Burns.

Walt Whitman himself could not have told you why the poem was good. Had he had any intimation of the true reason, he would have spoiled the poem. The recurrence and antiphony of the thrush, the lilac, the thought of death, the beauty of nature, are in a balance and dream of natural symmetry such as no cunning could come at, no conscious art could do other than spoil.

It is ungrateful to note Whitman's limitations, his lack of human passion, the falseness of many of his notions about the American people. The man knew the world merely as an observer, he was never a living part of it, and no mere observer can understand the life about him. Even his work during the war was mainly the work of an observer, and his poems and notes upon the period are picturesque. As to his talk about comrades and Manhattanese car-drivers, and brass-founders displaying their brawny arms around each other's brawny necks, all this gush and sentiment in Whitman's poetry is false to life. It has a lyrical value, as representing Whitman's personal feelings, but no one else in the country was ever found who felt or acted like this.

In fact, in all that concerns the human relations Walt Whitman is as unreal as, let us say, William Morris, and the American mechanic would probably prefer Sigurd the Volsung, and understand it better than Whitman's poetry.

This falseness to the sentiment of the American is interwoven with such wonderful descriptions of American sights and scenery, of ferryboats, thoroughfares, cataracts, and machine-shops that it is not strange the foreigners should have accepted the gospel.

On the whole, Whitman, though he solves none of the problems of life and throws no light on American civilization, is a delightful appearance, and a strange creature to come out of our beehive. This man committed every unpardonable sin against our conventions, and his whole life was an outrage. He was neither chaste, nor industrious, nor religious. He patiently lived upon cold pie and tramped the earth in triumph.

He did really live the life he liked to live, in defiance of all men, and this is a great desert, a most stirring merit. And he gave, in his writings, a true picture of himself and of that life,—a picture which the world had never seen before, and which it is probable the world will not soon cease to wonder at.

—John Jay Chapman, "Walt Whitman,"
Emerson and Other Essays, 1898

JENNETTE BARBOUR PERRY "WHITMANIA" (1898)

It is a curious phase of Whitman's greatness—this intense personal following. There has been nothing like it in the history of letters. Johnson had only one Boswell. No man, apparently, could come near Whitman without being swayed from his own orbit. John Burroughs appears to be almost the only man who, knowing him very well, is able to stand up straight after it. The rest—some of them more and some of them less—have lost their sense of proportion. They have fallen into an embarrassing habit of referring to Whitman and Jesus of Nazareth in the same breath. (Implication in favor of Whitman.) We are willing that the Whitman buttons should be irradiated. It is harmless enough; but when we are obliged to see the buttons eclipse the person of Whitman, and the person of Whitman eclipse the personality, we are roused to mild resentment. It is, of course, a matter of some public interest to know how many times a day Mr. Whitman washed his hands, but we confess to a much larger curiosity as to the attitude of Walt Whitman the man towards comradship and life. Even the reiterated statement of his "cheerfulness" can hardly be said to be exhaustive.

A friend of mine, a man-of-letters, is wont to say that he "only hopes to live long enough to see that Whitman bubble burst." Anyone can recall more than one contemporary critic who will charge across a whole field in pursuit of any ragtag of Whitman that flutters in sight. Even the journals take sides. It would not be difficult to draw up two lists headed "Whitmanite" and "Anti-Whitmanite," and assign to one or the other almost every critical journal of the day. The situation is not to be solved by a sneer. One can only observe respectfully and ponder. There is something a little uncanny about the intense seriousness of the two sides. If the Whitmanites lay themselves open to ridicule by their assertive self-effacement, the Anti-Whitmanites come dangerously near the grotesque in their scathing contempt for this inoffensive man who only wished to "loafe and invite his soul."

"I am not a Comtist nor a Buddhist nor a Whitmanite," a friend writes me. Is the shade of ridicule towards the last class a figment of the fancy? A Whitmanite, it is to be feared, no matter how dignified his bearing, is never taken quite seriously. Perhaps it is the "ite," the remnant of the prejudice that hovers in the minds of men over the Hittites, Kenites, Perizzites, Jebusites. Perhaps it is phonetic. While Whitman lived he was never, in spite of the well-intentioned efforts of his friends, a ridiculous figure. The robustness and breeziness of the man put sentimentality where it belonged, and turned childish adulation into decent praise. Even the charity that his admirers brought upon him he accepted with sturdy good humor—and opened a bank-account. But now that Whitman is dead, all this is changed. Now that the head is gone, the decapitated body waves wild members, and calls it eulogy. First there was *In Re,* a volume that some of us who admire Whitman's genius cannot even yet open without qualms; and then *Whitman the Man,* and then *The Pete Letters,* and now, worse and most persistent of all, this Whitman journal. Is it any wonder that Whitman had the foresight to enter protest:

> I call the world to distrust the accounts of my friends, but listen to my
>   enemies, as I myself do.
> I charge you forever reject those who would expound me, for I cannot
>   expound myself.
> I charge that there be no theory or school founded out of me,
> I charge you to leave all free, as I have left all free.

—Jennette Barbour Perry, "Whitmania,"
Critic, February 26, 1898, pp. 137–38

THOMAS WENTWORTH HIGGINSON
"WHITMAN" (1899)

In this critical assessment, Thomas Wentworth Higginson claims Whitman's poetry suffers from several flaws and one major, fatal defect that prevent him from securing literary immortality. Best known as a correspondent, mentor, and editor of the American poet Emily Dickinson, Higginson finds Whitman's lyricism flawed by an impersonal sensuality, a lack of philosophical structure, and a dandyish use of foreign terms. Whitman's sensuality is "the blunt, undisguised attraction of sex to sex," lacking the idealism of the American poet Edgar Allan Poe or the mixture of the spiritual and the carnal found in the work of the English poet Christina Rossetti. Higginson wonders why Whitman cannot write a love poem dignified by feelings for a specific woman, suggesting his misunderstanding of Whitman's sexuality. Acknowledging that individual lines in Whitman's poems are touched with inspiration, Higginson questions the seriousness of Whitman's pro-American sentiments, noting how his borrowings from foreign languages call into question his nationalist project. Yet, more than inconsistency, Higginson claims, Whitman's work suffers most from inauthenticity. Whitman writes of laborers, he claims, like one who has never labored, and of war like one who has never served and fought.

Higginson's discussion will prove useful to explorations of how Whitman's audience responded to his sensual poetry, as well as to the common image of him as a libertine. Did Whitman's frankness make audiences more receptive, or did the caricature of Whitman as an ignorant, indecorous, lustful laborer interfere with this liberation in the years immediately following his death? Students comparing Whitman to later poets might focus on the topic of desire and ask to what extent Whitman's poetry provided a model for their own. Lastly, students writing about Whitman's representations of labor and war and his relation to the laboring classes may find Higginson's charge of inauthenticity a good counterexample of many common views. Readers might ask to what extent Whitman's various professions provided him a solid base of imagery and diction for depicting labor. Did other critics seem to agree with Higginson's charge? Why or why not? To what extent are Whitman's depictions of labor or of war historically accurate?

Whitman can never be classed, as Spinoza was by Schleiermacher, among "God-intoxicated" men; but he was early inebriated with two potent draughts—himself and his country:—

One's self I sing, a simple separate person,
Yet utter the word Democratic, the word, En Masse.

With these words his collected poems open, and to these he has always been true. They have brought with them a certain access of power, and they have also implied weakness; on the personal side leading to pruriency and on the national side to rant. For some reason or other our sexual nature is so ordained that it is very hard for a person to dwell much upon it, even for noble and generous purposes, without developing a tendency to morbidness; the lives of philanthropists and reformers have sometimes shown this; and when one insists on this part of our nature for purposes of self-glorification, the peril is greater. Whitman did not escape the danger; it is something that he outgrew it; and it is possible that if let entirely alone, which could hardly be expected, he might have dropped *Children of Adam,* and some of the more nauseous passages in other effusions, from his published works. One thing which has always accentuated the seeming grossness of the sensual side of his poems has been the entire absence of that personal and ideal side of passion which alone can elevate and dignify it. Probably no poet of equal pretensions was ever so entirely wanting in the sentiment of individual love for woman; not only has he given us no love-poem, in the ordinary use of that term, but it is as difficult to conceive of his writing one as of his chanting a serenade beneath the window of his mistress. His love is the blunt, undisguised attraction of sex to sex; and whether this appetite is directed towards a goddess or a streetwalker, a Queensbury or a handmaid, is to him absolutely unimportant. This not only separates him from the poets of thoroughly ideal emotion, like Poe, but from those, like Rossetti, whose passion, though it may incarnate itself in the body, has its sources in the soul.

As time went on, this less pleasing aspect became softened; his antagonisms were disarmed by applauses; although this recognition sometimes took a form so extreme and adulatory that it obstructed his path to that simple and unconscious life which he always preached but could not quite be said to practice. No one can be said to lead a noble life who writes puffs of himself and offers them to editors, or who borrows money of men as poor as himself and fails to repay it. Yet his career purified itself, as many careers do, in the alembic of years, and up to the time of his death (March 26, 1892) he gained constantly both in friends and in readers. Intellectually speaking, all critics now admit that he shows in an eminent degree that form of the ideal faculty which Emerson conceded to Margaret Fuller—he has "lyric glimpses." Rarely constructing anything, he is yet singularly gifted in phrases, in single cadences, in casual wayward strains as from an Aeolian harp. It constantly happens that the titles or catch-words of his poems are better than the poems themselves; as we sometimes hear it said in praise of a clergyman that he has beautiful texts. "Proud Music of the Storm," "When lilacs last in the door-yard bloomed," and others, will readily occur to memory. Often, on the other hand, they are inflated, as "Chanting the Square Deific," or affected and feeble, as "Eidolons." One of the most curiously un-American traits in a poet professedly so national is his way of interlarding foreign, and especially French, words to a degree that recalls the fashionable novels of the last generation, and gives an incongruous effect comparable only to Theodore Parker's description of an African chief seen by some one at Sierra Leone,—"With the exception of a dress-coat, his Majesty was as naked as a pestle." In the opening lines, already quoted from one of his collected volumes (ed. 1881), Whitman defines "the word Democratic, the word En Masse;" and everywhere French phrases present themselves. The vast sublimity of night on the prairies only suggests to him "how plenteous! how spiritual! how *resume*," whatever that may mean; he talks of "*Melange* mine own, the seen and the unseen;" writes poems "with reference to *ensemble*;" says "the future of the States I *harbinge* glad and sublime;" and elsewhere, "I blow through my *embouchures* my loudest and gayest for them." He is "the extolled of *amies*,"—meaning apparently mistresses; and says that neither youth pertains to him, "nor *delicatesse*." Phrases like these might be multiplied indefinitely, and when he says, "No dainty *dolce affettuoso* I," he seems vainly to disclaim being exactly what he is. He cannot even introduce himself to the audience without borrowing a foreign word,—"I, Walt Whitman, one of the roughs, a kosmos,"—and really stands in this respect on a plane not much higher than that of those young girls at boarding-school who commit French phrases to memory in order to use them in conversation and give a fancied tone of good society.

But after all, the offense, which is a trivial affectation in a young girl, has a deeper foundation in a man who begins his literary career at thirty-seven. The essential fault of Whitman's poetry was well pointed out by a man of more heroic nature and higher genius, Lanier, who defined him as a dandy. Of all our poets, he is really the least simple, the most meretricious; and this is the reason why the honest consciousness of the classes which he most celebrates,—the drover, the teamster, the soldier,—has never been reached by his songs. He talks of labor as one who has never really labored; his *Drum-Taps* proceed from one who has never personally responded to the tap of the drum. This is his fatal and insurmountable defect; and it is because his own countrymen instinctively recognize this, and foreigners do not, that his following has always been larger abroad than at home. But it is also true that he has, in a fragmentary and disappointing way, some of the very highest ingredients of a poet's nature: a keen eye, a ready sympathy, a strong touch, a vivid but not shaping imagination. In his cyclopaedia of epithets, in his accumulated directory of details, in his sandy wastes of iteration, there are many scattered particles of gold—never sifted out by him, not always abundant enough to pay for the sifting, yet unmistakable gold. He has something of the turgid wealth, the self-conscious and mouthing amplitude of Victor Hugo, and much of his broad, vague, indolent desire for the welfare of the whole human race; but he has none of Hugo's structural power, his dramatic or melodramatic instinct, and his occasionally terse and brilliant condensation. It is not likely that he will ever have that place in the future which is claimed for him by his English admirers or even by the more cautious indorsement of Mr. Stedman; for, setting aside all other grounds of criticism, he has phrase, but not form—and without form there is no immortality.

—Thomas Wentworth Higginson, "Whitman,"
Contemporaries, 1899, pp. 79–84

J.A. MacCulloch "Walt Whitman: The Poet of Brotherhood" (1899)

To many intellectual and cultured readers this latest prophet of brotherhood will seem a mere unintelligible babbler, because of the form of his verse, so alien to all the traditions of poetry. We can conceive the admirers of Pope's balanced couplets, or the lovers of Tennyson's mellifluous lines, turning up their noses at these shaggy and amorphous verses. Yet, for the passionate ardours with which he has fired so many readers, for his heroic strength, his creative impulse, his noble hopes, much may be forgiven to this herald of a new epoch. When such men as Tennyson, Ruskin, and Carlyle could find in him a kindred soul, his position cannot so easily be sneered away. For, in truth, his poems have the smack of life, of action, of hope; they were never written in a mock twilight by some peevish scribbler, whose verses are a penance to read, and their existence a slander upon human nature. They may, it is conceivable, disappoint those who think of poetry as mere candied sugar,

sweeter than the lids of Juno's eyes
Or Cytherea's breath.

Yet to those who love the sunlight and the breeze, and who cherish the hopes that make us manful, they will always be beloved and turned to as a source of inspiration and of strength.

—J.A. MacCulloch, "Walt Whitman: The Poet of Brotherhood,"
Westminster Review, November 1899, pp. 563–64

WILLIAM JAMES "A CONTEMPORARY POET" (1899)

Psychologist, philosopher, and a brother of novelist Henry James, William James praises Whitman's all-encompassing imagination, which finds terms of praise for everything in the world, and the goodness of his character, which seems untainted by misery, anger, or anxiety. James claims that Whitman, utterly untouched by evil, exemplifies "healthy-mindedness." This excerpt provides an excellent discussion of the psychology of Whitman's poetry.

Walt Whitman, for instance, is accounted by many of us a contemporary prophet. He abolishes the usual human distinctions, brings all conventionalisms into solution, and loves and celebrates hardly any human attributes save those elementary ones common to all members of the race. For this he becomes a sort of ideal tramp, a rider on omnibus-tops and ferry-boats, and, considered either practically or academically, a worthless, unproductive being. His verses are but ejaculations—things mostly without subject or verb, a succession of interjections on an immense scale. He felt the human crowd as rapturously as Wordsworth felt the mountains, felt it as an overpoweringly significant presence, simply to absorb one's mind in which should be business sufficient and worthy to fill the days of a serious man. . . .

When your ordinary Brooklynite or New Yorker, leading a life replete with too much luxury, or tired and careworn about his personal affairs, crosses the ferry or goes up Broadway, his fancy does not thus 'soar away into the colors of the sunset' as did Whitman's [in "Crossing Brooklyn Ferry"] nor does he inwardly realize at all the indisputable fact that this world never did anywhere or at any time contain more of essential divinity, or of eternal meaning, than is embodied in the fields of vision over which his eyes so carelessly pass. There is life; and there, a step away, is death. There is the only kind of beauty there ever was. There is the old human struggle and its fruits together. There is the text and the sermon, the real and the ideal in one. But to the jaded and unquickened eye it is all dead and common, pure vulgarism, flatness, and disgust. 'Hech! it is a sad sight!' says Carlyle, walking at night with some one who appeals to him to note the splendor of the stars. And that very repetition of the scene to new generations of men in *secula seculorum*, that eternal recurrence of the common order, which so fills a Whitman with mystic satisfaction, is to a Schopenhauer, with the emotional anaesthesia, the feeling of 'awful inner emptiness' from out of which he views it all, the chief ingredient of the tedium it instils. What is life on the largest scale, he asks, but the same recurrent inanities, the same dog barking, the same fly buzzing, forevermore? Yet of the kind of fibre of which such *inanities* consist is the material woven of all the excitements, joys, and *meanings* that ever were, or ever shall be, in this world.

—William James, "A Contemporary Poet,"
Talks to Teachers of Psychology, New York, 1899.
Reprinted 1913, pp. 248–54

GEORGE SANTAYANA "THE POETRY OF BARBARISM: II. WALT WHITMAN" (1900)

The Spanish-born philosopher, poet, and scholar George Santayana shows his ambivalent, but ultimately affirming, attitude toward Whitman in this essay. Disparaging Whitman as a thinker and as a poet of the people, Santayana nevertheless praises the elemental force of his poetry. Ungoverned by any preexisting principles or system of belief, Whitman's poems are his own unadorned perceptions, and thus a perfectly primitive art. Like the Bible's Adam, who names the animals in the Garden of Eden, Whitman regards creation and the work of human life from a fresh, pure perspective. Yet, according to Santayana, Whitman mistakenly believes that the common, laboring classes that exemplify and experience this elemental existence would cherish it; Whitman thus appeals most to intellectuals and foreigners whose lives are removed from the basic concerns of the pioneer. When Whitman elevated political democracy to a moral principle, Santayana argues, the poet excluded ideals that would prove antithetical to what he believed was America's essential egalitarian, pioneering spirit. Still, Santayana finds that Whitman's vigorous, inclusive, joyous spirit provides affirmation and companionship for readers afflicted by the disappointments and despair of conventional day-to-day life.

An important figure in American philosophy, Santayana was deeply interested in the connections among art, literature, religion, and philosophy. His claim that Whitman appeals to a "sensuality touched with mysticism" anticipates the twentieth-century writer Malcolm Cowley's introduction to Whitman's 1855 *Leaves of Grass*, which emphasized Whitman's mysticism, but could leave readers wondering to what extent Santayana focuses on the spiritual impulse in Whitman's poetry, and to what extent the re-creation and intensification of sensory experience. Like many other readers, Santayana discusses Whitman's political values, attention to nature and the senses, and evocation of the chaos and diversity of nineteenth-century American society, but curiously, Santayana is less attentive to Whitman's themes of mortality and the afterlife. Readers might ask if this omission reflects a change in literary values between the nineteenth and twentieth centuries, particularly coming from Santayana, whose ideas influenced such modernist writers as T.S. Eliot and Wallace Stevens.

The works of Walt Whitman offer an extreme illustration of this phase of genius (barbarism), both by their form and by their substance. It was the singularity of his literary form—the challenge it threw to the conventions of verse and of language—that first gave Whitman notoriety: but this notoriety has become fame, because those incapacities and solecisms which glare at us from his pages are only the obverse of a profound inspiration and of a genuine courage. Even the idiosyncrasies of his style have a side which is not mere perversity or affectation; the order of his words, the procession of his images, reproduce the method of a rich, spontaneous, absolutely lazy fancy. In most poets such a natural order is modified by various governing motives—the thought, the metrical form, the echo of other poems in the memory. By Walt Whitman these conventional influences are resolutely banished. We find the swarms of men and objects rendered as they might strike the retina in a sort of waking dream. It is the most sincere possible confession of the lowest—I mean the most primitive—type of perception. All ancient poets are sophisticated in comparison and give proof of longer intellectual and moral training. Walt Whitman has gone back to the innocent style of Adam, when the animals filed before him one by one and he called each of them by its name.

In fact, the influences to which Walt Whitman was subject were as favourable as possible to the imaginary experiment of beginning the world over again. Liberalism and transcendentalism both harboured some illusions on that score; and they were in the air which our poet breathed. Moreover he breathed this air in America, where the newness of the material environment made it easier to ignore the fatal antiquity of human nature. When he afterward became aware that there was or had been a world with a history, he studied that world with curiosity and spoke of it not without a certain shrewdness. But he still regarded it as a foreign world and imagined, as not a few Americans have done, that his own world was a fresh creation, not amenable to the same laws as the old. The difference in the conditions blinded him, in his merely sensuous apprehension, to the identity of the principles.

His parents were farmers in central Long Island and his early years were spent in that district. The family seems to have been not too prosperous and somewhat nomadic; Whitman himself drifted through boyhood without much guidance. We find him now at school, now helping the labourers at the farms, now wandering along the beaches of Long Island, finally at Brooklyn working in an apparently desultory way as a printer and sometimes as a writer for a local newspaper. He must have read or heard something, at this early period, of the English classics; his style often betrays the deep effect made upon him by the grandiloquence of the Bible, of Shakespeare, and of Milton. But his chief interest, if we may trust his account, was already in his own sensations. The aspects of Nature, the forms and habits of animals, the sights of cities, the movement and talk of common people, were his constant delight. His mind was flooded with these images, keenly felt and afterward to be vividly rendered with bold strokes of realism and imagination.

Many poets have had this faculty to seize the elementary aspects of things, but none has had it so exclusively; with Whitman the surface is absolutely all and the underlying structure is without interest and almost without existence. He had had no education and his natural delight in imbibing sensations had not been trained to the uses of practical or theoretical intelligence. He basked in the sunshine of perception and wallowed in the stream of his own sensibility, as later at Camden in the shallows of his favourite brook. Even during the civil war, when he heard the drum-taps so clearly, he could only gaze at the picturesque and terrible aspects of the struggle, and linger among the wounded day after day with a canine devotion; he could not be aroused either to clear thought or to positive action. So also in his poems; a multiplicity of images pass before him and he yields himself to each in turn with absolute passivity. The world has no inside; it is a phantasmagoria of continuous visions, vivid, impressive, but monotonous and hard to distinguish in memory, like the waves of the sea or the decorations of some barbarous temple, sublime only by the infinite aggregation of parts.

This abundance of detail without organization, this wealth of perception without intelligence and of imagination without taste, makes the singularity of Whitman's genius. Full of sympathy and receptivity, with a wonderful gift of graphic characterization and an occasional rare grandeur of diction, he fills us with a sense of the individuality and the universality of what he describes—it is a drop in itself yet a drop in the ocean. The absence of any principle of selection or of a sustained style enables him to render aspects of things and of emotion which would have eluded a trained writer. He is, therefore, interesting even where he is grotesque or perverse. He has accomplished, by the sacrifice of almost every other good quality, something never so well done before. He has approached common life without bringing in his mind any higher standard by which to criticise it; he has seen it, not in contrast with an ideal, but as the expression of forces more indeterminate and elementary than itself; and the vulgar, in this cosmic setting, has appeared to him sublime.

There is clearly some analogy between a mass of images without structure and the notion of an absolute democracy. Whitman, inclined by his genius and habits to see life without relief or organization, believed that his inclination in this respect corresponded with the spirit of his age and country, and that Nature and society, at least in the United States, were constituted after the fashion of his own mind. Being the poet of the average man, he wished all men to be specimens of that average, and being the poet of a fluid Nature, he believed that Nature was or should be a formless flux. This personal bias of Whitman's was further encouraged by the actual absence of distinction in his immediate environment. Surrounded by ugly things and common people, he felt himself happy, ecstatic, overflowing with a kind of patriarchal love. He accordingly came to think that there was a spirit of the New World which he embodied, and which was in complete opposition to that of the Old, and that a literature upon novel principles was needed to express and strengthen this American spirit.

Democracy was not to be merely a constitutional device for the better government of given nations, not merely a movement for the material improvement of the lot of the poorer classes. It was to be a social and a moral democracy and to involve an actual equality among all men. Whatever kept them apart and made it impossible for them to be messmates together was to be discarded. The literature of democracy was to ignore all extraordinary gifts of genius or virtue, all distinction drawn even from great passions or romantic adventures. In Whitman's works, in which this new literature is foreshadowed, there is accordingly not a single character nor a single story. His only hero is Myself, the "single separate person," endowed with the primary impulses, with health, and with sensitiveness to the elementary aspects of Nature. The perfect man of the future, the prolific begetter of other perfect men, is to work with his hands, chanting the poems of some future Walt, some ideally democratic bard. Women are to have as nearly as possible the same character as men: the emphasis is to pass from family life and local ties to the friendship of comrades and the general brotherhood of man. Men are to be vigorous, comfortable, sentimental, and irresponsible.

This dream is, of course, unrealized and unrealizable, in America as elsewhere. Undeniably there are in America many suggestions of such a society and such a national character. But the growing complexity and fixity of institutions necessarily tends to obscure these traits of a primitive and crude democracy. What Whitman seized upon as the promise of the future was in reality the survival of the past. He sings the song of pioneers, but it is in the nature of the pioneer that the greater his success the quicker must be his transformation into something different. When Whitman made the initial and amorphous phase of society his ideal, he became the prophet of a lost cause. That cause was lost, not merely when wealth and intelligence began to take shape in the American Commonwealth, but it was lost at the very foundation of the world, when those laws of evolution were established which Whitman, like Rousseau, failed to understand. If we may trust Mr. Herbert Spencer, these laws involve a passage from the homogeneous to the heterogeneous, and a constant progress at once in differentiation and in organization—all, in a word, that Whitman systematically deprecated or ignored. He is surely not the spokesman of the tendencies of his country, although he describes some aspects of its past and present condition: nor does he appeal to those whom he describes, but rather to the *dilettanti* he despises. He is regarded as representative chiefly by foreigners, who look for some grotesque expression of the genius of so young and prodigious a people.

Whitman, it is true, loved and comprehended men; but this love and comprehension had the same limits as his love and comprehension of Nature. He observed truly and responded to his observation with genuine and pervasive emotion. A great gregariousness, an innocent tolerance of moral weakness, a genuine admiration for bodily health and strength, made him bubble over with affection for the generic human creature. Incapable of an ideal passion, he was full of the milk of human kindness. Yet, for all his acquaintance with the ways and thoughts of the common man of his choice, he did not truly understand him. For to understand people is to go much deeper than they go themselves; to penetrate to their characters and disentangle their inmost ideals. Whitman's insight into man did not go beyond a sensuous sympathy; it consisted in a vicarious satisfaction in their pleasures, and an instinctive love of their persons. It never approached a scientific or imaginative knowledge of their hearts.

Therefore Whitman failed radically in his dearest ambition: he can never be a poet of the people. For the people, like the early races whose poetry was ideal, are natural believers in perfection. They have no doubts about the absolute desirability of wealth and learning and power, none about the worth of pure goodness and pure love. Their chosen poets, if they have any, will be always those who have known how to paint these ideals in lively even if in gaudy colours. Nothing is farther from the common people than the corrupt desire to be primitive. They instinctively look toward a more exalted life, which they imagine to be full of distinction and pleasure, and the idea of that brighter existence fills them with hope or with envy or with humble admiration.

If the people are ever won over to hostility to such ideals, it is only because they are cheated by demagogues who tell them that if all the flowers of civilization were destroyed its fruits would become more abundant. A greater share of happiness, people think, would fall to their lot could they destroy everything beyond their own possible possessions. But they are made thus envious and ignoble only by a deception: what they really desire is an ideal good for themselves which they are told they may secure by depriving others of their preeminence. Their hope is always to enjoy perfect satisfaction themselves; and therefore a poet who loves the picturesque aspects of labour and vagrancy will hardly be the poet of the poor. He may have described their figure and occupation, in neither of which they are much interested; he will not have read their souls. They will prefer to him any sentimental story-teller, any sensational dramatist, any moralizing poet; for they are hero-worshippers by temperament, and are too wise or too unfortunate to be much enamoured of themselves or of the conditions of their existence.

Fortunately, the political theory that makes Whitman's principle of literary prophecy and criticism does not always inspire his chants, nor is it presented, even in his prose works, quite bare and unadorned. In *Democratic Vistas* we find it clothed with something of the same poetic passion and lighted up with the same flashes of intuition which we admire in the poems. Even there the temperament is finer than the ideas and the poet wiser than the thinker. His ultimate appeal is really to something more primitive and general than any social aspirations, to something more elementary than an ideal of any kind. He speaks to those minds and to those moods in which sensuality is touched with mysticism. When the intellect is in abeyance, when we would "turn and live with the animals, they are so placid and self-contained," when we are weary of conscience and of ambition, and would yield ourselves for a while to the dream of sense, Walt Whitman is a welcome companion. The images he arouses in us, fresh, full of light and health and of a kind of frankness and beauty, are prized all the more at such a time because they are not choice, but drawn perhaps from a hideous and sordid environment. For this circumstance makes them a better means of escape from convention and from that fatigue and despair which lurk not far beneath the surface of conventional life. In casting off with self-assurance and a sense of fresh vitality the distinctions of tradition and reason a man may feel, as he sinks back comfortably to a lower level of sense and instinct, that he is returning to Nature or escaping into the infinite. Mysticism makes us proud and happy to renounce the work of intelligence, both in thought and in life, and persuades us that we become divine by remaining imperfectly human. Walt Whitman gives a new expression to this ancient and multiform tendency. He feels his own cosmic justification and he would lend the sanction of his inspiration to all loafers and holiday-makers. He would be the congenial patron of farmers and factory hands in their crude pleasures and pieties, as Pan was the patron of the shepherds of Arcadia: for he is sure that in spite of his hairiness and animality, the gods will acknowledge him as one of themselves and smile upon him from the serenity of Olympus.

—George Santayana, "The Poetry of Barbarism:
II. Walt Whitman," *Interpretations of Poetry and Religion*,
1900, pp. 177–87

William P. Trent (1903)

He seems to be as much the victim of jargon as of cant. His catalogues, his trailing lines, his blundering foreign locutions are as little spontaneous, as little appropriate to his purposes and subjects, as any mannerisms known to the student of pedantic epochs. They are scarcely signs of decadence, as we have seen, nor are they to be set down as mere affectations. They are far more probably effects of an inborn want of art, of a combination of overearnestness and underculture. It is worth noting, however, that they seem to produce on some readers a sort of hypnotic effect, and that during the latter half of Whitman's career he appeared to slough them off to a fair extent. For this reason a beginner in Whitman might almost be advised to read *Leaves of Grass* backward. However this may be, it is surely a mistake to suppose that Whitman is throughout his work the cataloguer in jargon that so jostles the poet of "Starting from Paumanok" and "I Sing the Body Electric." As for his free rhythm, it must suffice to say that this too has its hypnotic effects, and that it is on the whole satisfactory to many cultivated ears. Whitman loved music, and there is music in his best verse, which, if not precisely metrical, is not altogether lawless. That the compositions couched in it are entitled to the name of poems seems obvious, not merely on account of their emotional and imaginative power when the poet is at his best, but also because they do not often suggest the rhythm of prose. At least it is apparent to the student of Whitman's prose that its rhythmical qualities are different from those of his hypothetical verse.

—William P. Trent, A *History of American Literature,*
1903, pp. 493–94

G.K. CHESTERTON
"CONVENTIONS AND THE HERO" (1904)

The cynics (pretty little lambs) tell us that experience and the advance of years teach us the hollowness and artificiality of things. In our youth, they say, we imagine ourselves among roses, but when we pluck them they are red paper. Now, I believe everybody alive knows that the reverse of this is the truth. We grow conservative as we grow old, it is true. But we do not grow conservative because we have found so many new things spurious. We grow conservative because we have found so many old things genuine. We begin by thinking all conventions, all traditions, false and meaningless. Then one convention after another, one tradition after another, begins to explain itself, begins to beat with life under our hand. We thought these things were simply stuck on to human life; we find that they are rooted. We thought it was only a tiresome regulation that we should take off our hats to a lady; we find it is the pulse of chivalry and the splendour of the West. We thought it was artificial to dress for dinner. We realize that the festive idea, the idea of the wedding garment, is more natural than Nature itself. As I say, the precise opposite of the cynical statement is the truth. Our ardent boyhood believes things to be dead; and graver manhood discovers them to be alive. We waken in our infancy and believe ourselves surrounded by red paper. We pluck at it and find that it is roses.

A good instance may be found in the case of a great man who has been the sole spiritual support of me and many others, who will remain one of our principal spiritual supports. Walt Whitman is, I suppose, beyond question the ablest man America has yet produced. He also happens to be, incidentally, one of the greatest men of the nineteenth century. Ibsen is all very well, Zola is all very well and Maeterlinck is all very well; but we have begun already to get to the end of them. And we have not yet begun to get to the beginning of Whitman. The egoism of which men accuse him is that sense of human divinity which no one has felt since Christ. The baldness of which men accuse him is simply that splendidly casual utterance which no sage has used since Christ. But all the same, this gradual and glowing conservatism which grows upon us as we live leads us to feel that in just those points in which he violated the chief conventions of poetry, in just those points he was wrong. He was mistaken in abandoning metre in poetry, not because in forsaking it he was forsaking anything ornamental or anything civilized, as he himself thought. In forsaking metre he was forsaking something quite wild and barbarous, something as instinctive as anger and as necessary as meat. He forgot that all real things move in a rhythm, that the heart beats in harmony, that the seas rise and ebb in harmony. He forgot that any child who shouts falls into some sort of repetition and assonance, that the wildest dancing is at the bottom monotonous. The whole of Nature moves in a recurrent music; it is only with a considerable effort of civilization that we can contrive to be other than musical. The whole world talks poetry; it is only we who, with elaborate ingenuity, manage to talk prose.

The same that is true of Whitman's violation of metre is true, though in a minor degree, of his violation of what is commonly called modesty. Decorum itself is of little social value; sometimes it is a sign of social decay. Decorum is the morality of immoral societies. The people who care most about modesty are often those who care least about chastity; no better examples could be given than oriental Courts or the west-end drawing-rooms. But all the same Whitman was wrong. He was wrong because he had at the back of his mind the notion that modesty or decency was in itself an artificial thing. This is quite a mistake. The roots of modesty, like the roots of mercy or of any other traditional virtue, are to be found in all fierce and primitive things. A wild shyness, a fugitive self-possession, belongs to all simple creatures. It belongs to children; it belongs to savages; it belongs even to animals.

To conceal something is the first of Nature's lessons; it is far less elaborate than to explain everything. And if women are, as they certainly are, much more dignified and much more modest than men, if they are more reticent, and, in the excellent current phrase, 'keep themselves to themselves' much more, the reason is very simple; it is because women are much more fierce and much more savage than men. To be thoroughly immodest is an exceedingly elaborate affair. To have complete self-revelation one must have complete self-consciousness. Thus it is that while from the beginning of the world men have had the most exquisite philosophies and social arrangements, nobody ever thought of complete indecency, indecency on principle, until we reached a high and complex state of civilization. To conceal some things came to us like eating bread. To talk about everything never appeared until the age of the motor-car.

—G.K. Chesterton, "Conventions and the Hero," 1904

EZRA POUND "WHAT I FEEL ABOUT WALT WHITMAN" (1909)

The galvanizing force behind modernism, the American poet, translator, and literary theorist Ezra Pound admitted his reluctant debt to Walt Whitman in his poem "A Pact," claiming that "It was you [Whitman] that broke the new wood, / Now is a time for carving." The following essay, characterized by Pound's evocation of the spoken voice through intentional misspellings and grammatical elisions, further explores his ambivalent attitude toward Whitman. For Pound, Whitman mirrors America exactly, to the point where "He *is* America" in all its crudeness and philistinism. Yet while Pound finds Whitman "disgusting," Pound cannot help but praise his predecessor's genius. Pound hails Whitman as the father of American poetry, both because he achieved his visionary goal of embodying all America in poetry, and because like Dante he was the first to write in the "vulgar" or common language of his nation. Moreover, Pound acknowledges that he now sees Whitman as a figure of world importance precisely because he is a quintessentially American poet, a profound achievement given the longstanding influence of European culture on America. Yet because Whitman's America was a young country, so Whitman's poetry is a profound beginning for later poets to follow, but not a final masterpiece.

As much as Pound is concerned with the influence of Whitman's genius on future poetry, he is also reflecting on Whitman's particular influence on his own work. Early in the essay, Pound identifies himself as a world citizen rather than as an American, and this distance enables him to detail and discuss Whitman's achievements without having to participate in the divisive arguments characteristic of earlier Whitman criticism. Reflecting on his artistic relationship to Whitman, Pound distinguishes between the poet's "Tricks" and his "message." Pound refuses to appropriate Whitman's tricks, which would likely include the long-lined free verse, sublime egotism, and incantatory rhythms of *Leaves of Grass*. Nevertheless Pound shares in Whitman's message, which Pound takes to be the appreciation of beauty as well as the reassertion of art's central place in all human existence, including history, politics, philosophy, and economics.

Pound's essay represents an important shift in Whitman criticism and scholarship, and students exploring changing attitudes toward Whitman might reflect on the changes represented by this essay, written seventeen years after Whitman's death. Instead of concerning himself with Whitman's personal character, with his relative place in the literary canon, or even with particular passages from his poetry, Pound writes about Whitman as a resource for future artists, as well as a world figure whose profundity can be measured by his influence on society. Students writing about Whitman's relationship to modernism will find Pound's essay an essential starting point, for his criticism and praise alike reveal many of the principles of literary modernism, most importantly the paradox of Pound's injunction to "Make it new!" and the profound engagement with Western civilization in the works of such poets as Pound himself, T.S. Eliot, H.D. (Hilda Doolittle), Hart Crane, and even the most Whitmanlike modernist, William Carlos Williams. Finally, students wishing to make a direct comparison of the two poets should consider Pound's decision to single out Whitman's "To the Sunset Breeze" and attempt to explain why Pound would favor that particular poem.

⸻ ⸻ ⸻

From this side of the Atlantic I am for the first time able to read Whitman, and from the vantage of my education and—if it be permitted a man of my scant years—my world citizenship: I see him America's poet. The only Poet before the artists of the Carmen-Hovey [*sic*] period, or better, the only one of the conventionally recognized 'American Poets' who is worth reading.

He *is* America. His crudity is an exceeding great stench, but it *is* America. He is the hollow place in the rock that echo, with his time. He *does* 'chant the crucial stage' and he is the 'voice triumphant.' He is disgusting. He is an exceedingly nauseating pill, but he accomplishes his mission.

Entirely free from the renaissance humanist ideal of the complete man or from the Greek idealism, he is content to be what he is, and he is his time and his people. He is a genius because he has vision of what he is and of his function. He knows that he is a beginning and not a classically finished work.

I honor him for he prophesied me while I can only recognize him as a forebear of whom I ought to be proud.

In America there is much for the healing of the nations, but woe unto him of the cultured palate who attempts the dose.

As for Whitman, I read him (in many parts) with the acute pain, but when I write of certain things I find myself using his rhythms. The expression of certain things related to cosmic consciousness seems tainted with this maramis.

I am (in common with every educated man) an heir of the ages and I demand my birth-right. Yet if Whitman represented his time in language acceptable to one accustomed to my standard of intellectual-artistic living he would belie his time and nation. And yet I am but one of his 'ages and ages encrustations' or to be exact an encrustation of the next age. The vital part of my message, taken from the sap and fibre of America, is the same as his.

Mentally I am a Walt Whitman who has learned to wear a collar and a dress shirt (although at times inimical to both). Personally I might be very glad to conceal my relationship to my spiritual father and brag about my more congenial ancestry—Dante, Shakespeare, Theocritus, Villon, but the descent is a bit difficult to establish. And, to be frank, Whitman is to my fatherland (Patriam quam odi et amo for no uncertain reasons) what Dante is to Italy and I at my best can only be a strife for a renaissance in America of all the lost or temporarily mislaid beauty, truth, valor, glory of Greece, Italy, England and all the rest of it.

And yet if a man has written lines like Whitman's to the 'Sunset breeze' one has to love him. I think we have not yet paid enough attention to the deliberate artistry of the man, not in details but in the large.

I am immortal even as he is, yet with a lesser vitality as I am the more in love with beauty (If I really do love it more than he did). Like Dante he wrote in the 'vulgar tongue', in a new metric. The first great man to write in the language of his people.

Et ego Petrarca in lingua vetera scribo, and in a tongue my people understand not.

It seems to me I should like to drive Whitman into the old world. I sledge, he drill—and to scourge America with all the old beauty. (For Beauty is an accusation) and with a thousand thongs from Homer to Yeats, from Theocritus to Marcel Schwob. This desire is because I am young and impatient, were I old and wise I should content myself in seeing and saying that these things will come. But now, since I am by no means sure it would be true prophecy, I am fain set my own hand to the labour.

It is a great thing, reading a man to know, not 'His Tricks are not as yet my Tricks, but I can easily make them mine' but 'His message is my message. We will see that men hear it.'

—Ezra Pound, "What I Feel About
Walt Whitman," February 1, 1909

Virginia Woolf
"Visits to Walt Whitman" (1918)

In this essay appreciation, the twentieth-century English novelist, feminist author, and literary theorist Virginia Woolf explores the ties between
Whitman's personal character and the quality of his poetic "voice,"
which she characterizes as humane, pleasure seeking, and optimistic. Recounting the history of how Whitman's poetry was brought to
England, Woolf remarks on the pleasure of finding and reading the
work of an author not yet discovered or championed by literary critics,
suggesting that Whitman's poetry provides a perennial freshness for
any reader. She then describes Whitman's personal deportment, depicting somewhat pleasurably his messy home arrangements and his soft,
working-class attire, which she associates with Whitman's own cham-
pioning of the "common" American. Woolf marvels at how Whitman
addresses writers of world stature such as Shakespeare and Aeschylus
with the almost gossipy familiarity reserved for friends and colleagues,
rather than literary figures. Finally, Woolf compares him with the English
writer Thomas Carlyle, finding the latter irrevocably dismal and unhappy
while emphasizing the ever-increasing blissfulness and happiness of
Whitman's voice.

This essay is most useful for students exploring the links between
Whitman's biography or personal character and his poetry, or for
those seeking ways to characterize the voice in his poetry. While Woolf
compares Whitman to several other literary figures, these associations are
made mostly in passing, and thus offer little material for a comparison.
The extended contrast with Carlyle, however, offers possibilities for
an analysis of the two authors, particularly in terms of their response
to modernization, a discussion that might be further enlightened by
considering Whitman's relation to Ralph Waldo Emerson, the American
author who was most responsible for the transcendental movement.
Emerson was an important supporter of Whitman's early work and was,
despite his own optimistic nature, a close friend of Carlyle's.

The great fires of intellectual life which burn at Oxford and at Cambridge are
so well tended and long established that it is difficult to feel the wonder of
this concentration upon immaterial things as one should. When, however,
one stumbles by chance upon an isolated fire burning brightly without
associations or encouragement to guard it, the flame of the spirit becomes a
visible hearth where one may warm one's hands and utter one's thanksgiving.

It is only by chance that one comes upon them; they burn in unlikely places. If asked to sketch the condition of Bolton about the year 1885 one's thoughts would certainly revolve round the cotton market, as if the true heart of Bolton's prosperity must lie there. No mention would be made of the group of young men—clergymen, manufacturers, artisans, and bank clerks by profession—who met on Monday evenings, made a point of talking about something serious, could broach the most intimate and controversial matters frankly and without fear of giving offence, and held in particular the view that Walt Whitman was 'the greatest epochal figure in all literature'. Yet who shall set a limit to the effect of such talking? In this instance, besides the invaluable spiritual service, it also had some surprisingly tangible results. As a consequence of those meetings two of the talkers crossed the Atlantic; a steady flow of presents and messages set in between Bolton and Camden; and Whitman as he lay dying had the thought of 'those good Lancashire chaps' in his mind. The book recounting these events has been published before, but it is well worth reprinting for the light it sheds upon a new type of hero and the kind of worship which was acceptable to him.

To Whitman there was nothing unbefitting the dignity of a human being in the acceptance either of money or of underwear, but he said that there is no need to speak of these things as gifts. On the other hand, he had no relish for a worship founded upon the illusion that he was somehow better or other than the mass of human beings. 'Well,' he said, stretching out his hand to greet Mr Wallace, 'you've come to be disillusioned, have you?' And Mr Wallace owned to himself that he was a little disillusioned. Nothing in Walt Whitman's appearance was out of keeping with the loftiest poetic tradition. He was a magnificent old man, massive, shapely, impressive by reason of his power, his delicacy, and his unfathomable depths of sympathy. The disillusionment lay in the fact that 'the greatest epochal figure in all literature' was 'simpler, homelier, and more intimately related to myself than I had imagined'. Indeed, the poet seems to have been at pains to bring his common humanity to the forefront. And everything about him was as rough as it could be. The floor, which was only half carpeted, was covered with masses of papers, eating and washing things mixed themselves with proofs and newspaper cuttings in such ancient accumulations that a precious letter from Emerson dropped out accidentally from the mass after years of interment. In the midst of all this litter Walt Whitman sat spotlessly clean in his rough grey suit, with much more likeness to a retired farmer whose working days are over; it pleased him to talk of this man and of that, to ask questions about their children and their land; and, whether it was the result of thinking back over places and human beings rather than over books and thoughts, his mood was uniformly benignant. His temperament, and no sense of duty, led him to this point of view, for in his opinion it behoved him to 'give out or express what I really was, and, if I felt like the Devil, to say so!'

And then it appeared that this wise and free-thinking old farmer was getting letters from Symonds and sending messages to Tennyson, and was indisputably, both in his opinion and in yours, of the same stature and importance as any of the heroic figures of the past or present Their names dropped into his talk as the names of equals. Indeed, now and then something seemed 'to set him apart in spiritual isolation and to give him at times an air of wistful sadness', while into his free and easy gossip drifted without effort the phrases and ideas of his poems. Superiority and vitality lay not in a class but in the bulk; the average of the American people, he insisted, was immense, 'though no man can become truly heroic who is really poor'. And 'Shakespeare and suchlike' come in of their own accord on the heels of other matters. 'Shakespeare is the poet of great personalities.' As for passion, 'I rather think Aeschylus greater'. 'A ship in full sail is the grandest sight in the world, and it has never yet been put into a poem.' Or he would throw off comments as from an equal height upon his great English contemporaries. Carlyle, he said, 'lacked amorousness'. Carlyle was a growler. When the stars shone brightly—'I guess an exception in that country'—and some one said 'It's a beautiful sight', Carlyle said, 'It's a sad sight' . . . 'What a growler he was!'

It is inevitable that one should compare the old age of two men who steered such different courses until one saw nothing but sadness in the shining of the stars and the other could sink into a reverie of bliss over the scent of an orange. In Whitman the capacity for pleasure seemed never to diminish, and the power to include grew greater and greater, so that although the authors of this book lament that they have only a trivial bunch of sayings to offer us, we are left with a sense of an 'immense background or vista' and stars shining more brightly than in our climate.

—Virginia Woolf, "Visits to Walt Whitman,"
Times Literary Supplement, January 3, 1918

D.H. LAWRENCE "POETRY OF THE PRESENT" (1920)

The unrestful, ungraspable poetry of the sheer present, poetry whose very permanency lies in its wind-like transit. Whitman's is the best poetry of this kind. Without beginning and without end, without any base and pediment, it sweeps past for ever, like a wind that is forever in passage, and unchainable. Whitman truly looked before and after. But he did not sigh for what is not. The clue to all his utterance lies in the sheer appreciation of the instant moment, life surging itself into utterance at its very well-head. Eternity is only an abstraction from the actual present. Infinity is only a great reservoir of recollection, or a reservoir of aspiration: titan-made. The quivering nimble hour of the present, this is the quick of Time. This is the immanence. The quick of the universe is the pulsating *carnal self*, mysterious and palpable. So it is always.

Because Whitman put this into his poetry, we fear him and respect him so profoundly. We should not fear him if he sang only of the 'old unhappy far-off things', or of the 'wings of the morning'. It is because his heart beats with the urgent, insurgent Now, which is even upon us all, that we dread him. He is so near the quick. . . .

Such is the rare new poetry. One realm we have never conquered: the pure present. One great mystery of time is *terra incognita* to us: the instant. The most superb mystery we have hardly recognized: the immediate, instant self. The quick of all time is the instant. The quick of all the universe, of all creation, is the incarnate, carnal self. Poetry gave us the clue: free verse: Whitman. Now we know.

—D.H. Lawrence, "Poetry of the Present,"
Intro. to American edition of *New Poems*, 1920

D.H. LAWRENCE "WHITMAN" (1921)

Prolific and controversial, the English novelist, poet, and essayist D.H. Lawrence was profoundly influenced by Whitman's poetry, particularly its celebration of human sexuality and its evocation of a cosmic consciousness. In this excerpt from his landmark work on American literature, Lawrence praises Whitman's intensity, his vast sympathies (which erase all false divisions between, for example, good and evil, man and woman), and his ultimate unification of life and death in one "mystic circuit."

Lawrence claims that Whitman's identification with mankind as a whole paradoxically proves to be a form of self-expression, for Whitman's personal self is reasserted rather than lost in this cosmic extension. Yet Lawrence criticizes Whitman for constantly striving after universality instead of periodically withdrawing into solitary selfhood, a healthy antidote that Lawrence likens to the systole and diastole of the human pulse. Nevertheless, Lawrence affirms Whitman's attempt to embrace life and death absolutely in his poetry, claiming that such harmony is essential to the future of all nations, all literature, all ties among human beings, and to existence itself.

In somewhat veiled language in the latter part of the essay, Lawrence explores Whitman's idealization of homosexuality in the relationship of "comrades." While Lawrence claims Whitman is wrong to exclude heterosexual love and marriage from the process of ultimate human fulfillment, he is nevertheless correct in representing that final state as a quasi-platonic relationship that surpasses the bonds of sexuality but does not reject them. Hailing him as the greatest modern poet, Lawrence criticizes the American public for failing to appreciate the profound humanity of Whitman's art, which for Lawrence signals a new dawn in human existence.

Students using psychoanalytical and existential approaches to Whitman's poetry will find this essay essential reading. Lawrence's observations about Whitman's development of the higher consciousness through his embrace of the lower dimensions of the human psyche correspond to Freud's divisions of the id, ego, and superego. Lawrence's emphasis on Whitman's intensity, which he often likens to Dionysian ecstasy, illustrates the existential philosopher Friedrich Nietzsche's concepts of the übermensch or superman. Lawrence's views on comradeship and marriage will supply useful material for any discussion of Whitman's sexuality, his ideas of friendship, or his treatment of the relation between eros and platonic love. Students writing about Whitman's influence on modern poetry will find a wealth of material in this essay. Given Lawrence's own Whitmanlike cadences, readers might explore the relation between his poetry and the themes he finds in Whitman's, or contrast instead Lawrence's response to Whitman's influence with Ezra Pound's ("What I Feel about Walt Whitman").

━━━◈━━ ━━◈━━ ━━◈━━

Whitman is the greatest of the Americans. One of the greatest poets of the world, in him an element of falsity troubles us still. Something is wrong; we cannot be quite at ease in his greatness.

This may be our own fault. But we sincerely feel that something is overdone in Whitman; there is something that is too much. Let us get over our quarrel with him first.

All the Americans, when they have trodden new ground, seem to have been conscious of making a breach in the established order. They have been self-conscious about it. They have felt that they were trespassing, transgressing, or going very far, and this has given a certain stridency, or portentousness, or luridness to their manner. Perhaps that is because the steps were taken so rapidly. From Franklin to Whitman is a hundred years. It might be a thousand.

The Americans have finished in haste, with a certain violence and violation, that which Europe began two thousand years ago or more. Rapidly they have returned to lay open the secrets which the Christian epoch has taken two thousand years to close up.

With the Greeks started the great passion for the ideal, the passion for translating all consciousness into terms of spirit and ideal or idea. They did this in reaction from the vast old world which was dying in Egypt. But the Greeks, though they set out to conquer the animal or sensual being in man, did not set out to annihilate it. This was left for the Christians.

The Christians, phase by phase, set out actually to *annihilate* the sensual being in man. They insisted that man was in his reality *pure* spirit, and that he was perfectible as such. And this was their business, to achieve such a perfection.

They worked from a profound inward impulse, the Christian religious impulse. But their proceeding was the same, in living extension, as that of the Greek esoterics, such as John the Evangel or Socrates. They proceeded, by will and by exaltation, to overcome all the passions and all the appetites and prides.

Now, so far, in Europe, the conquest of the lower self has been objective. That is, man has moved from a great impulse within himself, unconscious. But once the conquest has been effected, there is a temptation for the conscious mind to return and finger and explore, just as tourists now explore battlefields. This self-conscious mental provoking of sensation and reaction in the great affective centres is what we call sentimentalism or sensationalism. The mind returns upon the affective centres, and sets up in them a deliberate reaction.

And this is what all the Americans do, beginning with Crèvecoeur, Hawthorne, Poe, all the transcendentalists, Melville, Prescott, Wendell Holmes, Whitman, they are all guilty of this provoking of mental reactions in the physical self, passions exploited by the mind. In Europe, men like Balzac and Dickens, Tolstoi and Hardy, still act direct from the passional motive, and not inversely, from mental provocation. But the aesthetes and symbolists, from Baudelaire and Maeterlinck and Oscar Wilde onwards, and nearly all later Russian, French, and English novelists set up their reactions in the mind and reflect them by a secondary process down into the body. This makes a vicious living and a spurious art. It is one of the last and most fatal effects of idealism. Everything becomes self-conscious and spurious, to the pitch of madness. It is the madness of the world of today. Europe and America are all alike; all the nations self-consciously provoking their own passional reactions from the mind, and *nothing* spontaneous.

And this is our accusation against Whitman, as against the others. Too often he deliberately, self-consciously *affects* himself. It puts us off, it makes us dislike him. But since such self-conscious secondariness is a concomitant of all American art, and yet not sufficiently so to prevent that art from being of rare quality, we must get over it. The excuse is that the Americans have had to perform in a century a curve which it will take Europe much longer to finish, if ever she finishes it.

Whitman has gone further, in actual living expression, than any man, it seems to me. Dostoevsky has burrowed underground into the decomposing psyche. But Whitman has gone forward in life-knowledge. It is he who surmounts the grand climacteric of our civilization.

Whitman enters on the last phase of spiritual triumph. He really arrives at that stage of infinity which the seers *sought*. By subjecting the deepest centres of the lower self, he attains the maximum consciousness in the higher self: a degree of extensive consciousness greater, perhaps, than any man in the modern world.

We have seen Dana and Melville, the two adventurers, setting out to conquer the last vast *element*, with the spirit. We have seen Melville touching at last the far end of the immemorial, prehistoric Pacific civilization, in 'Typee.' We have seen his terrific cruise into universality.

Now we must remember that the way, even towards a state of infinite comprehension, is through the externals towards the quick. And the vast elements, the cosmos, the big things, the universals, these are always the externals. These are met first and conquered first. That is why science is so much easier than art. The quick is the living being, the quick of quicks is the individual soul. And it is here, at the quick, that Whitman proceeds to find the experience of infinitude, his vast extension, or concentrated intensification into Allness. He carries the conquest to its end.

If we read his paeans, his chants of praise and deliverance and accession, what do we find? All-embracing, indiscriminate, passional acceptance; surges of chaotic vehemence of invitation and embrace, catalogues, lists, enumerations. 'Whoever you are, to you endless announcements! . . .' 'And of these one and all I weave the song of myself.' 'Lovers, endless lovers.'

Continually the one cry: I am everything and everything is me. I accept everything in my consciousness; nothing is rejected:

I am he that aches with amorous love;
Does the earth gravitate? does not all matter, aching; attract all matter?
So the body of me to all I meet or know.

At last everything is conquered. At last the lower centres are conquered. At last the lowest plane is submitted to the highest. At last there is nothing more to conquer. At last all is one, all is love, even hate is love, even flesh is spirit. The great oneness, the experience of infinity, the triumph of the living spirit, which at last includes everything, is here accomplished.

It is man's accession into wholeness, his knowledge in full. Now he is united with everything. Now he embraces everything into himself in a oneness. Whitman is drunk with the new wine of this new great experience, really drunk with the strange wine of infinitude. So he pours forth his words, his chants of praise and acclamation. It is man's maximum state of consciousness, his highest state of spiritual being. Supreme spiritual consciousness, and the divine drunkenness of supreme consciousness. It is reached through embracing love. 'And whoever walks a furlong without sympathy walks to his own funeral dresst in his shroud.' And this supreme state, once reached, shows us the One Identity in everything, Whitman's cryptic *One Identity*.

Thus Whitman becomes in his own person the whole world, the whole universe, the whole eternity of time. Nothing is rejected. Because nothing opposes him. All adds up to one in him. Item by item he identifies himself with the universe, and this accumulative identity he calls Democracy. En Masse, One Identity, and so on.

But this is the last and final truth, the last truth is at the quick. And the quick is the single individual soul, which is never more than itself, though it embrace eternity and infinity, and never *other* than itself, though it include all men. Each vivid soul is unique, and though one soul embrace another, and include it, still it cannot *become* that other soul, or livingly dispossess that other soul. In extending himself, Whitman still remains himself; he does not become the other man, or the other woman, or the tree, or the universe: in spite of Plato.

Which is the maximum truth, though it appears so small in contrast to all these infinites, and En Masses, and Democracies, and Almightynesses. The essential truth is that a man is himself, and only himself, throughout all his greatnesses and extensions and intensifications.

The second truth which we must bring as a charge against Whitman is the one we brought before, namely, that his Allness, his One Identity, his En masse, his Democracy, is only a half-truth—an enormous half-truth. The other half is Jehovah, and Egypt, and Sennacherib: the other form of Allness, terrible and grand, even as in the Psalms.

Now Whitman's way to Allness, he tells us, is through endless sympathy, merging. But in merging you must merge away from something, as well as towards something, and in sympathy you must depart from one point to arrive at another. Whitman lays down this law of sympathy as the one law, the direction of merging as the one direction. Which is obviously wrong. Why not a right-about-turn? Why not turn slap back to the point from which you started to merge? Why not *that* direction, the reverse of merging, back to the single and overweening self? Why not, instead of endless dilation of sympathy, the retraction into isolation and pride?

Why not? The heart has its systole diastole, the shuttle comes and goes, even the sun rises and sets. We know, as a matter of fact, that all life lies between two poles. The direction is twofold. Whitman's one direction becomes a hideous tyranny once he has attained his goal of Allness. His One Identity is a prison of horror, once realized. For identities are manifold and each jewel like, different as a sapphire from an opal. And the motion of merging becomes at last a vice, a nasty degeneration, as when tissue breaks down into a mucous slime. There must be the sharp retraction from isolation, following the expansion into unification, otherwise the integral being is overstrained and will break, break down like disintegrating tissue into slime, imbecility, epilepsy, vice, like Dostoevsky.

And one word more. Even if you reach the state of infinity, you can't sit down there. You just physically can't. You either have to strain still further into universality and become vaporish, or slimy: or you have to hold your toes and sit tight and practise Nirvana; or you have to come back to common dimensions, eat your pudding and blow your nose and be just yourself, or die and have done with it. A grand experience is a grand experience. It brings a man to his maximum. But even at his maximum a man is not more than himself. When he is infinite he is still himself. He still has a nose to wipe. The state of infinity is *only* a state, even if it be the supreme one.

But in achieving this state Whitman opened a new field of living. He drives on to the very centre of life and sublimates even this into consciousness. Melville hunts the remote white whale of the deepest passional body, tracks it down. But it is Whitman who captures the whale. The pure sensual body of man, at its deepest remoteness and intensity, this is the White Whale. And this is what Whitman captures.

He seeks his consummation through one continual ecstacy, the ecstacy of *giving himself*, and of being taken. The ecstacy of his own reaping and merging with another, with others; the sword-cut of sensual death. Whitman's motion is always the motion of *giving himself*. This is my body—take, and eat. It is the great sacrament. He knows nothing of the other sacrament, the sacrament in pride, where the communicant envelops the victim and host in a flame of ecstatic consuming, sensual gratification, and triumph.

But he is concerned with others beside himself: with woman, for example. But what is woman to Whitman? Not much? She is a great function—no more. Whitman's 'athletic mothers of these States' are depressing. Muscles and wombs: functional creatures—no more.

> As I see my soul reflected in Nature,
> As I see through a mist, One with inexpressible completeness,
>   sanity, beauty,
> See the bent head and areas folded over the breast, the Female I see.

That is all. The woman is reduced, really, to a submissive function. She is no longer an individual being with a living soul. She must fold her arms and bend her head and submit to her functioning capacity. Function of sex, function of birth.

> This the nucleus—after the child is born of woman, man is born
>   of woman,
> This the bath of birth, this the merge of small and large, and the outlet
>   again—

Acting from the last and profoundest centres, man acts womanless. It is no longer a question of race continuance. It is a question of sheer, ultimate being, the perfection of life, nearest to death. Acting from these centres, man is an extreme being, the unthinkable warrior, creator, mover and maker.

And the polarity is between man and man. Whitman alone of all moderns has known this positively. Others have known it negatively, *pour épater les bourgeois*. But Whitman knew it positively, in its tremendous knowledge, knew the extremity, the perfectness, and the fatality.

Even Whitman becomes grave, tremulous, before the last dynamic truth of life. In *Calamus* he does not shout. He hesitates: he is reluctant, wistful. But none the less he goes on. And he tells the mystery of manly love, the love of comrades. Continually he tells us the same truth: the new world will be built upon the love of comrades, the new great dynamic of life will be manly love. Out of this inspiration the creation of the future.

The strange Calamus has its pink-tinged root by the pond, and it sends up its leaves of comradeship, comrades at one root, without the intervention of woman, the female. This comradeship is to be the final cohering principle of the new world, the new Democracy. It is the cohering principle of perfect soldiery, as he tells in *Drum Taps*. It is the cohering principle of final *unison* in creative activity. And it is extreme and alone, touching the confines of death. It is something terrible to bear, terrible to be responsible for. It is the soul's last and most vivid responsibility, the responsibility for the circuit of final friendship, comradeship, manly love.

> Yet you are beautiful to me you faint-tinged roots, you make
>   me think of death,
> Death is beautiful from you, (what indeed is finally beautiful except
>   death and love?)
> O I think it is not for life I am chanting here my chant of lovers, I think
>   it must be for death.
> For how calm, how solemn it grows to ascend to the atmosphere
>   of lovers,
> Death or life I am then indifferent, my soul declines to prefer,
> (I am not sure but the high soul of lovers welcomes death most,)
> Indeed O death, I think now these leaves mean precisely the same as you
>   mean—

Here we have the deepest, finest Whitman, the Whitman who knows the extremity of life, and of the soul's responsibility. He has come near now to death, in his creative life. But creative life must come near to death, to link up the mystic circuit. The pure warriors must stand on the brink of death. So must the men of a pure creative nation. We shall have no beauty, no dignity, no essential freedom otherwise. And so it is from Sea-Drift, where the male bird sings the lost female: not that she is lost, but lost to him who has had to go beyond her, to sing on the edge of the great sea, in the night. It is the last voice on the shore.

> Whereto answering; the sea,
> Delaying not, hurrying not,
> Whisper'd to me through the night, and very plainly before daybreak,
> Lisp'd to me the low and delicious word death,
> And again death, death, death, death,

Hissing melodious, neither like the bird nor like my arous'd child's heart,
But edging near as privately for me rustling at my feet,
Creeping thence steadily up to my ears and laving me softly all over,
Death, death, death, death, death—

What a great poet Whitman is: great like a great Greek. For him the last enclosures have fallen, he finds himself on the shore of the last sea. The extreme of life: so near to death. It is a hushed, deep responsibility. And what is the responsibility? It is for the new great era of mankind. And upon what is this new era established? On the perfect circuits of vital flow between human beings. First, the great sexless normal relation between individuals, simple sexless friendships, unison of family, and clan, and nation, and group. Next, the powerful sex relation between man and woman, culminating in the eternal orbit of marriage. And, finally, the sheer friendship, the love between comrades, the manly love which alone can create a new era of life.

The one state, however, does not annul the other, it fulfils the other. Marriage is the great step beyond friendship, and family, and nationality, but it does not supersede these. Marriage should only give repose and perfection to the great previous bonds and relationships. A wife or husband who sets about to annul the old, pre-marriage affections and connections ruins the foundations of marriage. And so with the last, extremest love, the love of comrades. The ultimate comradeship which sets about to destroy marriage destroys its own *raison d'être*. The ultimate comradeship is the final progression from marriage; it is the last seedless flower of pure beauty, beyond purpose. But if it destroys marriage it makes itself purely deathly. In its beauty, the ultimate comradeship flowers on the brink of death. But it flowers from root of all life upon the blossoming tree of life.

The life-circuit now depends entirely upon the sex-unison of marriage. This circuit must never be broken. But it must be still surpassed. We cannot help the laws of life.

If marriage is sacred, the ultimate comradeship is utterly sacred, since it has no ulterior motive whatever, like procreation. If marriage is eternal, the great bond of life, how much more is this bond eternal, being the great life-circuit which borders on death in all its round. The new, extreme, the sacred relationship of comrades awaits us, and the future of mankind depends on the way in which this relation is entered upon by us. It is a relation between fearless, honorable, self-responsible men, a balance in perfect polarity.

The last phase is entered upon, shakily, by Whitman. It will take us an epoch to establish the new, perfect circuit of our being. It will take an epoch to establish the love of comrades, as marriage is really established now. For fear of going on, forwards, we turn round and destroy, or try to destroy, what lies behind. We are trying to destroy marriage, because we have not the courage to go forward from marriage to the new issue. Marriage must never be wantonly attacked. True marriage is eternal; in it we have our consummation and being. But the final consummation lies in that which is beyond marriage.

And when the bond, or circuit of perfect comrades is established, what then, when we are on the brink of death, fulfilled in the vastness of life? Then, at last, we shall know a starry maturity.

Whitman put us on the track years ago. Why has no one gone on from him? The great poet, why does no one accept his greatest word? The Americans are not worthy of their Whitman. They take him like a cocktail, for fun. Miracle that they have not annihilated every word of him. But these miracles happen.

The greatest modern poet! Whitman, at his best, is purely himself. His verse springs sheer from the spontaneous sources of his being. Hence its lovely, lovely form and rhythm: at the best. It is sheer, perfect, human spontaneity, spontaneous as a nightingale throbbing, but still controlled, the highest loveliness of human spontaneity, undecorated, unclothed. The whole being is there, sensually throbbing, spiritually quivering, mentally, ideally speaking. It is not, like Swinburne, an exaggeration of the one part of being. It is perfect and whole. The whole soul speaks at once, and is too pure for mechanical assistance of rhyme and measure. The perfect utterance of a concentrated, spontaneous soul. The unforgettable loveliness of Whitman's lines:

Out of the cradle endlessly rocking.
Ave America!

—D.H. Lawrence, "Whitman," *The Nation & Athenaeum,*
July 23, 1921, pp. 616–19

WORKS

This section features some of the most widely known writings on *Leaves of Grass*. Whitman's poetic career was marked by celebration and controversy from its inception, and these writings not only charted the oscillations of Whitman's reputation, but often contributed to them. In general, the authors excerpted here focus less on Whitman's personal character than on the poems themselves, and this critical position makes the entries valuable for students developing text-focused arguments rather than biographical ones. The poetic persona of *Leaves of Grass* (or the figure of the poet who speaks through the poems) is often discussed, though at times the collection is seemingly treated as an individual, with virtues worth emulating and foibles worth mocking, suggesting both the fullness of the persona behind Whitman's poetic voice and the tendency of nineteenth-century critics to view works of literature as unified texts, with all discrepancies, errors, and oversights viewed as intrinsic, if not explainable. Directly or indirectly, the essays included here give voice to many nineteenth-century aesthetic theories, and students writing about the aesthetics underlying the various responses to Whitman's poetry, or about Whitman's influence on those aesthetic theories, will find the readings essential.

Readers examining the various responses to the general themes of *Leaves of Grass* will also find much of value, especially important pieces by the transcendentalist authors Ralph Waldo Emerson and Henry David Thoreau, as well as two reviews of the book by Whitman himself, one an early anonymous review that served as Whitman's *ars poetica*, or statement of his personal aesthetic, the other a somber reflection on the relative success of *Leaves of Grass* as an American work of literature and as an inspiration for democratic art. While the tone of these essays is largely praising, the authors focus on a variety of topics, including mysticism, the nature of American art, the canonical status of *Leaves of Grass*, Whitman's affinities with transcendentalism and Hinduism, and concepts of love. The introductions to the individual essays offer a number of research questions and applications for these pieces, but students might also examine the full selection of essays to discuss how Whitman's poetic reputation was established, what general affinities his writings bore to the works of the transcendentalists, and how *Leaves of Grass* was both defined as and helped to define authentic American literature.

Students writing on the major poems and sections of *Leaves of Grass* will find some of the longer essays more contentious and textually focused than the general overviews. Writing about the Calamus poems, John Addington Symonds advances the first theory about Whitman's implicit homosexuality, an idea that has gained scholarly credibility and that now informs many central discussions of Whitman's poetry. Students examining issues of Whitman's sexual identity must contend with Symonds's arguments, which have not only acquired the force of gospel, but which indirectly indicate, in the courteous ambivalence of the conclusion, nineteenth-century America's intense social rejection of nontraditional relationships. Students writing about Whitman's influence on later authors may find Symonds's essay particularly useful in explaining why Whitman was seen as a liberating figure not only by homosexual writers such as Allen Ginsberg and Michael Cunningham, but also by heterosexual writers such as Pablo Neruda and Galway Kinnell.

The American novelists Henry James and William Dean Howells each criticize *Drum-Taps*, Whitman's collection of Civil War–inspired poems, for its proselike reportorial style. Their essays exemplify the negative reactions to Whitman's stylistic experiments and provide excellent material for discussions of the relative appropriateness of Whitman's style for representing the new face of war, which the Civil War ushered in. In addition, James's and Howells's essays help contrast Whitman's war poetry with the work of other war poets from his time, such as Henry Timrod or Herman Melville, though James's later recantation offers its own poignant and telling counterargument.

In their discussions of Whitman's individual long poems "Out of the Cradle Endlessly Rocking," "Passage to India," and "Song of Myself," Stephen Whicher, V.K. Chari, and Leslie Fiedler offer important twentieth-century responses, each more speculative and text- and archive-based and less evaluative than their nineteenth-century counterparts. This approach is partially exemplified by Walker Kennedy's highly polemical, ad hominem attack on Whitman's poetic persona. Key thematic topics such as love, death, solipsism, loneliness and alienation, and the nature of the self and the self's encounter with the nonself (or Other) preoccupy Whicher and Fiedler. Students writing about how those topics pertain to Whitman's poetry in general, or to "Out of the Cradle Endlessly Rocking" and "Song of Myself" in particular, will find rich support for their arguments here.

For students curious about how Whitman's revisions to the poems in *Leaves of Grass* altered their themes, Whicher's comparison of the original and final versions of "Out of the Cradle Endlessly Rocking" provides rich material and a model approach. Whicher indicates that in seeking to suggest a greater sense of self-control during his most intense imaginative experiences, Whitman removed from his poem the sense of desperation and the dramatic confrontation with the reality of mortality that made the original version so visceral and spiritually potent. Students might take Whicher's findings and see if they pertain or can be applied to other poems Whitman revised. Alternately, students might position themselves against Whicher and argue on behalf of the "deathbed" versions of the poems, an approach Whicher himself implicitly supports.

The brief excerpt from V.K. Chari's essay on Whitman's relation to Hinduism provides a starting point for research on that topic, but it also raises the issue of literary influence in Whitman's own poetry. Noting that, as an autodidact and an editor, Whitman was a voracious reader and so could very well have been influenced by the Hindu texts with which he shares such spiritual affinity, Chari nevertheless admits that Whitman's overt references to India prove vague, thus rendering the issue of literary influence uncertain (an object lesson, perhaps, for students seeking to make such an argument).

Finally, Walker Kennedy's uniformly derisive essay will be useful for students writing critical assessments of Whitman's poetry and in need of well-turned satirical claims. Kennedy's sentiments will prove just as effective for students setting up their arguments as counters to other positions. Kennedy's insistence on Whitman's lunacy, while medically unsound, may prove useful for students making comparisons between Whitman's poetry and that of other experimental poets deemed alternately "mystical" and "insane," including Christopher Smart, William Blake, and Allen Ginsberg. In connection to Chari's essay, Kennedy's frequent criticism of Whitman's seemingly contradictory or nonsensical statements may offer valuable support for arguments about the philosophical debt Whitman owes to Eastern thought, particularly Hinduism, which often proves frustratingly illogical for Western rationalism.

LEAVES OF GRASS

Ralph Waldo Emerson (1855)

This personal letter from Ralph Waldo Emerson, perhaps the most important figure in American transcendentalism, was famously (or perhaps notoriously) reprinted by Whitman in the second edition of *Leaves of Grass*. An essayist, a poet, and a former Unitarian minister, Emerson argued that divinity was present throughout the physical world and that all humans were equally miracles of creation, ideas that find a striking parallel in Whitman's poetry. While Whitman later disavowed the influence of Emerson's writings on his own, he proclaimed his indebtedness to and his spiritual affinity with Emerson early in his career, though Whitman remained distinct from Emerson in continuing to celebrate the human body as coequal with the soul.

Emerson praises Whitman on three main points. First, Emerson singles out *Leaves of Grass* as the most authentically American work of literature yet to have been written, no small praise given Emerson's ongoing search for distinctly American talent. Second, he praises the originality of Whitman's free verse, its perceptions and its memorable expressions, noting the great pleasure given by Whitman's treatment of his subjects. Lastly, Emerson argues that *Leaves of Grass* is the work of no mere newcomer, but of a literary talent whose personal and intellectual backgrounds enabled him to produce a major work of literature.

This letter could be used in a variety of comparisons of Whitman and Emerson, including the influence of Emerson's writings on Whitman's poetry, Whitman's link to American transcendentalism, and Whitman's quintessentially American characteristics, as defined by Emerson. This latter topic invites further analysis of the link between American nationalism and expansionism and the drive among American intellectuals to create or discover works of art free of European influence and heritage. Students interested in Whitman's emerging status as a national literary figure could examine the impact this letter had on Whitman's place in the American literary canon, while students writing about the rich and complex publishing history of *Leaves of Grass* could examine the effects of Whitman's commercial use of this private correspondence. Students exploring notions of artistic genius, a subject of great interest to Emerson, might reflect on the ways Whitman corresponded to Emerson's ideas about genius, and the ways he helped shape them.

I am not blind to the worth of the wonderful gift of *Leaves of Grass*. I find it the most extraordinary piece of wit & wisdom that America has yet contributed. I am very happy in reading it, as great power makes us happy. It meets the demand I am always making of what seemed the sterile & stingy Nature, as if too much handiwork or too much lymph in the temperament were making our western wits fat & mean.

I give you joy of your free & brave thought. I have great joy in it. I find incomparable things said incomparably well, as they must be. I find the courage of *treatment,* which so delights us, & which large perception only can inspire.

I greet you at the beginning of a great career, which yet must have had a long foreground somewhere, for such a start. I rubbed my eyes a little to see if this sunbeam were no illusion; but the solid sense of the book is a sober certainty. It has the best merits, namely, of fortifying & encouraging.

I did not know until I, last night, saw the book advertised in a newspaper, that I could trust the name as real & available for a Post-office. I wish to see my benefactor, & have felt much like striking my tasks, & visiting New York to pay you my respects.

—Ralph Waldo Emerson, Letter to Walt Whitman
(July 21, 1855)

Charles A. Dana (1855)

His *Leaves of Grass* are doubtless intended as an illustration of the natural poet. They are certainly original in their external form, have been shaped on no pre-existent model out of the author's own brain. Indeed, his independence often becomes coarse and defiant. His language is too frequently reckless and indecent though this appears to arise from a naïve unconsciousness rather than from an impure mind. His words might have passed between Adam and Eve in Paradise, before the want of fig-leaves brought no shame; but they are quite out of place amid the decorum of modern society, and will justly prevent his volume from free circulation in scrupulous circles. With these glaring faults, the *Leaves of Grass* are not destitute of peculiar poetic merits, which will awaken an interest in the lovers of literary curiosities. They are full of bold, stirring thoughts—with occasional passages of effective description, betraying a genuine intimacy with Nature and a keen appreciation of beauty—often presenting a rare felicity of diction, but so disfigured with eccentric fancies as to prevent a consecutive perusal without offense, though no impartial reader can fail to be impressed with the vigor and quaint beauty of isolated portions.

—Charles A. Dana, *New York Tribune,* July 23, 1855, p. 3

WALT WHITMAN (1855)

While the idea of reviewing one's own book may seem comical, if not absurd, Walt Whitman's anonymous assessment of *Leaves of Grass* is quite serious, and represents part of Whitman's early effort to construct and develop his literary persona. Claiming that the author himself is incarnate in the poems of *Leaves of Grass*, Whitman anonymously emphasizes his American identity and his separateness from European culture, calling himself a "rude child of the people!" Using the same catalogue technique employed in many of his poems, Whitman details the various sights and sensations in the author's daily life, characterizing him as a common man of natural ease and great emotional intimacy with his fellow men. In response to criticism of the egotism detectable in *Leaves of Grass*, Whitman argues that the focus on the individual self is in fact a celebration of the "natural propensities" that join humankind, "the singularity which consists in no singularity," so that the author of *Leaves of Grass* is not a model for a new type of American, but an illustration of that type.

This essay offers excellent material for arguments about Whitman's concept of the self, from his rejection of the stigma associated with egotism to his assertion of the universality of human nature. Likewise, Whitman's anonymous review lists the general qualities he values in American society, useful material in any discussion of his definition of America and his preference for the pioneering character. Students examining Whitman's style should note how he uses catalogues and apostrophe similarly in this essay and in his poetry. Such similarities lend support to arguments both about the proselike quality of Whitman's verse and for the formal consistency Whitman retains throughout his thematically varied poetry and prose.

To give judgment on real poems, one needs an account of the poet himself. Very devilish to some, and very divine to some, will appear the poet of these new poems, the *Leaves of Grass;* an attempt, as they are, of a naïve, masculine, affectionate, contemplative, sensual, imperious person, to cast into literature not only his own grit and arrogance, but his own flesh and form, undraped, regardless of models, regardless of modesty or law, and ignorant or slightly scornful, as at first appears, of all except his own presence and experience, and all outside the fiercely loved land of his birth and the birth of his parents, and their parents for several generations before him. Politeness this man has none, and regulation he has none. A rude child of the people!—no imitation—

no foreigner—but a growth and idiom of America. No discontented—a careless slouch, enjoying today. No dilettante democrat—a man who is part-and-part with the commonalty, and with immediate life—loves the streets—loves the docks—loves the free rasping talk of men—likes to be called by his given name, and nobody at all need Mr. Him—can laugh with laughers—likes the ungenteel ways of laborers—is not prejudiced one mite against the Irish—talks readily with them—talks readily with niggers—does not make a stand on being a gentleman, nor on learning or manners—eats cheap fare, likes the strong flavored coffee of the coffee-stands in the market, at sunrise—likes a supper of oysters fresh from the oyster-smack—likes to make one at the crowded table among sailors and workpeople—would leave a select soiree of elegant people any time to go with tumultuous men, roughs, receive their caresses and welcome, listen to their noise, oaths, smut, fluency, laughter, repartee—and can preserve his presence perfectly among these, and the like of these. The effects he produces in his poems are no effects of artists or the arts, but effects of the original eye or arm, or the actual atmosphere, or tree, or bird. You may feel the unconscious teaching of a fine brute, but will never feel the artificial teaching of a fine writer or speaker.

Other poets celebrate great events, personages, romances, wars, loves, passions, the victories and power of their country, or some real or imagined incident—and polish their work, and come to the conclusions, and satisfy the reader. This poet celebrates natural propensities in himself; and that is the way he celebrates all. He comes to no conclusions, and does not satisfy the reader. He certainly leaves him what the serpent left the woman and the man, the taste of the Paradisaic tree of the knowledge of good and evil, never to be erased again.

What good is it to argue about egotism? There can be no two thoughts on Walt Whitman's egotism. That is avowedly what he steps out of the crowd and turns and faces them for. Mark, critics! Otherwise is not used for you the key that leads to the use of the other keys to this well-enveloped man. His whole work, his life, manners, friendships, writings, all have among their leading purposes an evident purpose to stamp a new type of character, namely his own, and indelibly fix it and publish it, not for a model but an illustration, for the present and future of American letters and American young men, for the South the same as the North, and for the Pacific and Mississippi country, and Wisconsin and Texas and Kansas and Canada and Havana and Nicaragua, just as much as New York and Boston. Whatever is needed toward this achievement he puts his hand to, and lets imputations take their time to die.

First be yourself what you would show in your poem—such seems to be this man's example and inferred rebuke to the schools of poets. He makes no allusions to books or writers; their spirits do not seem to have touched him; he has not a word to say for or against them, or their theories or ways. He never offers others; what he continually offers is the man whom our Brooklynites know so well. Of pure American breed, large and lusty—age thirty-six years (1855)—never once using medicine—never dressed in black, always dressed freely and clean in strong clothes—neck open, shirt-collar flat and broad, countenance tawny transparent red, beard well-mottled with white, hair like hay after it has been mowed in the field and lies tossed and streaked—his physiology corroborating a rugged phrenology—a person singularly beloved and looked toward, especially by young men and the illiterate—one who has firm attachments there, and associates there—one who does not associate with literary people—a man never called upon to make speeches at public dinners—never on platforms amid the crowds of clergymen, or professors, or aldermen, or congressmen—rather down in the bay with pilots in their pilot-boat—or off on a cruise with fishers in a fishing-smack—or riding on a Broadway omnibus, side by side with the driver—or with a band of loungers over the open grounds of the country—fond of New York and Brooklyn—fond of the life of the great ferries—one whom, if you should meet, you need not expect to meet an extraordinary person—one in whom you will see the singularity which consists in no singularity—whose contact is no dazzle or fascination, nor requires any deference, but has the easy fascination of what is homely and accustomed—as of something you knew before, and was waiting for—there you have Walt Whitman, the begetter of a new offspring out of literature, taking with easy nonchalance the chances of its present reception, and, through all misunderstandings and distrusts, the chances of its future reception.

—Walt Whitman, *Brooklyn Daily Times*, September 29, 1855

Rufus W. Griswold (1855)

An unconsidered letter of introduction has oftentimes procured the admittance of a scurvy fellow into good society, and our apology for permitting any allusion to the above volume in our columns is, that it has been unworthily recommended by a gentleman of wide repute, and might, on that account, obtain access to respectable people, unless its real character were exposed.

Mr Ralph Waldo Emerson either recognizes and accepts these 'leaves,' as the gratifying result of his own peculiar doctrines, or else he has hastily indorsed them, after a partial and superficial reading. If it is of any importance he may extricate himself from the dilemma. We, however, believe that this book does express the bolder results of a certain transcendental kind of thinking, which some may have styled philosophy.

As to the volume itself, we have only to remark, that it strongly fortifies the doctrines of the Metempsychosists, for it is impossible to imagine how any man's fancy could have conceived such a mass of stupid filth, unless he were possessed of the soul of a sentimental donkey that had died of disappointed love. This *poet*(?) without wit, but with a certain vagrant wildness, just serves to show the energy which natural imbecility is occasionally capable of under strong excitement.

There are too many persons, who imagine they demonstrate their superiority to their fellows, by disregarding all the politeness and decencies of life, and, therefore, justify themselves in indulging the vilest imaginings and shamefullest license. But nature, abhorring the abuse of the capacities she has given to man, retaliates upon him, by rendering extravagant indulgence in any direction followed by an insatiable, ever-consuming. and never to be appeased passion.

Thus, to these pitiful beings, virtue and honor are but names. Bloated with self-conceit, they strut abroad unabashed in the daylight, and expose to the world the festering sores that overlay them, like a garment. Unless we admit this exhibition to be beautiful, we are at once set down for non-progressive conservatives, destitute of the 'inner light,' the far-seeingness which, of course, characterizes those gifted individuals. Now, any one who has noticed the tendency of thought in these later years, must be aware that a quantity of this kind of nonsense is being constantly displayed. The immodesty of presumption exhibited by those *seers*; their arrogant pretentiousness; the complacent smile with which they listen to the echo of their own braying, should be, and we believe is, enough to disgust the great majority of sensible folks; but, unfortunately, there is a class that, mistaking sound for sense, attach some importance to all this rant and cant. These candid, these ingenuous, these honest 'progressionists;' these human diamonds without flaws; these men that have *come*—detest furiously all shams; 'to the pure, all things are pure;' they are pure, and, consequently, must thrust their reeking presence under every man's now.

They seem to think that man has no instinctive delicacy, is not imbued with a conservative and preservative modesty, that acts as a restraint upon the violence of passions, which for a wise purpose, have been made so strong. No! these fellows have no secrets, no disguises; no, indeed! But they do have, conceal it by whatever language they choose, a degrading, beastly sensuality, that is fast rotting the healthy core of all the social virtues.

There was a time when licentiousness laughed at reproval; now it writes essays and delivers lectures. Once it shunned the light; now it courts attention, writes books showing how grand and pure it is, and prophesies from its lecherous lips its own ultimate triumph.

Shall we argue with such men? Shall we admit them into our houses, that they may leave a foul odor, contaminating the pure, healthful air? Or shall they be placed in the same category with the comparatively innocent slave of poverty, ignorance, and passion that skulks along in the shadows of byways; even in her deep degradation possessing some sparks of the Divine light, the germ of good that reveals itself by a sense of shame?

Thus, then, we leave this gathering of muck to the laws which, certainly, if they fulfil their intent, must have power to suppress such obscenity. As it is entirely destitute of wit, there is no probability that any would, after this exposure, read it in the hope of finding that; and we trust no one will require further evidence—for, indeed, we do not believe there is a newspaper so vile that would print confirmatory extracts.

In our allusion to this book, we have found it impossible to convey any, even the most faint idea of its style and contents, and of our disgust and detestation of them, without employing language that cannot be pleasing to ears polite; but it does seem that some one should, under circumstances like these, undertake a most disagreeable, yet stern duty. The records of crime show that many monsters have gone on in impunity, because the exposure of their vileness was attended with too great indelicacy. *Peccatum illud horribile, inter Christianos non nominandum.*[1]

Note

1. 'That horrible sin not to be mentioned among Christians.'

—Rufus W. Griswold, *New York Criterion*, November 10, 1855

EDWARD EVERETT HALE (1856)

Sympathetic and unqualifiedly praising, the Reverend Edward Everett Hale's anonymous review of the 1855 edition of *Leaves of Grass* was the first to assert Whitman's status as the founding figure in American poetry, an opinion that shaped and defined much of the critical discussion of Whitman in the nineteenth century. Hale hails Whitman's originality, freshness, and spontaneity, qualities that evoke a true and optimistic perception of reality. No criticisms are offered, save a friendly jab at Whitman for having been perhaps too cautious, rather than reckless, with his notorious use of indelicate phrases, which the noted essayist and Unitarian minister finds no more "indelicate" than anything in Homer.

Since Hale was the first reviewer to praise Whitman in such absolute terms, students examining the history of Whitman's canonization will find this review a touchstone for those discussions, with many of the points of critical praise—originality, naturalness, hopefulness, distinct and accurate observation—first articulated by Hale. Hale's description of the book's publication history supplies important background information, but the review's great value is as evidence of the originality and unconventional nature of Whitman's poetry, which was so new and innovative that traditional publishing houses wouldn't print it and traditional bookstores wouldn't carry it. A notable topic arises with Hale's assertion that the preface's discussion of American genius represents the best part of *Leaves of Grass*. Students exploring the ideas of American genius or the nature of genuinely American art might compare relevant passages from "Song of Myself" to the preface to clarify Whitman's analysis of genius and explain why Hale seems to privilege the preface.

⸺⧓⧓⸺ ⸺⧓⧓⸺ ⸺⧓⧓⸺

Everything about the external arrangement of this book was odd and out of the way. The author printed it himself, and it seems to have been left to the winds of heaven to publish it. So it happened that we had not discovered it before our last number, although we believe the sheets had then passed the press. It bears no publisher's name, and, if the reader goes to a bookstore for it, he may expect to be told at first, as we were, that there is no such book, and has not been. Nevertheless, there is such a book, and it is well worth going twice to the bookstore to buy it. Walter Whitman, an American—one of the roughs—no sentimentalist,—no stander above men and women, or apart from them, no more modest than immodest,—has tried to write down here, in a sort of prose poetry, a good deal of what he has seen, felt, and guessed at in a pilgrimage of some thirty-five years. He has a horror of conventional language of any kind. His theory of expression is, that, 'to speak in literature with the perfect rectitude and *insouciance* of the movements of animals, is the flawless triumph of art.' Now a great many men have said this before. But generally it is the introduction to something more artistic than ever,—more conventional and strained. Antony began by saying he was no orator, but none the less did an oration follow. In this book, however, the prophecy is fairly fulfilled in the accomplishment. 'What I experience or portray shall go from my composition without a shred of my composition. You shall stand by my side and look in the mirror with me.'

So truly accomplished is this promise,—which anywhere else would be a flourish of trumpets,—that this thin quarto deserves its name. That is to say, one reads and enjoys the freshness, simplicity, and reality of what he reads, just as the tired man, lying on the hill-side in summer, enjoys the leaves of grass around him,—enjoys the shadow,—enjoys the flecks of sunshine,—not for what they 'suggest to him,' but for what they are.

So completely does the author's remarkable power rest in his simplicity, that the preface to the book—which does not even have large letters at the beginning of the lines, as the rest has—is perhaps the very best thing in it. We find more to the point in the following analysis of the 'genius of the United States', than we have found in many more pretentious studies of it.

> Other states indicate themselves in their deputies, but the genius of the United States is not best or most in its executive or legislatures, nor in its ambassadors or authors or colleges or churches or parlors, nor even in its newspapers or inventors;—but always most in the common people.

. . . The book is divided into a dozen or more sections, and in each one of these some thread of connection may be traced, now with ease, now with difficulty,—each being a string of verses, which claim to be written without effort and with entire *abandon*. So the book is a collection of observations, speculations, memories, and prophecies, clad in the simplest, truest, and often the most nervous English,—in the midst of which the reader comes upon something as much out of place as a piece of rotten wood would be among leaves of grass in the meadow, if the meadow had no object but to furnish a child's couch. . . .

Claiming . . . a personal interest in every thing that has ever happened in the world, and, by the wonderful sharpness and distinctness of his imagination, making the claim effective and reasonable, Mr 'Walt Whitman' leaves it a matter of doubt where he has been in this world, and where not. It is very clear, that with him, as with most other effective writers, a keen, absolute memory, which takes in and holds every detail of the past,—as they say the exaggerated power of the memory does when a man is drowning,—is a gift of his organization as remarkable as his vivid imagination. What he has seen once, he has seen for ever. And thus there are in this curious book little thumbnail sketches of life in the prairie, life in California, life at school, life in the nursery,—life, indeed, we know not where not,—which, as they are unfolded one after another, strike us as real,—so real that we wonder how they came on paper.

For the purpose of showing that he is above every conventionalism, Mr Whitman puts into the book one or two lines which he would not address to a woman nor to a company of men. There is not anything, perhaps, which *modern* usage would stamp as more indelicate than are some passages in Homer. There is not a word in it meant to attract readers by its grossness, as there is in half the literature of the last century, which holds its place unchallenged on the tables of our drawing-rooms. For all that, it is a pity that a book where everything else is natural should go out of the way to avoid the suspicion of being prudish.

—Edward Everett Hale, *North American Review*,
LXXXII, 170, January 1856, pp. 275–77

DANTE GABRIEL ROSSETTI (1856)

How I loathe *Wishi-washi,*—of course without reading it. I have not been so happy in loathing anything for a long while—except, I think, *Leaves of Grass,* by that Orson of yours. I should like just to have the writing of a valentine to him in one of the reviews.

—Dante Gabriel Rossetti,
Letter to William Allingham (April 1856)

ANONYMOUS (1856)

So, then, these rank *Leaves* have sprouted afresh, and in still greater abundance. We hoped that they had dropped, and we should hear no more of them. But since they thrust themselves upon to again, with a pertinacity that is proverbial of noxious weeds, and since these thirty-two poems (!) threaten to become 'several hundred,—perhaps a thousand,'—we can no longer refrain from speaking of them as we think they deserve. For here is not a question of literary opinion principally, but of the very essence of religion and morality. The book might pass for merely hectoring and ludicrous, if it were not something a great deal more offensive. We are bound in conscience to call it impious and obscene. *Punch* made sarcastic allusion to it some time ago, as a specimen of American literature. We regard it as one of its worst disgraces. Whether or not the author really bears the name he assumes,—whether or not the strange figure opposite the title-page resembles him, or is even intended for his likeness—whether or not he is considered among his friends to be of a sane mind, whether he is in earnest, or only playing off some disgusting burlesque,—we are hardly sure yet. We know only, that, in point of style, the book is an impertinence towards the English language; and in point of sentiment, an affront upon the recognized morality of respectable people. Both its language and thought seem to have just broken out of Bedlam. It sets off upon a sort of distracted philosophy, and openly deifies the bodily organs, senses, and appetites, in terms that admit of no double sense. To its pantheism and libidinousness it adds the most ridiculous swell of self-applause; for the author is 'one of the roughs, a kosmos, disorderly, fleshy, sensual, divine inside and out. This head more than churches or bibles or creeds. The scent of these arm-pits an aroma finer than prayer. If I worship any particular thing, it shall be some of the spread of my body.' He leaves 'washes and razors for foofoos;' thinks the talk 'about virtue and about vice' only 'blurt,' he being above and indifferent to both of them; and he himself, 'speaking the password primeval, By God! will accept nothing which all cannot have the counterpart of on the same terms.' These quotations are made with cautious delicacy. We pick our way as cleanly as we can between other passages which are more detestable.

A friend whispers as we write, that there is nevertheless a vein of benevolence running through all this vagabondism and riot. Yes; there is plenty of that philanthropy, which cares as little for social rights as for the laws of God. This Titan in his own esteem is perfectly willing that all the rest of the world should be as frantic as himself. In fact, he has no objection to any persons whatever, unless they wear good clothes, or keep themselves tidy. Perhaps it is not judicious to call any attention to such a prodigious impudence. Dante's guide through the infernal regions bade him, on one occasion, Look and pass on. It would be a still better direction sometimes, when in neighborhoods of defilement and death, to pass on without looking. Indeed, we should even now hardly be tempted to make the slightest allusion to this crazy outbreak of conceit and vulgarity, if a sister Review had not praised it, and even undertaken to set up a plea in apology for its indecencies. We must be allowed to say, that it is not good to confound the blots upon great compositions with the compositions that are nothing but a blot. It is not good to confound the occasional ebullitions of too loose a fancy or too wanton a wit, with a profession and 'illustrated' doctrine of licentiousness. And furthermore, it is specially desirable to be able to discern the difference between the nudity of a statue and the gestures of a satyr; between the plain language of a simple state of society, and the lewd talk of the opposite state, which a worse than heathen lawlessness has corrupted; between the 'εὐνῇ καὶ ψιλότητι', or 'ψιλότητι καὶ εὐνῇ μιγῆναι,'[1] of the *Iliad* and *Odyssey*, and an ithyphallic audacity that insults what is most sacred and decent among men.

There is one feature connected with the second edition of this foul work to which we cannot feel that we do otherwise than right in making a marked reference, because it involves the grossest violation of literary comity and courtesy that ever passed under our notice. Mr Emerson had written a letter of greeting to the author on the perusal of the first edition, the warmth and eulogium of which amaze us. But 'Walt Whitman' has taken the most emphatic sentence of praise from this letter, and had it stamped in gold, signed 'R. W. Emerson,' upon the back of his *second* edition. This second edition contains some additional pieces, which in their loathsomeness exceed any of the contents of the first. Thus the honored name of Emerson, which has never before been associated with anything save refinement and delicacy in speech and writing, is made to indorse a work that teems with abominations.

Note
1. 'In love and marriage', and 'to join in love and intercourse'.

—Anonymous, *Christian Examiner*, Boston, June 1856

HENRY DAVID THOREAU (1856)

In this letter, major transcendentalist Henry David Thoreau, author of *Walden* and "Civil Disobedience," praises Whitman's personal character and the power of his poems to make the reader ready to witness wonders, especially in the poems that would later become "Song of Myself" and "Crossing Brooklyn Ferry." Yet Thoreau also criticizes Whitman's poetry for its sensuality, which Thoreau finds an impediment to the development of authentic love and an unfortunate but potentially serious liability if Whitman is to attain a broader audience.

Thoreau's letter compares Whitman's poetry to the literature of "the Orientals," by which he means the religious poetry and writings of Hinduism in particular. While Whitman proclaimed his ignorance of these writings to Thoreau, his own notebooks and poems indicate otherwise, revealing at the very least Whitman's familiarity with Hinduism, and in some cases his direct incorporation of its philosophical tenets. Students writing on the relation between Whitman's poetry and Hinduism will find Thoreau's support for this comparison in the letter, and an even fuller enumeration of the links between transcendentalism and Hinduism in *Walden*. Whitman's denial of familiarity with Hindu writings reveals an interesting pattern of self-revision in Whitman's life, where the elder Whitman denies the influence and even the knowledge of certain authors and texts that greatly affected the composition of the different editions of *Leaves of Grass* from 1855 to 1865. Students writing about the creation of Whitman's public persona through his writings, his interactions with other intellectuals, and through anecdotes about Whitman told by friends and followers, will find much to consider in Thoreau's letter.

⸻ ⸺ ⸺

That Walt Whitman, of whom I wrote to you, is the most interesting fact to me at present. I have just read his second edition (which he gave me), and it has done me more good than any reading for a long time. Perhaps I remember best the poem of *Walt Whitman, an American,* and the "Sun-Down Poem." There are two or three pieces in the book which are disagreeable, to say the least; simply sensual. He does not celebrate love at all. It is as if the beasts spoke. I think that men have not been ashamed of themselves without reason. No doubt there have always been dens where such deeds were unblushingly recited, and it is no merit to compete with their inhabitants. But even on this side he has spoken more truth than any American or modern that I know. I have found his poem exhilarating, encouraging. As for its sensuality,—and it may turn out to be less sensual than it appears,—I do not so much wish that those parts were not written, as that men and women were so pure that they could read them without harm, that is, without understanding them. One woman told me that no woman could read it,—as if a man could read what a woman could not. Of course Walt Whitman can communicate to us no experience, and if we are shocked, whose experience is it that we are reminded of?

On the whole, it sounds to me very brave and American, after whatever deductions. I do not believe that all the sermons, so called, that have been preached in this land put together are equal to it for preaching.

We ought to rejoice greatly in him. He occasionally suggests something a little more than human. You can't confound him with the other inhabitants of Brooklyn or New York. How they must shudder when they read him! He is awfully good.

To be sure I sometimes feel a little imposed on. By his heartiness and broad generalities he puts me into a liberal frame of mind prepared to see wonders,—as it were, sets me upon a hill or in the midst of a plain,—stirs me well up, and then—throws in a thousand of brick. Though rude, and sometimes ineffectual, it is a great primitive poem,—an alarum or trumpet-note ringing through the American camp. Wonderfully like the Orientals, too, considering that when I asked him if he had read them, he answered, "No: tell me about them."

I did not get far in conversation with him,—two more being present,—and among the few things which I chanced to say, I remember that one was, in answer to him as representing America, that I did not think much of America or of politics, and so on, which may have been somewhat of a damper to him.

Since I have seen him, I find that I am not disturbed by any brag or egoism in his book. He may turn out the least of a braggart of all, having a better right to be confident.

He is a great fellow.

—Henry David Thoreau, Letter to Harrison Blake
(December 7, 1856)

WILLIAM ALLINGHAM (1857)

I've read *Leaves of Grass*, and found it rather pleasant, but little new or original; the portrait the best thing. Of course, to call it poetry, in any sense, would be mere abuse of language. In poetry there is a special freedom, which, however, is *not* lawlessness and incoherence.

—William Allingham, Letter to
Dante Gabriel Rossetti (April 10, 1857)

ANONYMOUS "INNATE VULGARITY" (1859)

Nothing can more clearly demonstrate the innate vulgarity of our American people, their radical immodesty, their internal licentiousness, their unchastity of heart, their foulness of feeling, than the tabooing of Walt Whitman's *Leaves of Grass*. It is quite impossible to find a publisher for the new edition which has long since been ready for the press, so measureless is the depravity of public taste. There is not an indecent word, an immodest expression, in the entire volume; not a suggestion which is not purity itself, and yet it is rejected on account of its indecency! So much do I think of this work by the healthiest and most original poet America has produced, so valuable a means is it of rightly estimating character, that I have been accustomed to try with it of what quality was the virtue my friends possessed. How few stood the test I shall not say. Some did, and praised it beyond measure. These I set down without hesitation as radically pure, as 'born again,' and fitted for the society of heaven and the angels. And this test I would recommend to every one. Would you, reader, male or female, ascertain if you be actually modest, innocent, pure-minded? read the *Leaves of Grass*. If you find nothing improper there, you are one of the virtuous and pure. If, on the contrary, you find your sense of decency shocked, then is that sense of decency an exceedingly foul one, and you, man or woman, a very vulgar, dirty person.

The atmosphere of the *Leaves of Grass* is as sweet as that of a hayfield. Its pages exhale the fragrance of nature. It takes you back to man's pristine state of innocence in paradise, and lifts you Godwards. It is the healthiest book, morally, this century has produced: and if it were reprinted in the form of a cheap tract, and scattered broadcast over the land, put into the hands of youth, and into the hands of men and women everywhere, it would do more towards elevating our nature, towards eradicating this foul, vulgar, licentious, sham modesty, which so degrades our people now, than any other means within my knowledge. What we want is not outward, but inward modesty, not external, but internal virtue, not silk and broad-cloth decency, but a decency infused into every organ of the body and faculty of the soul. Is modesty a virtue? Is it then worn in clothes? Does it hang over the shoulders, or does it live and breathe in the heart? Our modesty is a Jewish phylactery sewed up in the padding of a coat, and stitched into a woman's stays.

—Anonymous, "Innate Vulgarity,"
Fourteen Thousand Miles Afoot, 1859

ANONYMOUS (1860)

Of all the writers we have ever perused Walt Whitman is the most silly, the most blasphemous, and the most disgusting. If we can think of any stronger epithets we will print them in a second edition.

—Anonymous, *Literary Gazette*, London, July 7, 1860

ANONYMOUS (1860)

In no other modern poems do we find such a lavish outpouring of wealth. It is as if, in the midst of a crowd of literati bringing handfuls of jewels, a few of pure metal elaborately wrought, but the rest merely pretty specimens of pinchbeck, suddenly a herculean fellow should come along with an entire gold mine. Right and left he scatters the glittering dust,—and it is but dust in the eyes of those who look only for pleasing trinkets. Out of his deep California sacks, mingled with native quartz and sand, he empties the yellow ore,—sufficient to set up fifty small practical jewellers dealing in galvanized ware, if they were not too much alarmed at the miner's rough garb to approach and help themselves. Down from his capacious pockets tumble astonishing nuggets,—but we, who are accustomed to see the stuff never in its rude state, but only in fashionable shapes of breastpins, or caneheads, start back with affright, and scream for our toes.

It is much to be regretted that treasures of such rare value are lost to the age through the strange form and manner in which they are presented. But it is time lost blaming the miner. Perhaps he could have done differently, perhaps not; at all events, we must take him as he is, and if we are wise, make the best of him.

The first and greatest objection brought against Walt Whitman and his *Leaves of Grass* is their indecency. Nature is treated here without fig leaves; things are called by their names, without any apparent sense of modesty or shame. Of this peculiarity—so shocking in an artificial era—the dainty reader should be especially warned. But it is a mistake to infer that the book is on this account necessarily immoral. It is the poet's design, not to entice to the perversion of Nature, which is vice, but to lead us back to Nature, which in his theory is the only virtue. His theory may be wrong, and the manner in which he carried it out repulsive, but no one who reads and understands him will question the sincerity of his motives, however much may be doubted the wisdom of attempting in this way to restore mankind to the days of undraped innocence.

In respect of plain speaking, and in most respects, the *Leaves* more resemble the Hebrew Scriptures than do any other modern writings. The style is wonderfully idiomatic and graphic. The commonest daily objects and the most exalted truths of the soul, this bard of Nature touches with the ease and freedom of a great master. He wonders at all things, he sympathizes with all things and with all men. The nameless something which makes the power and spirit of music, of poetry, of all art, throbs and whirls under and through his verse, affecting us we know not how, agitating and ravishing the soul. And this springs so genuinely from the inmost nature of the man, that it always appears singularly in keeping even with that extravagant egotism, and with those surprisingly quaint or common expressions, at which readers are at first inclined only to laugh. In his frenzy, in the fire of his inspiration, are fused and poured out together elements hitherto considered antagonistic in poetry—passion, arrogance, animality, philosophy, brag, humility, rowdyism, spirituality, laughter, tears, together with the most ardent and tender love, the most comprehensive human sympathy which ever radiated its divine glow through the pages of poems.

—Anonymous, *Cosmopolite*, Boston, August 4, 1860

GEORGE SAINTSBURY (1874)

In this review of the fifth edition of *Leaves of Grass*, the English critic and scholar of French literature George Saintsbury examines the changes Whitman had made to the new edition, and from these changes offers important generalizations about Whitman as a poet. Saintsbury avoids engaging in the divisive debates over Whitman's subjects and his status as a poet, arguing that such issues are often marred by misunderstandings and biases among Whitman's detractors and supporters alike. Instead, Saintsbury argues for the power of Whitman's manner of expression, almost regardless of the subject matter, thus attempting to reclaim Whitman's status as poet rather than as a prophet or creator of scandal. The new edition, Saintsbury notes, features changes to individual poem titles, to the titles of sections in the volume, and even to the material design of the book, indicating an increasing conventionality in Whitman's once-revolutionary poetics, though only on a superficial level. Saintsbury reserves his praise for the strength, freshness, strangeness, and originality of Whitman's style, which remains focused on developing new poetic rhythms even as it forsakes conventional rhyme and meter. Yet for all his focus on Whitman's style, Saintsbury still acknowledges the importance of several subjects for Whitman, including the sea, sexual passion, and death, arguing that their commonality links all mankind, elevating and solemnizing human existence.

Saintsbury's discussion of the latter themes may prove most fruitful for students writing on such poems as "Out of the Cradle Endlessly Rocking," "As I Ebb'd with the Ocean of Life," and "I Sing the Body Electric." For students writing about Whitman's poetics, particularly the nature of his rhythms and his free use of prosodic devices, Saintsbury's essay offers much to consider. It represents an early attempt to define and discuss "free verse," and any reader seeking to explore in greater depth Whitman's free verse would do well to reflect on Saintsbury's comparison of Whitman's attempt to create a highly rhythmic free verse with the French poet Charles Baudelaire's cultivation of prosaic rhythms in his prose poems. Though admittedly more concerned with Whitman's manner than his subject matter, Saintsbury nevertheless claims that Whitman's ideal of a "universal republic, or rather brotherhood of men" is the central thesis of his "poetical gospel." While not unique in claiming this, Saintsbury distinctly connects Whitman's democratic ideal with his style, and students approaching Whitman's poetry through the close reading practices of New Criticism may find Saintsbury's blend of formal focus and thematic generalization salient. Finally, Saintsbury's observations about and assessments of the changes Whitman made between the fourth and fifth editions of *Leaves of Grass* will prove helpful in a comparative analysis of different versions of Whitman's poems. Saintsbury notes the inclusion of *Drum-Taps*, and his examination of Whitman's treatment of death as both common and profound may be of interest to students writing about Whitman's experience as a Civil War nurse, about his representation of death before and after the Civil War, and about his response to Abraham Lincoln's assassination in "When Lilacs Last in the Dooryard Bloom'd."

—◊◊◊◊◊◊—   —◊◊◊◊◊◊—   —◊◊◊◊◊◊—

Several years have now passed since Walt Whitman's poetical works and claims were first brought before the notice of Englishmen of letters, yet it is more than doubtful whether, even among this class, there is any clear and decided view of his merits to be found prevailing. His poems have suffered the usual fate of such abnormal productions; it has been considered that admiration of them must be a kind of voluntary eccentricity, a gratuitous flourish in the face of respectability and orthodoxy. And it cannot be denied that he has not altogether escaped that worst of all calamities to a literary man, the admiration of the incompetent. It is true that he has been praised, with discrimination as well as with emphasis, by Mr. Swinburne; but unfortunately Mr. Swinburne's praise is mainly a passport to the favour of those who would be likely to appreciate Whitman without any passport at all. The testimony of his other panegyrists has been not a little weakened: in some by supposed national or political prejudices; in others, as already mentioned, by notorious literary incompetence.

It is very much to be hoped that the publication of this new edition of the *Leaves of Grass* may be the occasion of a deeper and wider study of the American poet, a study which may be carried on purely as a matter of literature, and not with any lurking intention to illustrate preconceived ideas as to the merits or demerits of Walt Whitman's principles, practice, or mode of expression.

The volume now before us is very different in outward appearance from the edition of fourteen years ago, which has so long caught the eye by its dissimilarity to its brother occupants of the bookshelf. The old cloth boards, deeply and mystically stamped with strange emblems, have given way to an outer coat of sober and decent green suitable to any modern English poem. Thick paper and bold type have yielded to the exigencies of increased matter. The very titles of some of the poems have made concessions to conventionality. *Enfants d'Adam* have transplanted themselves into plain English; "Proto-Leaf" has disappeared from the contents; and "A Boston Ballad the 78th year T. S.," which used to excite vague and uncomfortable chronological uncertainties, has become, to the great solace of the reader, "A Boston Ballad, 1854." Altogether the book might seem to a too-fanciful critic to have abandoned, at least in externals, its former air of youthful and exuberant provocation, and to demand, more soberly if not less confidently, the maturer consideration of the student of letters.

But it is still as ever far more easy to argue for or against the book than to convey a clear account of it to persons not acquainted with it. Although the contents are divided and subdivided by the headings which the author has prefixed, yet these headings convey but little idea of what comes under them, sometimes indeed have very little reference to it. Nor is the connection of the different divisions of the work and their interdependence more obvious. It may be easy to explain the meaning of *Children of Adam,* of "Passage to India," and some others; but what shall we make of *Calamus,* or of *Leaves of Grass* itself? For the answers we must refer the reader to the book that it may give its own reply.

Moreover, the poet has in this edition availed himself of the incorporation of *Drum-taps* and other recently published matter, to dispose the whole contents of the volume in a new order, and to make many additions, alterations, and transpositions in individual poems. These changes are for the most part, as it appears to us, decided improvements, and the whole work possesses at present a unity and a completeness which are no small advantage. There are few poets who require to be studied as a whole so much as Walt Whitman—quotations and even tolerably extensive selections will not do—and it is a great gain to be directed by the author himself as to the order in which he would have us conduct the study.

It is not difficult to point out the central thesis of Walt Whitman's poetical gospel. It is briefly this: the necessity of the establishment of a universal republic, or rather brotherhood of men. And to this is closely joined another, or rather a series of others, indicating the type of man of which this universal republic is to consist, or perhaps which it is to produce. The poet's language in treating the former of these two positions is not entirely uniform; sometimes he speaks as of a federation of nations, sometimes as if mankind at large were to gravitate towards the United States, and to find in them the desired Utopia. But the constitution of the United States, at least that constitution as it ought to be, is always and uniformly represented as a sufficient and the only sufficient political means of attaining this Utopia, nay, as having to some extent already presented Utopia as a fact. Moreover, passing to the second point, the ideal man is imaged as the ideal Yankee, understanding that word of course as it is understood in America, not in Europe. He is to be a rather magnificent animal, almost entirely uncultured (this is not an unfair representation, although there are to be found certain vague panegyrics on art, and especially on music), possessing a perfect *physique,* well nourished and clothed, affectionate towards his kind, and above all things firmly resolved to admit no superior. As is the ideal man, so is the ideal woman to be. Now it may be admitted frankly and at once, that this is neither the creed nor the man likely to prove attractive to many persons east of the Atlantic. If it be said that the creed is a vague creed, and the man a detestable man, there will be very little answer attempted. Many wonderful things will doubtless happen "when," as the poet says, "through these States walk a hundred millions of superb persons;" but it must be allowed that there is small prospect of any such procession. One is inclined for very many sound reasons, and after discarding all prejudices, to opine that whatever salvation may await the world may possibly come from quarters other than from America. Fortunately, however, admiration for a creed is easily separable from admiration for the utterance and expression of that creed, and Walt Whitman as a poet is not difficult to disengage from Walt Whitman as an evangelist and politician. The keyword of all his ideas and of all his writings is universality. His Utopia is one which shall be open to everybody; his ideal of man and woman one which shall be attainable by everybody; his favourite scenes, ideas, subjects, those which everybody, at least to some extent, can enjoy and appreciate. He cares not that by this limitation he may exclude thoughts and feelings, at any rate phases of thought and feeling, infinitely choicer and higher than any which he admits. To express this striving after universality he has recourse to methods both unusual and (to most readers) unwelcome. The extraordinary jumbles and strings of names, places, employments, which deface his pages, and which have encouraged the profane to liken them to auctioneers' catalogues or indexes of encyclopedias, have no other object than to express this universal sympathy, reaching to the highest and penetrating to the lowest forms of life. The exclusion of culture, philosophy, manners, is owing also to this desire to admit nothing but what is open to every human being of ordinary faculty and opportunities. Moreover it is to this that we may fairly trace the prominence in Whitman's writings of the sexual passion, a prominence which has given rise, and probably will yet give rise, to much unphilosophical hubbub. This passion, as the poet has no doubt observed, is almost the only one which is peculiar to man as man, the presence of which denotes virility if not humanity, the absence of which is a sign of abnormal temperament. Hence he elevates it to almost the principal place, and treats of it in a manner somewhat shocking to those who are accustomed to speak of such subjects (we owe the word to Southey) *enfarinhadamente*. As a matter of fact, however, the treatment, though outspoken, is eminently "clean," to use the poet's own word; there is not a vestige of prurient thought, not a syllable of prurient language. Yet it would be a great mistake to suppose that sexual passion occupies the chief place in Whitman's estimation. There is according to him something above it, something which in any ecstasies he fails not to realize, something which seems more intimately connected in his mind with the welfare of mankind, and the promotion of his ideal republic. This is what he calls "robust American love." He is never tired of repeating "I am the poet of comrades"—Socrates himself seems renascent in this apostle of friendship. In the ears of a world (at least on this side the Atlantic) incredulous of such things, he reiterates the expressions of Plato to Aster, of Socrates respecting Charmides, and in this respect fully justifies (making allowance for altered manners) Mr. Symonds' assertion of his essentially Greek character, an assertion which most students of Whitman will heartily endorse. But we must again repeat that it is not so much in the matter as in the manner of his Evangel that the strength of Whitman lies. It is impossible not to notice his exquisite descriptive faculty, and his singular felicity in its use. Forced as he is, both by natural inclination and in the carrying out of his main idea, to take note of "the actual earth's equalities," he has literally filled his pages with the song of birds, the hushed murmur of waves, the quiet and multiform life of the forest and the meadow. And in these descriptions he succeeds in doing what is most difficult, in giving us the actual scene or circumstance as it impressed him, and not merely the impression itself. This is what none but the greatest poets have ever save by accident done, and what Whitman does constantly and with a sure hand. "You shall," he says at the beginning of his book:

> You shall no longer take things at second or third hand, nor look
>   through the eyes of the dead, nor feed on the spectres in books:
> You shall not look through my eyes either, nor take things from me:
> You shall listen to all sides and filter them from yourself.

But affluent as his descriptions are, there are two subjects on which he is especially eloquent, which seem indeed to intoxicate and inspire him the moment he approaches them. These are Death and the sea. In the latter respect he is not, indeed, peculiar, but accords with all poets of all times, and especially of this time. But in his connection of the two ideas (for the one always seems to suggest the other to him), and in his special devotion to Death, he is more singular. The combined influence of the two has produced what is certainly the most perfect specimen of his work, the "Word out of the Sea" (in this edition it has, we are sorry to see, lost its special title, and become the first merely of *Sea-Shore Memories).* Unfortunately it is indivisible, and its length precludes the possibility of quotation. But there is another poem almost equally beautiful, which forms part of "President Lincoln's Burial Hymn," and for this space may perhaps be found:—

DEATH-CAROL
Come, lovely and soothing Death,
Undulate round the world serenely arriving, arriving,
In the day, in the night, to all, to each,
Sooner or later, delicate Death.

Prais'd be the fathomless universe,
For life and joy, and for objects and knowledge curious;
And for love, sweet love. But praise! praise! praise!
For the sure-enwinding arms of cool-enfolding Death.

Dark Mother, always gliding near, with soft feet,
Have none chanted for thee a chant of fullest welcome?
Then I chant it for thee—I glorify thee above all;
I bring thee a song that when thou must indeed come, come
    unfalteringly.

Approach, strong Deliveress!
When it is so—when thou hast taken them, I joyously sing the dead,
Lost in the loving, floating ocean of thee,
Laved in the flood of thy bliss, O Death.

From me to thee glad serenades,
Dances for thee I propose, saluting thee—adornments and feastings for
    thee;
And the sights of the open landscape and the high spread sky are fitting,
And life and the fields and the huge and thoughtful night.

The night, in silence under many a star;
The ocean-shore, and the husky whispering wave whose voice I know;
And the soul turning to thee, O vast and well-veiled death,
And the body gratefully nestling close to thee.

Over the tree-tops I float thee a song!
Over the rising and sinking waves—over the myriad fields and the prairies
    wide;
Over the dense-packed cities all and the teeming wharves and ways,
I float this carol with joy, with joy to thee, O Death!

It is easy enough to connect this cultus of Death, and the pantheism which necessarily accompanies it, with the main articles of Whitman's creed. Death is viewed as the one event of great solemnity and importance which is common to all—the one inevitable, yet not commonplace incident in every life, however commonplace; and, further, it must not be overlooked that Death is pre-eminently valuable in such a system as this, in the capacity of reconciler, ready to accommodate all difficulties, to sweep away all rubbish. The cheeriest of optimists with the lowest of standards cannot pretend to assert or expect that everyone will live the ideal life—but Death pays all scores and obliterates all mistakes.

There remains, however, still to be considered a point not least in importance—the vehicle which Whitman has chosen for the conveyance of these thoughts. He employs, as most people know who know anything at all about him, neither rhyme nor even regular metre; the exceptions to this rule occurring among his more recent poems are few and insignificant. A page of his work has little or no look of poetry about it; it is not, indeed, printed continuously, but it consists of versicles, often less in extent than a line, sometimes extending to many lines. Only after reading these for some time does it become apparent that, though rhyme and metre have been abandoned, rhythm has not; and, moreover, that certain figures and tricks of language occur which are generally considered more appropriate to poetry than to prose. The total effect produced is dissimilar to that of any of the various attempts which have been made to evade the shackles of metre and rhyme, while retaining the other advantages of poetical form and diction. Whitman's style differs very much from that of such efforts as Baudelaire's *Petits Poemes en prose,* for from these all rhythm, diction, and so forth not strictly appropriate to prose is conscientiously excluded. It is more like the polymeters of the poet's namesake Walt in Richter's *Flegeljahre,* except that these latter being limited to the expression of a single thought are not divided into separate limbs or verses. Perhaps the likeness which is presented to the mind most strongly, is that which exists between our author and the verse divisions of the English Bible, especially in the poetical books, and it is not unlikely that the latter did actually exercise some influence in moulding the poet's work. It is hard to give a fair specimen of it in the way of quotation—that already given is not representative, being too avowedly lyrical—and the rhythm is as a rule too varying, complex, and subtle to be readily seized except from a comparison of many instances. Perhaps, however, the following stanza from *Children of Adam* may convey some idea of it:—

> I have perceived that to be with those I like is enough;
> To stop in company with the rest at evening is enough;
> To be surrounded by beautiful, curious, breathing, laughing flesh is
>   enough;
> To pass among them, or touch any one, or rest my arm ever so lightly
>   round his or her neck for a moment—what is this then?
> I do not ask any more delight—I swim in it as in a sea.
> There is something in staying close to men and women, and looking
>   on them, and in the
> contact and odour of them, that pleases the soul well;
> All things please the soul—but these please the soul well.

It will be observed that the rhythm is many-centred, that it takes fresh departures as it goes on. The poet uses freely alliteration, chiasmus, antithesis, and especially the retention of the same word or words to begin and end successive lines, but none of these so freely as to render it characteristic. The result, though perhaps uncouth at first sight and hearing, is a medium of expression by no means wanting in excellence, and certainly well adapted for Whitman's purposes. Strange as it appears to a reader familiarised with the exquisite versification of modern England or France, it is by no means in disagreeable contrast therewith, being at least in its earlier forms (for in some of the later poems reminiscences of the English heroic, of Longfellow's hexameters, and even of Poe's stanzas occur) singularly fresh, light, and vigorous. Nor should the language pass unmentioned—for though of course somewhat Transatlantic in construction and vocabulary, it is not offensively American. The chief blemish in the eyes of the sensitive critic is an ugly trick of using foreign words, such as "Libertad" for liberty, *"habitan* of the Alleghanies," "to become *eleve* of mine," 'with reference to *ensemble,"* and so forth; but even this does not occur very frequently. Few books abound more in "jewels five words long;" it is hardly possible to open a page without lighting upon some happy and memorable conceit, expression, thought, such as this of the grass:

> It is the handkerchief of the Lord;
> A scented gift and remembrance designedly dropt,
> Bearing the owner's name someway in the corners,
> that we may see and remark, and say Whose?

Or this of children's love to a father:

> They did not love him by allowance, they loved him
> with personal love.

Or again of the grass:

> And now it seems to me the beautiful uncut hair
> of graves.

Such in matter and in manner are Walt Whitman's *Leaves of Grass,* and there only remains to be added one recommendation to their study. The book, aggressive and vainglorious as it seems, is in reality remarkably free from vituperativeness of tone. Hardly to some "eunuchs, consumptive and genteel persons" is strong language used, and after all it rests with every reader whether he chooses to class himself with these. Amid all the ecstatic praise of America there is no abuse of England; amid all the excitement of the poems on the War there is little personal abuse of the Secessionists. No Englishman, no one indeed, whether American or Englishman, need be deterred from reading this book, a book the most unquestionable in originality, if not the most unquestioned in excellence, that the United States have yet sent us.

—George Saintsbury, *Academy,* October 10, 1874, pp. 398–400

SIDNEY LANIER (1878)

I read through the three volumes on Sunday: and upon a sober comparison I think Walt Whitman's *Leaves of Grass* worth at least a million of *Among My Books* and *Atalanta in Calydon.* In the two latter I could not find anything which has not been much better said before: but *Leaves of Grass* was a real refreshment to me—like rude salt spray in your face—in spite of its enormous fundamental error that a thing is good because it is natural, and in spite of the world-wide difference between my own conceptions of art and its author's.

—Sidney Lanier, Letter to Bayard Taylor (February 3, 1878)

EDWIN P. WHIPPLE
"AMERICAN LITERATURE" (1886)

Walt Whitman, who originally burst upon the literary world as "one of the roughs," and whose "barbaric yawp" was considered by a particular class of English critics as the first original note which had been struck in American poetry, and as good as an Indian war-whoop. Wordsworth speaks of Chatterton as "the marvellous boy;" Walt Whitman, in his first *Leaves of Grass,* might have been styled the marvellous "b'hoy." Walt protested against all convention, even all forms of conventional verse; he seemed to start up from the ground, an earth-born son of the soil, and put to all cultivated people the startling question, "What do you think of Me?" They generally thought highly of him as an original. Nothing is more acceptable to minds jaded with reading works of culture than the sudden appearance of a strong, rough book, expressing the habits, ideas, and ideals of the uncultivated; but, unfortunately, Whitman declined to listen to the suggestion that his daring disregard of convention should have one exception, and that he must modify his frank expression of the relations of the sexes. The author refused, and the completed edition of the *Leaves of Grass* fell dead from the press. Since that period he has undergone new experiences; his latest books are not open to objections urged against his earliest; but still the *Leaves of Grass,* if thoroughly cleaned, would even now be considered his ablest and most original work. But when the first astonishment subsides of such an innovation as Walt Whitman's, the innovator pays the penalty of undue admiration by unjust neglect.

—Edwin P. Whipple, "American Literature" (1886),
American Literature and Other Papers, 1887, pp. 112–14

WALTER LEWIN "*LEAVES OF GRASS*" (1887)

Every sincere and capable writer puts himself into his books, impressing even quotations and translations with his personality, but *Leaves of Grass* contains more than this. It is a unique autobiography. Many persons have written down the story of their lives, so far as, in their old age, they could recollect it. Looking back upon their career as a whole, they necessarily give to the record the impress of their later judgment. Usually such works are filled with incidents, though, here and there,—notably in the case of John Stuart Mill—they present a photograph of the mind. Walt Whitman did not wait until his later years to begin his autobiography. Life seemed a wondrous experience to him, worth putting on record while it was passing. He jotted down what he saw and heard and felt, while the events were still fresh and alive and in instant relation to himself. In *Leaves of Grass* Whitman has bodied forth a biography of the human soul; of his own ostensibly, of all souls really, for the experience of the individual is simply the experience of the race in miniature. *Leaves of Grass* is a record of the soul's voyage through life; a gathering of experience, of joy and sorrow, of feeling, emotion and thought. This gives to the book its power and charm, and also, in some aspects and to some persons, makes it repellent.

—Walter Lewin, *"Leaves of Grass,"*
Murray's Magazine, September 1887, pp. 327–28

JOHN ADDINGTON SYMONDS
"DEMOCRATIC ART" (1890)

A prominent Victorian poet, biographer, critic, researcher of homosexuality and eventual member of the homosexual community, John Addington Symonds was a longtime correspondent with Whitman. In 1890 he famously wrote Whitman to ask him about the homosexual imagery of Whitman's Calamus poems. Whitman flatly denied Symonds's analysis and claimed, as proof of his heterosexuality, to have fathered six illegitimate children, a fantastic if long-lived claim frequently invoked in discussions of Whitman's sexual identity.

In this essay, Symonds argues that Whitman's poetry is best encountered by readers and discussed by critics in its totality, for the problems of its vulgar diction and nonstandard grammar are exaggerated and exasperated by the selective sampling of quotation. After asserting that Whitman refigures political democracy as a moral, aesthetic, and spiritual ideal, Symonds offers what has become a bedrock view of Whitman as a mystic of the commonplace, one who finds divinity and miracle in the ordinary events of mundane reality.

Symonds focuses on Whitman as a religious iconoclast whose poetry nevertheless espouses a transcendentalist belief in the presence of God in all humankind and nature. Students writing about Whitman's mysticism or his affinities with American transcendentalism will find this essay essential. Likewise, students writing about the nature and origin of Whitman's democratic ideals will find that Symonds's essay raises important questions about whether Whitman's democracy is the political manifestation of his mysticism, or if his mysticism represents a metaphysical recasting of his political beliefs.

—◁◁◁— —◁◁◁— —◁◁◁—

Whitman offers enormous difficulties to the critic who wishes to deal fairly with him. The grotesqueness of his language and the uncouth structure of his sentences render it almost impossible to do justice to the breadth of his thought and the sublimity of his imagination. He ought to be taken in large draughts, to be lived with in long solitudes. His peculiar mode of utterance suffers cruelly by quotation. Yet it is needful to extract his very words, in order to escape from the vagueness of a summary.

The inscription placed upon the forefront of *Leaves of Grass* contains this phrase: "I speak the word of the modern, the word EN-MASSE." What this word means for Whitman is expressed at large throughout his writings. We might throw light upon it from the following passage:

> I speak the pass-word primeval—I give the sign of democracy;
> By God! I will accept nothing which all cannot have their counterpart of
>   on the same terms.

Thus Democracy implies the absolute equality of heritage possessed by every man and woman in the good and evil of this life. It also involves the conception that there is nothing beautiful or noble which may not be discovered in the simplest human being. As regards physical structure:

> Whoever you are! how superb and how divine is your body, or any part of it.
> As regards emotion and passions which throb and pulsate in the individual:
> Wherever the human heart beats with terrible throes out of its ribs.

"Whoever" and "wherever" are the emphatic words in these quotations. The human body in itself is august; the heart has tragedy implicit in its life-beats. It does not signify *whose* body, or *whose* heart. Here, there, and everywhere, the seeing eye finds majesty, the sentient intelligence detects the stuff of drama.

The same principle is applied to the whole sphere of nature. Miracles need not be sought in special occurrences, in phenomena which startle us out of our ordinary way of regarding the universe:

> To me, every hour of the light and dark is a miracle,
> Every inch of space is a miracle,
> Every square yard of the surface of the earth is spread with the same,
> Every cubic foot of the interior swarms with the same;
> Every spear of grass—the frames, limbs, organs of men and women,
>   and all that concern them,
> All these to me are unspeakable miracles.

At this point science shakes hands with the democratic ideal. We are not forced to gaze upon the starry heavens, or to shudder at islands overwhelmed by volcanic throes, in order to spy out the marvellous. Wonders are always present in the material world, as in the spiritual:

A morning-glory at my window satisfies me more than the metaphysics of books. The heroic lies within our reach, if we but stretch a finger forth to touch it:

> Lads ahold of fire-engines and hook-and-ladder ropes no less to me than
>   the Gods of the antique wars;
> Minding their voices peal through the crash of destruction,
> Their brawny limbs passing safe over charred laths, their white foreheads
>   whole and unhurt out of the flames.

Whitman expels miracles from the region of mysticism, only to find a deeper mysticism in the world of which he forms a part, and miracles in commonplace occurrences. He dethrones the gods of old pantheons, because he sees God everywhere around him. He discrowns the heroes of myth and romance; but greets their like again among his living comrades. What is near to his side, beneath his feet, upon the trees around him, in the men and women he consorts with, bears comparison with things far off and rarities imagined.

—John Addington Symonds, "Democratic Art"
Essays Speculative and Suggestive,
1890, Vol. 2, pp. 47–50

WALT WHITMAN
"AN OLD MAN'S REJOINDER" (1890)

Reflecting on his years composing and revising *Leaves of Grass*, Whitman here writes about the primary social, political, and historical influences on his poems: American individualism, westward expansion, and the Civil War. Yet while his poetry reflects the strengthening of American democracy, Whitman claims, it neither represents nor has inspired a truly "democratic art." The tone of this passage proves somber for Whitman, who cast himself as the prophet of American democracy. Students curious about the nature of democratic art would do well to read this essay along with Alexis de Tocqueville's discussion of the subject in *Democracy in America*. What is democratic art, according to de Tocqueville, and does Whitman's poetry correspond to his definition? If not, why not? Does Whitman's conception of democratic art differ from de Tocqueville's and, if so, how? Why does Whitman not credit his work as being democratic art?

No great poem or other literary or artistic work of any scope, old or new, can be essentially consider'd without weighing first the age, politics (or want of politics) and aim, visible forms, unseen soul, and current times, out of the midst of which it rises and is formulated: as the Biblic canticles and their days and spirit—as the Homeric, or Dante's utterance, or Shakspere's, or the old Scotch or Irish ballads, or Ossian, or Omar Khayyam. So I have conceiv'd and launch'd, and work'd for years at, my *Leaves of Grass*—personal emanations only at best, but with specialty of emergence and background—the ripening of the nineteenth century, the thought and fact and radiation of individuality, of America, the Secession war, and showing the democratic conditions supplanting everything that insults them or impedes their aggregate way. Doubtless my poems illustrate (one of novel thousands to come for a long period) those conditions; but 'democratic art' will have to wait long before it is satisfactorily formulated and defined—if it ever is.

—Walt Whitman, "An Old Man's Rejoinder"
(1890), *Good-Bye My Fancy*, 1891

John Burroughs
"His Ruling Ideas and Aims" (1896)

The American naturalist and author John Burroughs was a close friend of Walt Whitman's, and he was encouraged by Whitman to write about nature in prose that was both scientifically factual and poetically inspired. While Burroughs's first study of Whitman was extensively rewritten by the poet himself (part of Whitman's early effort to craft his literary persona), this second work reflects Burroughs's own style. Celebrating Whitman's art for its candor, oceanic power, and rejection of conventional literary technique (for which the poet was often criticized early in his career), Burroughs hails Whitman as a prophet of equality, arguing that the ideals of American democracy find a religious affirmation in Whitman's poetry. Burroughs praises the cosmic inclusiveness of *Leaves of Grass*, a book that refuses to leave out or denigrate any human experience, since every feature of existence is seen as corresponding with some feature of the poet's self.

Burroughs's study offers rich support for students interested in the links between Whitman's democratic and religious ideals, or for popular representations of Whitman as a prophetic rather than literary figure, though readers should be cautious when dealing with Burroughs's generally unequivocal praise of Whitman, since other supporters have been critical of Whitman's apparent rejection of more conventional literary modes of expression and literary subjects. For students approaching Whitman from a psychoanalytic standpoint, Burroughs's essay supports reading Whitman's catalogues as means of self-expression. Burroughs's indirect reference to three sources for Whitman's poetry—the U.S. Constitution, the prophetic books of the Bible, and Italian opera—will be of interest to students writing on the literary and cultural sources of Whitman's poetry. Burroughs's thorough analysis of the thematic influence of these sources offers much to consider.

I

Let me here summarize some of the ideas and principles in which *Leaves of Grass* has its root, and from which it starts. A collection of poems in the usual sense, a variety of themes artistically treated and appealing to our assthetic perceptibilities alone, it is not. It has, strictly speaking, but one theme,—personality, the personality of the poet himself. To exploit this is always the main purpose, and, in doing so, to make the book both directly and indirectly a large, impassioned utterance upon all the main problems of life and of nationality. It is primitive, like the early literature of a race or people, in that its spirit and purpose are essentially religious. It is like the primitive literatures also in its prophetic cry and in its bardic simplicity and homeliness, and unlike them in its faith and joy and its unconquerable optimism.

It has been not inaptly called the bible of democracy. Its biblical features are obvious enough with the darker negative traits left out. It is Israel with science and the modern added.

Whitman was swayed by a few great passions,—the passion for country, the passion for comrades, the cosmic passion, etc. His first concern seems always to have been for his country. He has touched no theme, named no man, not related in some way to America. The thought of it possessed him as thoroughly as the thought of Israel possessed the old Hebrew prophets. Indeed, it is the same passion, and flames up with the same vitality and power,—the same passion for race and nativity enlightened by science and suffused with the modern humanitarian spirit. Israel was exclusive and cruel. Democracy, as exemplified in Walt Whitman, is compassionate and all-inclusive:—

> My spirit has passed in compassion and determination around the whole
>   earth,
> I have looked for equals and lovers, and found them ready for me in all
>   lands;
> I think some divine rapport has equalized me with them.
> O vapors! I think I have risen with you, and moved away to distant
>   continents, and fallen down there, for reasons,
> I think I have blown with you, O winds,
> O waters, I have fingered every shore with you.

II

The work springs from the modern democratic conception of society,—of absolute social equality.

It embodies the modern scientific conception of the universe, as distinguished from the old theological conception,—namely, that creation is good and sound in all its parts.

It embodies a conception of evil as a part of the good, of death as the friend and not the enemy of life.

It places comradeship, manly attachment, above sex love, and indicates it as the cement of future states and republics.

It makes the woman the equal of the man, his mate and not his toy.

It treats sexuality as a matter too vital and important to be ignored or trifled with, much less perverted or denied. A full and normal sexuality,—upon this the race stands. We pervert, we deny, we corrupt sex at our peril. Its perversions and abnormalities are to be remedied by a frank and fervent recognition of it, almost a new priapism.

It springs from a conception of poetry quite different from the current conception. It aims at the poetry of things rather than of words, and works by suggestion and indirection rather than by elaboration.

It aims to project into literature a conception of the new democratic man,—a type larger, more copious, more candid, more religious, than we have been used to. It finds its ideals, not among scholars or in the parlor or counting-houses, but among workers, doers, farmers, mechanics, the heroes of land and sea.

Hence the atmosphere which it breathes and effuses is that of real things, real men and women. It has not the perfume of the distilled and concentrated, but the all but impalpable odor of the open air, the shore, the wood, the hilltop. It aims, not to be a book, but to be a man.

Its purpose is to stimulate and arouse, rather than to soothe and satisfy. It addresses the character, the intuitions, the ego, more than the intellect or the purely aesthetic faculties. Its end is not taste, but growth in the manly virtues and powers.

Its religion shows no trace of theology, or the conventional pietism.

It aspires to a candor and a directness like that of Nature herself.

It aims to let Nature speak without check, with original energy. The only checks are those which health and wholeness demand. Its standards are those of the natural universal.

Its method is egocentric. The poet never goes out of himself, but draws everything into himself and makes it all serve to illustrate his personality.

Its form is not what is called artistic. Its suggestion is to be found in organic nature, in trees, clouds, and in the vital and flowing currents.

In its composition the author was doubtless greatly influenced by the opera and the great singers, and the music of the great composers. He would let himself go in the same manner and seek his effects through multitude and the quality of the living voice.

Finally, *Leaves of Grass* is an utterance out of the depths of primordial, aboriginal human nature. It embodies and exploits a character not rendered anaemic by civilization, but preserving a sweet and sane savagery, indebted to culture only as a means to escape culture, reaching back always, through books, art, civilization, to fresh, unsophisticated nature, and drawing his strength from thence.

Another of the ideas that master Whitman and rule him is the idea of identity,—that you are you and I am I, and that we are henceforth secure whatever comes or goes. He revels in this idea; it is fruitful with him; it begets in him the ego-enthusiasm, and is at the bottom of his unshakable faith in immortality. It leavens all his work. It cannot be too often said that the book is not merely a collection of pretty poems, themes elaborated and followed out at long removes from the personality of the poet, but a series of *sorties* into the world of materials, the American world, piercing through the ostensible shows of things to the interior meanings, and illustrating in a free and large way the genesis and growth of a man, his free use of the world about him, appropriating it to himself, seeking his spiritual identity through its various objects and experiences, and giving in many direct and indirect ways the meaning and satisfaction of life. There is much in it that is not poetical in the popular sense, much that is neutral and negative, and yet is an integral part of the whole, as is the case in the world we inhabit. If it offends, it is in a wholesome way, like objects in the open air.

III

Whitman rarely celebrates exceptional characters. He loves the common humanity, and finds his ideals among the masses. It is not difficult to reconcile his attraction toward the average man, towards workingmen and "powerful, uneducated persons," with the ideal of a high excellence, because he finally rests only upon the most elevated and heroic personal qualities,—elevated but well grounded in the common and universal.

The types upon which he dwells the most fondly are of the common people. . . . All the *motifs* of his work are the near, the vital, the universal; nothing curious, or subtle, or farfetched. His working ideas are democracy, equality, personality, nativity, health, sexuality, comradeship, self-esteem, the purity of the body, the equality of the sexes, etc. Out of them his work radiates. They are the eyes with which it sees, the ears with which it hears, the feet upon which it goes. The poems are less like a statement, an argument, an elucidation, and more like a look, a gesture, a tone of voice.

"The word I myself put primarily for the description of them as they stand at last," says the author, "is the word Suggestiveness."

Leaves of Grass requires a large perspective; you must not get your face too near the book. You must bring to it a magnanimity of spirit,—a charity and faith equal to its own. Looked at too closely, it often seems incoherent and meaningless; draw off a little and let the figure come out. The book is from first to last a most determined attempt, on the part of a large, reflective, loving, magnetic, rather primitive, thoroughly imaginative personality, to descend upon the materialism of the nineteenth century, and especially upon a new democratic nation now in full career upon this continent, with such poetic fervor and enthusiasm as to lift and fill it with the deepest meanings of the spirit and disclose the order of universal nature. The poet has taken shelter behind no precedent, or criticism, or partiality whatever, but has squarely and lovingly faced the oceanic amplitude and movement of the life of his times and land, and fused them in his fervid humanity, and imbued them with deepest poetic meanings. One of the most striking features of the book is the adequacy and composure, even joyousness and elation, of the poet in the presence of the huge materialism and prosaic conditions of our democratic era. He spreads himself over it all, he accepts and absorbs it all, he rejects no part; and his quality, his individuality, shines through it all, as the sun through vapors. The least line, or fragment of a line, is redolent of Walt Whitman. It is never so much the theme treated as it is the man exploited and illustrated. Walt Whitman does not write poems, strictly speaking,—does not take a bit of nature or life or character and chisel and carve it into a beautiful image or object, or polish and elaborate a thought, embodying it in pleasing tropes and pictures. His purpose is rather to show a towering, loving, composite personality moving amid all sorts of materials, taking them up but for a moment, disclosing new meanings and suggestions in them, passing on, bestowing himself upon whoever or whatever will accept him, tossing hints and clues right and left, provoking and stimulating the thought and imagination of his reader, but finishing nothing for him, leaving much to be desired, much to be completed by him in his turn.

—John Burroughs, "His Ruling Ideas and Aims,"
Whitman: A Study, 1896, pp. 73–80

C.D. LANIER "WALT WHITMAN" (1902)

So bold and so varied are the eccentricities displayed in *Leaves of Grass* that one scarcely knows where to begin. What first strikes the superficial reader—and few readers have the courage to be anything more!—is the strange dithyrambic style of the so-called poems. A short line, or series of short lines, with no suspicion of meter, is suddenly followed by a long jumble of rough, jagged words, thrown higgledy-piggledy together, utterly without rhyme and often without reason. One of these enormities of verse will sometimes stretch, with its prolix enumerations and repetitions, to the length of a good-sized paragraph.

The portentous appearance sadly puzzled the reviewers, and, at first reading, one is surely apt to conclude that the author was mad as a March hare. At best it reminds one of the English translation of the Hindu epics, or an awkwardly rendered passage from the song of the Hebrew prophets. For these broken, passionate utterances, like the war poetry of Brihtnoth and the old Anglo-Saxon battle-ax swingers, did have strength and fire, whatever be their limitations considered as literature.

But the strange property of these wordy outpourings is that they actually begin to have a charm when one has fallen into some sympathy with Whitman. The very ruggedness and candid disclaiming of all title to esthetic beauty contain a certain fascination.

As to rhythm, it is not to be found at all until one has read conscientiously and painfully; then, with the composite effect of several pages in the mind, a sort of deep, weird rhythm does shape itself, how or whence one cannot tell. Mr. Stedman avers that these dithyrambs were carefully evolved according to some regular plan—which we take the liberty of doubting—and that Whitman's idea was to catch the deep underlying melodies of nature,—the break of the sea-surges, the rush of the winds, the cries of animals.

—C.D. Lanier, "Walt Whitman,"
Chautauquan, June 1902, p. 310

CALAMUS

JOHN ADDINGTON SYMONDS
"WALT WHITMAN: A STUDY" (1893)

A cornerstone of queer theory–based assessments of the homosexual content of Whitman's poetry, this essay by prominent Victorian critic and biographer John Addington Symonds contrasts the principle of adhesiveness, or love of man for fellow men, celebrated in the Calamus section of *Leaves of Grass* to the amative principle, or love of man for women, expressed in the notoriously sexual Children of Adam section. Arguing that the latter poems lacked passion and romantic sentiment, despite their subject matter, Symonds finds Whitman's expressions of comradeship in the Calamus poems vital, enthusiastic, tender, and of an intensity to which the modern world is unaccustomed. No other modern writer, he claims, has championed the spiritual superiority and greater lastingness of the adhesive principle over the amative principle like Whitman, to the point that Symonds sees it as the basis for America's enduring success as a nation. Symonds remains ambiguous about the issue of physical desire in Whitman's idea of adhesiveness, partly out of uncertainty, partly out of courtesy, given the general public's rejection of such passions. Symonds cites lines that suggest the poet may view such attraction as a tantalizing but dangerous possibility, writing that only the naïve would doubt at least the possibility of emotionally intense relations leading to physical passions. Taking pains to recount Whitman's disputation of this reading in Symond's private correspondence with him, Symonds nevertheless suggests himself unpersuaded.

Quite famously Whitman proclaimed Symonds's reading of the Calamus poems "damnable" and claimed in response that he had fathered six illegitimate children. The discussion of Whitman's sexuality has continued since, with current scholarship generally accepting that Whitman was homosexual in identity, if not lifestyle. Students will find this essay useful for discussions of Whitman's sexuality, and also in discussions of Whitman's incorporation of the language and ideas of phrenology into his poems. The essay also indirectly represents fin de siècle sexual mores and the coded language with which sexuality in general and homosexuality in particular had to be discussed. Given these existing social prohibitions, students may gain a better sense of how radical Whitman's Children of Adam and Calamus poems truly were by contrasting Symonds's guarded, almost coded, language with Whitman's more explicit language and imagery. Symonds's responses to the Calamus and Children of Adam poems also offer an excellent starting point for a comparison of the two sections, especially since he finds the former absent of romantic sentiment, the latter suffused with a startlingly fresh and original expression of love. Students writing about the relation between Whitman's politics and his sexuality will find D.H. Lawrence's essay fits nicely with Symonds's, since both authors find Whitman's adhesive passions truer than his amative ones, and both identify comradeship as the cornerstone of Whitman's democratic vision.

The section of Whitman's works which deals with adhesiveness, or the love of comrades, is fully as important, and in some ways more difficult to deal with, than his *Children of Adam*. He gave it the title *Calamus*, from the root of a water-rush, adopted by him as the symbol of this love.[1] Here the element of spirituality in passion, of romantic feeling, and of deep enduring sentiment, which was almost conspicuous by its absence from the section on sexual love, emerges into vivid prominence, and lends peculiar warmth of poetry to the artistic treatment. We had to expect so much from the poem quoted by me at the commencement of this disquisition. There Whitman described the love of man for woman as "fast-anchor'd, eternal"; the thought of the bride, the wife, as "more resistless than I can tell." But for the love of man for man he finds quite a different class of descriptive phrases: "separate, disembodied, another born, ethereal, the last athletic reality, my consolation." He hints that we have left the realm of sex and sense, and have ascended into a different and rarer atmosphere, where passion, though it has not lost its strength, is clarified. "Largior hie aether, et campos lumine vestit purpureo."

This emphatic treatment of an emotion which is usually talked about under the vague and formal term of friendship, gives peculiar importance to *Calamus*. No man in the modern world has expressed so strong a conviction that "manly attachment," "athletic love," "the high towering love of comrades," is a main factor in human life, a virtue upon which society will have to lay its firm foundations, and a passion equal in permanence, superior in spirituality, to the sexual affection. Whitman regards this emotion not only as the "consolation" of the individual, but also as a new and hitherto unapprehended force for stimulating national vitality.

There is no softness or sweetness in his treatment of this theme. His tone is sustained throughout at a high pitch of virile enthusiasm, which, at the same time, vibrates with acutest feeling, thrills with an undercurrent of the tenderest sensibility. Not only the sublimest thoughts and aspirations, but also the shyest, most shame-faced, yearnings are reserved for this love. At one time he exclaims:

> O I think it is not for life that I am chanting here my chant of lovers—I
> > think it must be for Death,
> For how calm, how solemn it grows, to ascend to the atmosphere of
> > lovers,
> Death or life I am then indifferent—my soul declines to prefer,
> I am not sure but the high soul of lovers welcomes death most;
> Indeed, O Death, I think now these leaves mean precisely the same
> > as you mean;
> Grow up taller, sweet leaves, that I may see! Grow up out of my breast!
> Spring away from the concealed heart there!
> Do not fold yourselves so, in your pink-tinged roots, timid leaves!
> Do not remain down there so ashamed, herbage of my breast!

The leaves are Whitman's emotions and the poems they engender; the root from which they spring is "manly attachment," "athletic love," symbolised for him in the blushing root of the pond-calamus which he plucked one day and chose to be the emblem of the love of lovers:

> O here I last saw him that tenderly loves me—and returns again, never
>   to separate from me,
> And this, O this shall henceforth be the token of comrades—this
>   Calamus-root shall,
> Interchange it, youths, with each other! Let none render it back!

At another time, in minor key, he writes as follows:

> O you when I often and silently come where you are, that I may be with you;
> As I walk by your side, or sit near, or remain in the same room with you,
> Little you know the subtle, electric fire that for your sake is playing
>   within me.

These extracts were necessary, because there is some misapprehension abroad regarding the precise nature of what Whitman meant by *Calamus*. His method of treatment has, to a certain extent, exposed him to misconstruction. Still, as his friend and commentator, Mr. Burroughs, puts it: "The sentiment is primitive, athletic, taking form in all manner of large and homely out-of-door images, and springs, as any one may see, directly from the heart and experience of the poet." The language has a passionate glow, a warmth of devotion, beyond anything to which the world is used in the celebration of friendship. At the same time the false note of insincerity or sensuousness is never heard. The melody is in the Dorian mood—recalling to our minds that fellowship in arms which flourished among the Dorian tribes, and formed the chivalry of pre-historic Hellas.

In the preface to the 1880 edition *of Leaves of Grass* and *Two Rivulets*, Whitman gives his own explanation of *Calamus*, and of the feelings which inspired that section of his work.

> Something more may be added—for, while I am about it, I would
> make a full confession. I also sent out *Leaves of Grass* to arouse and
> set flowing in men's and women's hearts, young and old, endless
> streams of living, pulsating love and friendship, directly from
> them to myself, now and ever. To this terrible, irrepressible yearning
> (surely more or less down underneath in most human souls), this

never-satisfied appetite for sympathy and this boundless offering of sympathy, this universal democratic comradeship, this old, eternal, yet ever-new interchange of adhesiveness, so fitly emblematic of America, I have given in that book, undisguisedly, declaredly, the openest expression. Besides, important as they are in my purpose as emotional expressions for humanity, the special meaning of the *Calamus,* cluster *of Leaves of Grass* (and more or less running through the book and cropping out in *Drum Taps),* mainly resides in its political significance. In my opinion, it is by a fervent accepted development of comradeship, the beautiful and sane affection of man for man, latent in all the young fellows, north and south, east and west—it is by this, I say, and by what goes directly and indirectly along with it, that the United States of the future (I cannot too often repeat) are to be the most effectually welded together, intercalated, annealed into a living union.

This being so, Whitman never suggests that comradeship may occasion the development of physical desire. On the other hand, he does not in set terms condemn desires, or warn his disciples against their perils. There is indeed a distinctly sensuous side to his conception of adhesiveness. To a Western Boy he says:

If you be not silently selected by lovers, and do not silently select lovers,
Of what use is it that you seek to become elect of mine?

Like Plato, in the *Phaedrus,* Whitman describes an enthusiastic type of masculine emotion, leaving its private details to the moral sense and special inclination of the individuals concerned.

The poet himself appears to be not wholly unconscious that there are dangers and difficulties involved in the highly-pitched emotions he is praising. The whole tenor of two carefully-toned compositions, entitled "Whoever you are, Holding me now in hand," and "Trickle, Drops," suggest an underlying sense of spiritual conflict. The following poem, again, is sufficiently significant and typical to call for literal transcription:

Earth, my likeness!
Though you look so impassive, ample and spheric there,
I now suspect that is not all;
I now suspect there is something fierce in you, eligible to burst forth;

For an athlete is enamoured of me—and I of him,
But toward him there is something fierce and terrible in me, eligible to
    burst forth,
I dare not tell it in word—not even in these songs.

The reality of Whitman's feeling, the intense delight which he derives from the personal presence and physical contact of a beloved man, find luminous expression in "A Glimpse," "Recorders ages hence," "When I heard at the Close of Day," "I saw in Louisiana a Live-Oak growing," "Long I thought that Knowledge alone would suffice me,"[2] "O Tan-faced Prairie-Boy," and "Vigil Strange I kept on the Field one Night."[3]

It is clear then that, in his treatment of comradeship, or the impassioned love of man for man, Whitman has struck a keynote, to the emotional intensity of which the modern world is unaccustomed. It therefore becomes of much importance to discover the poet-prophet's *Stimmung*—his radical instinct with regard to the moral quality of the feeling he encourages. Studying his works by their own light, and by the light of their author's character, interpreting each part by reference to the whole and in the spirit of the whole, an impartial critic will, I think, be drawn to the conclusion that what he calls the "adhesiveness" of comradeship is meant to have no interblending with the "amativeness" of sexual love. Personally, it is undeniable that Whitman possessed a specially keen sense of the fine restraint and continence, the cleanliness and chastity, that are inseparable from the perfectly virile and physically complete nature of healthy manhood. Still we have the right to predicate the same ground-qualities in the early Dorians, those founders of the martial institution of Greek love; and yet it is notorious to students of Greek civilisation that the lofty sentiment of their masculine chivalry was intertwined with much that is repulsive to modern sentiment.

Whitman does not appear to have taken some of the phenomena of contemporary morals into due account, although he must have been aware of them. Else he would have foreseen that, human nature being what it is, we cannot expect to eliminate all sensual alloy from emotions raised to a high pitch of passionate intensity, and that permanent elements within the midst of our society will imperil the absolute purity of the ideal he attempts to establish. It is obvious that those unenviable mortals who are the inheritors of sexual anomalies, will recognise their own emotion in Whitman's "superb friendship, exalte, previously unknown," which "waits, and has been always waiting, latent in all men," the "something fierce in me, eligible to burst forth," "ethereal comradeship," "the last athletic reality." Had I not the strongest proof in Whitman's private correspondence with myself that he repudiated any such deductions from his *Calamus,* I admit that I should have regarded them as justified; and I am not certain whether his own feelings upon this delicate topic may not have altered since the time when *Calamus* was first composed.

Notes

1. Its botanical name is Acorns Calamus. We call it "sweet-rush" or "sweet sedge."
2. Not included in the *Complete Poems and Prose.* It will be found in *Leaves of Grass,* Boston, 1860-61.
3. The two last are from *Drum-Taps.*

—John Addington Symonds,
Walt Whitman: A Study, 1893, pp. 67–76

DRUM-TAPS

Henry James
"Mr. Walt Whitman" (1865)

In this early book review, the American author Henry James (later known for such classic fictional works as "The Turn of the Screw," *The Portrait of a Lady,* and *The Wings of the Dove*) condemns Whitman's *Drum-Taps* as "an offense against art." Rejecting Whitman's prosaic style and eclecticism as mere novelty rather than artistic innovation, James claims that Whitman evokes the grandeur and tragedy of the Civil War from an artistically safe distance, and that he fails to plumb unexplored depths below the surface of observed details to reflect on the genuine emotions and experiences he relates. In this way, James writes, Whitman merely represents the general fashion in writing about the Civil War, but he proceeds to compare Whitman's poems unfavorably with other verse written in response to the war, noting that while the work of other poets "possessed a certain simple melody" in spite of their superficial treatment of their subject, *Drum-Taps* is "rough," "grim," "clumsy," and "monstrous because it pretends to persuade the soul while it slights the intellect."

For James, Whitman seems determined to offend refined artistic sensibilities "wilfully, consciously, arrogantly," and thus might be dismissed as little more than a literary sensationalist. James's criticism echoes two prevailing arguments in early Whitman criticism: namely, that Whitman is a decadent or perverse author, and that his decadence derives from a lack of formal education or artistic refinement. Finding the poems deliberately anti-intellectual, James rejects them not only as violations of artistic norms and social mores, but of the idea of art itself. Ironically, James would later renounce his early views and come to praise Whitman with equal zeal.

Students could cite this review in trying to explain the artistic criteria James uses to judge Whitman's poetry, contrasting passages from James's short fiction or novels with passages from Whitman's poetry and asking what features of Whitman's poetry lead to James's negative judgment. Readers might also try to explain how or whether the quoted passages warrant James's criticisms, or could examine how different passages from *Drum-Taps* might contradict James's judgment.

Students writing about Whitman in the context of other Civil War poets might compare the poems James quotes with examples of the poetry printed in newspapers during and after the Civil War. What is the "simple melody" James finds in the latter but not in Whitman's verse?

For students exploring the relation between literature and popular forms of writing such as book reviews, this essay offers an opportunity to investigate the availability and influence of periodicals like *The Nation*, in which this review first appeared, as well as the nature of book marketing in the nineteenth century. Did the negative review of *Drum-Taps* affect its sales, for instance? If so, how? A student might compare James's review with the negative review of *Drum-Taps* by the author William Dean Howells to construct a portrait of literary tastes in the mid-nineteenth century. This analysis might then help explain the ways in which Whitman came to be seen as a literary revolutionary.

—————

It has been a melancholy task to read this book; and it is a still more melancholy one to write about it. Perhaps since the day of Mr Tupper's *Philosophy* there has been no more difficult reading of the poetic sort. It exhibits the effort of an essentially prosaic mind to lift itself, by a prolonged muscular stain, into poetry. Like hundreds of other good patriots, during the last four years,

Mr Walt Whitman has imagined that a certain amount of violent sympathy with the great deeds and sufferings of our soldiers, and of admiration for our national energy, together with a ready command of picturesque language, are sufficient inspiration for a poet. If this were the case, we had been a nation of poets. The constant developments of the war moved us continually to strong feeling and to strong expression of it. But in those cases in which these expressions were written out and printed with all due regard to prosody, they failed to make poetry, as any one may see by consulting now in cold blood the back volumes of the *Rebellion Record*.

Of course the city of Manhattan, as Mr Whitman delights to call it, when regiments poured through it in the first months of the war, and its own sole god, to borrow the words of a real poet, ceased for a while to be the millionaire, was a noble spectacle, and a poetical statement to this effect is possible. *Of course* the tumult of a battle is grand, the results of a battle tragic, and the untimely deaths of young men a theme for elegies. But he is not a poet who merely reiterates these plain facts *ore rotundo*. He only sings them worthily who views them from a height. Every tragic event collects about it a number of persons who delight to dwell upon its superficial points—of minds which are bullied by the *accidents* of the affair. The temper of such minds seems to us to be the reverse of the poetic temper, for the poet, although he incidentally masters, grasps, and uses the superficial traits of his theme, is really a poet only in so far as he extracts its latent meaning and holds it up to common eyes. And yet from such minds most of our war-verses have come, and Mr Whitman's utterances, much as the assertion may surprise his friends, are in this respect no exception to general fashion. They are an exception, however, in that they openly pretend to be something better; and this it is that makes them melancholy reading.

Mr Whitman is very fond of blowing his own trumpet, and he has made very explicit claims for his books. 'Shut not your doors,' he exclaims at the outset—

Shut not your doors to me, proud libraries,
For that which was lacking among you all, yet needed most, I bring;
A book I have made for your dear sake, O soldiers,
And for you, O soul of man, and you, love of comrades;
The words of my book nothing; the life of it everything
A book separate not link'd with the rest, nor felt by the intellect;
But you will feel every word, O Libertad! arm'd Libertad!
It shall pass by the intellect to swim the sea, the air,
With joy with you, O soul of man.

These are great pretensions, but it seems to us that the following are even greater:

> From Paumanok starting I fly like a bird,
> Around and around to soar, to sing the idea of all;
> To the north betaking myself, to sing there arctic songs,
> To Kanada, till I absorb Kanada in myself—to Michigan then,
> To Wisconsin, Iowa, Minnesota, to sing their songs (they are inimitable);
> Then to Ohio and Indiana, to sing theirs—to Missouri and Kansas and
>   Arkansas to sing theirs,
> To Tennessee and Kentucky—to the Carolinas and Georgia, to sing theirs,
> To Texas, and so along up toward California, to roam accepted everywhere;
> To sing first (to the tap of the war-drum, if need be)
> The idea of ally—of the western world, one and inseparable,
> And then the song of each member of these States.

Mr Whitman's primary purpose is to celebrate the greatness of our armies; his secondary purpose is to celebrate the greatness of the city of New York. He pursues these objects through a hundred pages of matter which remind us irresistibly of the story of the college professor who, on a venturesome youth bringing him a theme done in blank verse, reminded him that it was not customary in writing prose to begin each line with a capital. The frequent capitals are the only marks of verse in Mr Whitman's writings. There is, fortunately, but one attempt at rhyme. We say fortunately, for if the inequality of Mr Whitman's lines were self-registering, as it would be in the case of an anticipated syllable at their close, the effect would be painful in the extreme. As the case stands, each line stands off by itself, in resolute independence of its companions, without a visible goal.

But if Mr Whitman does not write verse, he does not write ordinary prose. The reader has seen that liberty is 'libertad.' In like manner, comrade is 'camerado'; Americans are 'Americanos'; a pavement is a 'trottoir,' and Mr Whitman himself is a 'chansonnier.' If there is one thing that Mr Whitman is not, it is this, for Béranger was a *chansonnier*. To appreciate the force of our conjunction, the reader should compare his military lyrics with Mr Whitman's declamations. Our author's novelty, however, is not in his words, but in the form of his writing. As we have said, it begins for all the world like verse and turns out to be arrant prose. It is more like Mr Tupper's proverbs than anything we have met.

But what if, in form, it is prose? it may be asked. Very good poetry has come out of prose before this. To this we would reply that it must first have gone into it. Prose, in order to be good poetry, must first be good prose. As a general principle, we know of no circumstance more likely to impugn a writer's earnestness than the adoption of an anomalous style. He must have something very original to say if none of the old vehicles will carry his thoughts. Of course he may be surprisingly original. Still, presumption is against him. If on examination the matter of his discourse proves very valuable, it justifies, or at any rate excuses, his literary innovation.

But if, on the other hand, it is of a common quality, with nothing new about it but its manners, the public will judge the writer harshly. The most that can be said of Mr Whitman's vaticinations is, that, cast in a fluent and familiar manner, the average substance of them might escape unchallenged. But we have seen that Mr Whitman prides himself especially on the substance—the life—of his poetry. It may be rough, it may be grim, it may be clumsy—such we take to be the author's argument—but it is sincere, it is sublime, it appeals to the soul of man, it is the voice of a people. He tells us, in the lines quoted, that the words of his book are nothing. To our perception they are everything, and very little at that.

A great deal of verse that is nothing but words has, during the war, been sympathetically sighed over and cut out of newspaper corners, because it has possessed a certain simple melody. But Mr Whitman's verse, we are confident, would have failed even of this triumph, for the simple reason that no triumph, however small, is won but through the exercise of art, and that this volume is an offence against art. It is not enough to be grim and rough and careless; common sense is also necessary, for it is by common sense that we are judged. There exists in even the commonest minds, in literary matters, a certain precise instinct of conservatism, which is very shrewd in detecting wanton eccentricities.

To this instinct Mr Whitman's attitude seems monstrous. It is monstrous because it pretends to persuade the soul while it slights the intellect; because it pretends to gratify the feelings while it outrages the taste. The point is that it does this *on theory*, wilfully, consciously, arrogantly. It is the little nursery game of 'open your mouth and shut your eyes.' Our hearts are often touched through a compromise with the artistic sense, but never in direct violation of it. Mr Whitman sits down at the outset and counts out the intelligence. This were indeed a wise precaution on his part if the intelligence were only submissive! But when she is deliberately insulted, she takes her revenge by simply standing erect and open-eyed. This is assuredly the best she can do. And if she could find a voice she would probably address Mr Whitman as follows:

You came to woo my sister, the human soul. Instead of giving me a kick as you approach, you should either greet me courteously, or, at least, steal in unobserved. But now you have me on your hands. Your chances are poor. What the human heart desires above all is sincerity and you do not appear to me sincere. For a lover you talk entirely too much about yourself. In one place you threaten to absorb Kanada. In another you call upon the city of New York to incarnate you, as you have incarnated it. In another you inform us that neither youth pertains to you nor 'delicatesse,' that you are awkward in the parlour, that you do not dance, and that you have neither bearing, beauty, knowledge, nor fortune. In another place, by an allusion to your 'little songs,' you seem to identify yourself with the third person of the Trinity.

For a poet who claims to sing 'the idea of all,' this is tolerably egotistical. We look in vain, however, through your book for a single idea. We find nothing but flashy imitations of ideas. We find a medley of extravagances and commonplaces. We find art, measure, grace, sense sneered at on every page, and nothing positive given us in their stead. To be positive one must have something to say; to be positive requires reason, labour, and art; and art requires, above all things, a suppression of one's self, a subordination of one's self to an idea. This will never do for you, whose plan is to adapt the scheme of the universe to your own limitations. You cannot entertain and exhibit ideas; but, as we have seen, you are prepared to incarnate them. It is for this reason, doubtless, that when once you have planted yourself squarely before the public, and in view of the great service you have done to the ideal, have become, as you say, 'accepted everywhere,' you can afford to deal exclusively in words. What would be bald nonsense and dreary platitudes in any one else becomes sublimity in you.

But all this is a mistake. To become adopted as a national poet, it is not enough to discard everything in particular and to accept everything in general, to amass crudity upon crudity, to discharge the undigested contents of your blotting-book into the lap of the public. You must respect the public which you address; for it has taste, if you have not. It delights in the grand, the heroic, and the masculine; but it delights to see these conceptions cast into worthy form. It is indifferent to brute sublimity. It will never do for you to thrust your hands into your pockets and cry out that, as the research of form is an intolerable bore, the shortest and most economical way for the public to embrace its idols—for the nation to realise its genius—is in your own person.

This democratic, liberty-loving, American populace, this stern and war-tried people, is a great civiliser. It is devoted to refinement. If it has sustained a monstrous war, and practised human nature's best in so many ways for the last five years, it is not to put up with spurious poetry afterwards. To sing aright our battles and our glories it is not enough to have served in a hospital (however praiseworthy the task in itself), to be aggressively careless, inelegant, and ignorant, and to be constantly preoccupied with yourself. It is not enough to be rude, lugubrious, and grim. You must also be serious. You must forget yourself in your ideas. Your personal qualities—the vigour of your temperament, the manly independence of your nature, the tenderness of your heart—these facts are impertinent. You must be *possessed*, and you must thrive to possess your possession. If in your striving you break into divine eloquence, then you are a poet. If the idea which possesses you is the idea of your country's greatness, then you are a national poet; and not otherwise.

—Henry James, "Mr. Walt Whitman,"
The Nation, November 16, 1865, p. 626

WILLIAM DEAN HOWELLS
"DRUM-TAPS" (1865)

In this negative review of *Drum-Taps*, the American author William Dean Howells argues that Whitman's newest work conveys the pathos of the Civil War, but only with the same inarticulate expressions that Howells expects poetry to reshape into clear, tangible utterance. Unlike many of Whitman's critics, Howells does not attack Whitman in extreme terms, but with a slightly disapproving ironic tone, so that even his positive comments seem backhanded, as when he suggests that Whitman's command to himself in his own poems to give voice to the poetry of America is echoed by his audience. Howells finds *Drum-Taps* nearly identical in style to the first *Leaves of Grass*, excepting the absence of Whitman's notorious indecencies, which in fact only affected a small subset of society, Howells notes, another sign of Whitman's insignificance. The emotion behind these poems is sincere, notes Howells, and he accords

Whitman some personal respect for his service during the war, but in the end he finds that Whitman dwells in "mere consciousness," a state that may be affecting but which cannot be called poetry, however artful or consciously inartistic it may otherwise be.

Howells's review is an uncommon example of a moderately negative response to Whitman, and offers a good counterpoint to Henry James's review of the same book. Students examining how authors respond to fellow authors' works might contrast Howells's attitude toward Whitman, which was always respectful of his character but rather negative or at best indifferent to his work, with James's, which was initially zealous in its condemnations, but equally zealous later on in its praise. Students investigating the reception of Whitman's later work, or comparing responses to *Drum-Taps* and the first *Leaves of Grass*, particularly on the issues of formal versus free verse and emotional intensity, will find Howells's review useful, though perhaps less representative, given its reserved, moderately critical tone.

——————— ——————— ———————

Will saltpeter explode? Is Walt Whitman a true poet? Doubts to be solved by the wise futurity which shall pay off our national debt. Poet or not, however, there was that in Walt Whitman's first book which compels attention to his second. There are obvious differences between the two: this is much smaller than that; and whereas you had at times to hold your nose (as a great sage observed) in reading *Leaves of Grass*, there is not an indecent thing in *Drum-Taps*. The artistic method of the poet remains, however, the same, and we must think it mistaken. The trouble about it is that it does not give you sensation in a portable shape; the thought is as intangible as aroma; it is no more put up than the atmosphere.

We are to suppose that Mr Whitman first adopted his method as something that came to him of its own motion. This is the best possible reason, and only possible excuse, for it. In its way, it is quite as artificial as that of any other poet, while it is unspeakably inartistic. On this account it is a failure. The method of talking to one's self in rhythmic and ecstatic prose is one that surprises at first, but, in the end, the talker can only have the devil for a listener, as happens in other cases when people address their own individualities; not, however, the devil of the proverb, but the devil of reasonless, hopeless, all-defying egotism. An ingenious French critic said very acutely of Mr Whitman that he made you partner of the poetical enterprise, which is perfectly true; but no one wants to share the enterprise. We want its effect, its success; we do not want to plant corn, to hoe it, to drive the crows away, to gather it, husk it, grind it, sift it, bake it, and butter it, before eating it, and then take the risk of its being at last moldy in our mouths. And this is what you have to do in reading Mr Whitman's rhythm.

At first, a favorable impression is made by the lawlessness of this poet, and one asks himself if this is not the form which the unconscious poetry of American life would take, if it could find a general utterance. But there is really no evidence that such is the case. It is certain that among the rudest peoples the lurking sublimity of nature has always sought expression in artistic form, and there is no good reason to believe that the sentiment of a people with our high average culture would seek expression more rude and formless than that of the savagest tribes. It is not more probable that, if the passional principle of American life could find utterance, it would choose the lightest, least dubious, most articulate speech? Could the finest, most shapely expression be too good for it?

If we are to judge the worth of Mr Whitman's poetic theory (or impulse, or possession) by its popular success, we must confess that he is wrong. It is already many years since he first appeared with his claim of poet, and in that time he has employed criticism as much as any literary man in our country, and he has enjoyed the fructifying extremes of blame and praise. Yet he is, perhaps, less known to the popular mind, to which he has attempted to give an utterance, than the newest growth of the magazines and the newspaper notices. The people fairly rejected his former revelation, letter and spirit, and those who enjoyed it were readers with a cultivated taste for the quaint and the outlandish. The time to denounce or to ridicule Mr Whitman for his first book is past. The case of *Leaves of Grass* was long ago taken out the hands of counsel and referred to the great jury. They have pronounced no audible verdict; but what does their silence mean? There were reasons in the preponderant beastliness of that book why a decent public should reject it; but now the poet has cleansed the old channels of their filth, and pours through them a stream of blameless purity, and the public has again to decide, and this time more directly, on the question of his poethood. As we said, his method remains the same, and he himself declares that, so far as concerns it, he has not changed nor grown in anyway since we saw him last:

Beginning my studies, the first step pleased me so much,
The mere fact, consciousness—these forms—the power of motion,
The least insect or animal—the senses—eye-sight;
The first step, I say, aw'd me and pleas'd me so much,
I have never gone, and never wish'd to go, any further,
But stop and loiter all my life to sing it in ecstatic songs.

Mr Whitman has summed up his own poetical theory so well in these lines, that no criticism could possible have done it better. It makes us doubt, indeed, if all we have said in consideration of him has not been said idly, and certainly releases us from further explanation of his method.

In *Drum-Taps*, there is far more equality than in *Leaves of Grass*, and though the poet is not the least changed in purpose, he is certainly changed in fact. The pieces of the new book are nearly all very brief, but generally his expression is freer and fuller than ever before. The reader understands, doubtless, from the title, that nearly all these pieces relate to the war; and they celebrate many of the experiences of the author in the noble part he took in the war. One imagines the burly tenderness of the man who went to supply the

—*lack of woman's nursing*

that there was in the hospitals of the field, and woman's tears creep unconsciously to the eyes as the pity of his heart communicates itself to his readers. No doubt the pathos of many of the poems gains something from the quaintness of the poet's speech. One is touched in reading them by the same inarticulate feeling as that which dwells in music; and is sensible that the poet conveys to the heart certain emotions which the brain cannot analyze, and only remotely perceives. This is especially true of his inspirations from nature; memories and yearnings come to you folded, mute, and motionless in his verse, as they come in the breath of a familiar perfume. They give a strange, shadowy sort of pleasure, but they do not satisfy, and you rise from the perusal of this man's book as you issue from the presence of one whose personal magnetism is very subtle and strong, but who has not added to this tacit attraction the charm of spoken ideas. We must not mistake this fascination for a higher quality. In the tender eyes of an ox lurks a melancholy, soft and pleasing to the glance as the pensive sweetness of a woman's eyes; but in the orb of the brute there is no hope of expression, and in the woman's look there is the endless delight of history, the heavenly possibility of utterance.

Art cannot greatly employ itself with things in embryo. The instinct of the beast may interest science; but poetry, which is nobler than science, must concern itself with natural instincts only as they can be developed into the sentiments and ideas of the soul of man. The mind will absorb from nature all that is speechless in her influences; and it will demand from kindred mind those higher things which can be spoken. Let us say our say here against the nonsense, long current, that there is, or can be, poetry *between the lines*, as is often sillily asserted. *Expression* will always suggest; but mere *suggestion* in art is unworthy of existence, vexes the heart, and shall not live. Every man has tender, and beautiful, and lofty emotions; but the poet was sent into this world to give these a tangible utterance, and if he do not this, but only give us back dumb emotion for dumb emotion, he is a cumberer of the earth. There is a yearning, almost to agony at times, in the human heart, to throw off the burden of inarticulate feeling, and if the poet will not help it in this effort, if, on the contrary, he shall seek to weigh it and sink it down under heavier burdens, he has not any reason to be.

So long, then, as Mr Whitman chooses to stop at mere consciousness, he cannot be called a true poet. We all have consciousness; but we ask of art an utterance. We do not so much care in what way we get this expression; we will take it in ecstatic prose, though we think it is better subjected to the laws of prosody, since every good thing is subject to some law; but the expression we must have. Often, in spite of himself, Mr Whitman grants it in this volume, and there is some hope that he will hereafter grant it more and more. There are such rich possibilities in the man that it is lamentable to contemplate his error of theory. He has truly and thoroughly absorbed the idea of our American life, and we say to him as he says to himself, 'You've got enough in you, Walt; why don't you get it out?' A man's greatness is good for nothing folded up in him, and if emitted in barbaric yawps, it is not more filling than Ossian or the east wind.

—William Dean Howells, "Drum-Taps,"
Round Table, November 1865, pp. 147–48

"OUT OF THE CRADLE ENDLESSLY ROCKING"

STEPHEN E. WHICHER
"WHITMAN'S AWAKENING TO DEATH— TOWARD A BIOGRAPHICAL READING OF 'OUT OF THE CRADLE ENDLESSLY ROCKING'" (1960)

Claiming that revisions to later editions of *Leaves of Grass* concealed the profundity of Whitman's spiritual awakening in "Out of the Cradle Endlessly Rocking," Stephen E. Whicher examines the poem's 1859 version to evoke the profound moment of Whitman's poetic calling and his confrontation with the absolute reality of death. Alluding several times to a crisis of artistic faith suffered by the poet, and claiming that the boy's poetic calling parallels Whitman's later jubilation at the return of his imaginative powers, Whicher writes that later editions subdued Whitman's despair at losing the hopeful energies of "Song of Myself" in favor of a more tranquil reminiscence. Whicher returns to the earlier version of Whitman's encounter to evoke the dark, wounded reality the sea reveals, and thus to emphasize the remarkable, though limited, triumph of the poet's discovery of song.

Students writing about Whitman's symbolic and thematic use of nature and the sea will find Whicher's discussion of Whitman's dual awakening to life and death both detailed and vigorous, as will students writing about Whitman's treatment of the nature and duty of the poet. Whicher's secondary discussion of the sea as a maternal archetype will also interest students engaged with psychoanalytic, particularly Freudian, readings of Whitman. On the subject of Whitman's revisions, Whicher offers a model approach to comparison, and students examining different editions will profit both from his findings and his example. Whicher does not judge one version of the poem superior to the others, but explores the tonal and thematic differences resulting from these revisions. He does, however, acknowledge a greater dramatic intensity in the earlier, less controlled version, and students writing about the vitality of the earlier editions of *Leaves of Grass* will find that Whicher lends strong support to their claims.

It is still too little realized that, with the possible but not obvious exception of Melville, no American author has ever engaged in a more daring or eventful voyage of the mind than Whitman. In his later years Whitman himself for some reason attempted to hide its extent, retouched and toned down his most revealing poems and ingeniously fitted them together into a structure toward which he claimed he had been working all the time. This jerry-built monument to the aging Whitman, which remains to this day the basis of nearly all anthologies of his work and is still reverently toured by uncritical guides, is actually a major obstacle to the recognition of his trite stature. Fortunately a strong critical tradition has now for many years been working to lay bare for us the real structure of Whitman's work, the spiritual biography that emerges from a comparative reading of all the editions of his *Leaves*. In this paper I wish to re-examine some part of this story as it emerges from certain key poems of the 1853 and 1860 editions, in particular 'Out of the Cradle.' . . .

In 'Out of the Cradle' Whitman has contrived to tell his whole story and even to go beyond it. The long one-sentence 'pre-verse' is intended to establish the basic fiction of the poem. The poet will tell us of something long past, he suggests, which now for some reason comes over his memory. By this distancing device he contrives to win some artistic and personal control over his material. In most versions the distinction of the poet that is and the boy that was is made sharp and distinct:

I, chanter of pains and joys, uniter of here and hereafter . . .
A reminiscence sing.

Such a bardic line implies firm poetic control, emotion recollected in tranquillity. But neither this line nor the following one is in the 1859 version, where the poet therefore seems much more under the spell of the memories that have seized him:

A man—yet by these tears a little boy again,
Throwing myself on the sand, I,
Confronting the waves, sing.

What has actually seized him, of course, is the meaning now to him of these images, so much so that in the first version he has a hard time keeping the presentness of his feelings from bursting through and destroying his narrative fiction.

Nevertheless, the reminiscent mode of the poem greatly enlarges its range by permitting him to bring his whole life to bear on it. As a poem of loss and awakening it goes back even to his very earliest loss and awakening, the 'primal' separation of the child from the mother. Though this theme is stressed at once by the poet, especially in the original version, one must avoid reductiveness here. This layer of the poem underlies the whole and already predicts its shape, but it is not the complete structure. From it comes, however, a powerful metaphor for the awakening that is the main subject.

The boy, leaving his bed, finds himself wandering in a strange dark world like something out of Blake, a haunted borderland between shore and sea, here and hereafter, conscious and unconscious. In its troubled restlessness it resembles the moonlit swamp that is glimpsed for a moment in 'Song of Myself' or some of the dream-scenes in 'The Sleepers.' We sense here, especially in the 1859 version, which is more dark and troubled throughout than the final one, the same dumb, unassuageable grief as in 'As I Ebb'd.' It also is a wounded world, impotently twining and twisting with the pain of some obscure fatality. Here there is even less visible occasion for such agony, since the chief actor is not a broken poet but a curious child. The poem is heavy with the man's foreknowledge of what the child, now born, must go through. Like the star in 'When Lilacs Last,' however, the scene also has something to tell, some 'drowned secret' which it is struggling to utter. It does not merely mourn a loss, like the seascape in 'As I Ebb'd,' but also hints of something to be found.

What has drawn the boy from his infantile security into this parturient midnight is a bird. In a flashback the poet tells of the brief May idyll of Two Together. the sudden loss of the she-bird, and the wonderful song of woe that followed, drawing the boy back night after night to listen until the night came when he awakened to its meaning. Then it seemed to him that the bird was a messenger, an interpreter, singing on behalf of the new world he had entered to tell him its secret. This secret is really two secrets, that the meaning of life is love and that he is to be its poet. The song releases the love and the songs of love in his own heart, which he now realizes has long been ready and waiting for this moment; he awakes and ecstatically dedicates himself to this service.

Yet, bewilderingly, this discovery of what life means and what he is for at once plunges him into new trouble and doubt; he finds himself once more groping for something unknown, and is not released until the voice of the sea whispers him a very different secret, the word death. This *double* awakening provides criticism with its chief problem in this poem. It is true that the boy's spiritual development is dramatically consistent and requires no explanation from outside the poem, but it is complex and rapid, an extreme example of dramatic foreshortening. Since it is also intensely personal, the biographical framework I have sketched helps to make its meaning clear.

To put the matter summarily, in the boy's awakening Whitman has fused all his own awakenings together, with the result that his poem moves in one night over a distance which he had taken forty years of life to cover. The emotional foreground, of course, is occupied by the tragic awakening of 1859, the discovery of love not merely as a passion for one particular being rather than an appetite for everything in general, but also as inherently unsatisfied. Love and grief are one. The bird's story is Whitman's story, distanced and disguised, but it is also man's. The outsetting bard of love will be the bard of unsatisfied love because there is no other kind.

But here we encounter a difficulty, for in many of the other poems of 1859 Whitman had suggested that his awakening to love had stopped his poems and ended his poetic career. Of course he could hardly have overlooked the fact that his crisis did arouse him to new poems and to some of his best. Certainly he was proud of this poem, immediately printed it and followed it with one of his self-written reviews announcing that he would not be mute any more. Perhaps we may read a special meaning into his selection of this poem as the first public evidence of his return to song. In this 'reminiscence' of the birth of his poetic vocation he is actually celebrating its recovery. The process of relieving his pain in song has now proceeded so far, past 'death's outlet' songs like 'Hours Continuing Long' and 'As I Ebb'd,' past a poem of first recognition like 'Scented Herbage,' that he can now begin to see that the deathblow to his old 'arrogant poems' is proving to be a lifeblow to new and better if more sorrowful ones, and so for the first time, in the guise of a reminiscence, he can make not just his grief but its transmutation into the relief of song the subject of his singing.

In the measure that he recovers his poetic future he also recovers his past. His sense of returning powers naturally picks up and blends with his memories of that other awakening, whenever and whatever it was, that led to the poems of 1855. In the boy's joy he draws on and echoes his first awakening, the ecstatic union of self and soul celebrated in 'Song of Myself,' when he *had* felt a thousand songs starting to life within him in response to the 'Song of Two Together.' Overlaid on that is his second dark awakening to the truth of 'two together no more' which had at first appeared to end his singing. If we thus provisionally disentangle the strands that Whitman has woven together we can understand better why the song of the bird must plunge the boy almost simultaneously into ecstasy and despair.

The steps of this process are obscured for us in the final version by Whitman's deletion of a crucial stanza that explains why the boy needs a word from the sea when he already has so much from the bird. After the lines

O give me some clue!
O if I am to have so much, let me have more!

the original version continued as follows:

O a word! what is my destination?
O I fear it is henceforth chaos!
O how joys, dreads, convolutions, human shapes, and all shapes,
    spring as from graves around me!
O phantoms! You cover all the land and all the sea!
O I cannot see in the dimness whether you smile or frown upon me!
O vapor, a look, a word! O well-beloved!
O you dear women's and men's phantoms!

This stanza or something similar appears in all editions of 'Out of the Cradle' until the last version of 1881, when Whitman was twenty years away from his poem. Perhaps he dropped it then because he felt it spoke too plainly from the motions of 1859 and was not in keeping with what his poem had become. That it was not necessary to the success of the poem is proved by the success the poem has had without it, yet its omission greatly changes the total effect. The quality of the boy's need is lightened to a more usual adolescent distress and the sea's answer becomes the kind of grave reassurance characteristic of the later Whitman. In the original version the boy is not just distressed, he is desperate with the desperation of the man of 1859. The first act of his awakened poet's vision has been to abort and produce a frightening chaos. Instead of the triumphant vision of Life which Whitman himself had known, when the whole world smiled on its conquering lover, nothing rises now before the outsetting bard but a dim phantasmagoria of death-shapes. It is almost impossible not to read this passage as coming from the poet himself rather than from the boy—indeed. Whitman was right to cut it, it is out of keeping—for these 'dear women's and men's phantoms' are surely dear because they are those of the men and women and the whole world that had already started to life for him in his poems, their life the eddying of his living soul, but are now strengthless ghosts, like the power of vision from which their life had come. This is the 'terrible doubt of appearances' that had plagued him from the beginning, now revived and confirmed by his new crisis. Whitman here openly transfers to the boy the man's despair.

With this background it should not be hard to see that the answer the sea gives to the despair characteristic of 1859 is the answer characteristic of 1859. Its essential quality is the same tragic acceptance as in 'Scented Herbage,' a knowledge of death not as consolation or promise, still less as mere appearance, but as reality, the 'real reality' that completes the reality of love in the only way in which it can be completed. In the language of Thoreau, the sea is a 'realometer' that says, 'this is, and no mistake.' The lift her answer brings is like that of 'Scented Herbage,' the lift of naming the whole truth and so passing beyond illusion to a consent to fate. A sign that this is so is the sea's taciturnity. The thrush's beautiful song of death in 1865, weaving a veil of life-illusion over the same hard truth and so easing it for us, is not present here; simply the word, the thing itself. In this stark directness, again, the kinship is to 'Scented Herbage' rather than to 'When Lilacs Last.'

Yet certainly the fact that this word also, like the bird's song of love and the boy's despair, is ascribed to a dramatic character makes a profound difference. The sea as dramatic character in this poem has two phases. In the earlier part, before the boy turns to her for his answer, she is a background voice blending with the drama of bird and boy but essentially not a part of it. She has an ancient sorrow of her own which leaves her no grief to spare for this small incident on her shores. She does not share the egocentric fallacy of boy and bird, in which even moon, wind, and shadows join in futile sympathy. In this part of the poem she is the same sea as in 'As I Ebb'd', the 'fierce old mother' who 'endlessly cries for her castaways'—all her castaways, not just these—the deep ocean of life and death that rolls through all things.

Of course, behind every detail of the poem, including this one, we feel the poet's shaping power, creating a symbolical language for the life of his own mind. In this kind of subjective drama the author is all the characters; bird, boy, and sea are one and join in a grief that is at bottom the same because it is his own. But Whitman has now seen through the Emersonian illusion that the power of the poet prophesies a victory for the man. Where 'Song of Myself' had dramatized the omnipotence of bardic vision, 'Out of the Cradle' dramatizes the discovery that the power of the bard is only to sing his own limits. Like the bird in Marianne Moore's poem, his singing is mighty because he is caged. As a dramatic character, then, the sea is the Not-Me, Fate, Karma, that-which-cannot-be-changed. As such she dominates the scene, which is all, as Kenneth Burke would say, under her aegis, but she does not share in its temporal passions.

At the end, however, she condescends to reveal herself and changes from the ground of the question to the answer. The change is not so much in the sea as in the boy. As before, he hears when he is ready to listen; the sea has been speaking all the time. Even the bird, in the early version, heard her and responded with continued song. Before he can hear her the boy must finish his egocentric cycle and pass from his hybristic promise to sing 'clearer, louder, and more sorrowful' songs than the bird's to his despairing recognition that there is no good in him. The sign that he is ready is the question itself. Then the sea approaches and whispers as privately for him, revealing the secret which will release him from passion to perception. What she shows him is, I have suggested, no consoling revelation but simply reality. Yet the fact that this answer is now felt to come from the sea, from the heart of the Not-Me that has defeated Whitman's arrogant demands for another Me, suggests that the division between him and his world is not final after all, that the separation both have suffered can still be healed. The elemental forces of 'As I Ebb'd' have fused with the perception of reality of 'Scented Herbage' to form a new Thou, in Buber's language—no longer the tousled mistress Whitman had ordered around in 'Song of Myself,' certainly, but a goddess who will speak to him when he is ready to accept her on her own terms. Then he can hear in the voice of the sea the voice of a mother, a figure as we know 'always near and always divine' to him. The real reality of 'Scented Herbage' has acquired a local habitation and a name, has gathered around itself life and numenosity, and Whitman is well on his way by this dark path to replace the Comrade who had deserted him on the open road.

—Stephen E. Whicher, "Whitman's Awakening to Death— Toward a Biographical Reading of 'Out of the Cradle Endlessly Rocking,'" *Studies in Romanticism*, 1, 1960, pp. 9–10, 22–28

"PASSAGE TO INDIA"

V.K. CHARI
"WHITMAN AND INDIAN THOUGHT" (1959)

In this overview of the connections between Whitman's poetry and Hinduism, scholar V.K. Chari writes that no definitive evidence exists for Whitman's having read Hindu literature, pointing out that the vagueness of Whitman's references to India supports this point. Nevertheless, Chari also argues that Whitman was an extensive reader by nature and an editor by profession, and that his poetry bears too remarkable an affinity with Hindu thought to refute such an influence completely. Students writing about the possible influence of Hinduism on Whitman will ultimately find the matter unresolvable; however, they will find that Chari's essay offers support for the claim of influence while also exemplifying an even-handed approach to the dispute.

Whitman's references to India are altogether of a superficial nature, and his poem 'Passage to India,' which might have been the only direct evidence of Whitman's enthusiasm for India, reveals no precise knowledge about India and is the least Indian of his poems. But then it is to be wondered how without reading the Hindu books Whitman came unwittingly to exhibit such marked affinities with Hindu Vedantic thought. Romain Rolland, who doubted the Indian origin of Whitman's inspiration, was quick to perceive these affinities, but he attributed the poet's mystical experiences to his own subjective realization and partly to the predilections of his background and culture. Rolland's appraisal of Whitman completely underrates the importance of the role of books in the making of the poet. That Whitman was an indefatigable reader and that he passed through a long period of self-instruction before 'making' his poems is clear from his preparatory reading and thought. Books had a great deal more importance in Whitman's mental growth than has generally been estimated. They clarified his native visions and confirmed his intuitions; further they opened out to him new horizons of experience. The range of Whitman's knowledge was extraordinary to judge from his manuscript notebooks. Moreover, the comprehensive duties of an editor compelled him to read almost all important publications of his time and review them in his papers. Thus all the contemporary journalistic literature, the best plays, operas, sermons, lectures and articles were accessible to him.

—V.K. Chari, "Whitman and Indian Thought,"
Western Humanities, vol. XIII, 1959, 291–97

"SONG OF MYSELF"

WALKER KENNEDY "WALT WHITMAN" (1884)

Declaring that Whitman's poetry represents the antithesis of democracy in its rejection of common sense, clarity of expression, and consistency of thought, Walker Kennedy repeats many of the standard criticisms of Whitman in this essay written shortly after the poet's death. Frequently characterizing Whitman as a lunatic and his declarations as nonsense, Kennedy attempts to follow Whitman's prophetic and mystical rhetoric to its logical conclusions, belittling the poet as imprecise at best and incoherent at worst. Offended by Whitman's egotism, Kennedy suggests that Whitman has mistaken the maxim that a work of art reveals things about its creator to mean that a work of art should only be about its creator. His greatest disgust is reserved for Whitman's overt treatment of sexuality and the human body, which Kennedy deems unquotable, and he asserts that even with the loosest artistic standards, Whitman's unpolished, ungrammatical, self-consciously nonliterary writings fail to qualify as poetry.

Recognizing that the tone of nineteenth-century book reviews was often more derisive, satirical, and personal than most current reviews, students may glean a number of valuable literary insights from Kennedy's invective. While criticisms of Whitman's lack of artistry were common,

Kennedy identifies several literary devices as indications of this failing, including Whitman's catalogues, his hyperbole, and his juxtaposition of details without explanatory narrative. Students writing about Whitman as an experimental poet will find Kennedy's essay and the standards he enumerates an excellent example of the conventions Whitman rejected. Those exploring such a topic would do well to consider on what grounds the conventional literature Kennedy upholds would reject such devices. Toward the end of the essay, Kennedy negatively contrasts Whitman with a number of other artists, including Virgil, Dante, Shakespeare, and Goethe. Students writing about how literary canons are used to construct systems of artistic values and to exclude certain authors should reflect on the values Kennedy associates with these writers, perhaps with an eye to the artistic values that would eventually be reconstituted with Whitman's addition to the canon.

What is the *raison d'etre* of *Leaves of Grass?* Has the author ever stated in intelligible English the purpose of his book? Is its aim moral, political, scientific, aesthetic? Is it written in the interest of democracy, or of the intellectual classes? Very likely its author would claim that its purpose is collective. Has it inspired any one with greater love for humanity; has it caused the torch of patriotism in the hand of any individual to burn the brighter; has it lifted a single soul from its despair; has it brought sunshine to any heart; has it given new hopes; has it sweetened religion; has it encouraged science; has it given new wings to the imagination; has it led the intellect into new paths of light and knowledge; has it cleared up any of our doubts or thrown the slightest ray of helpful light upon our questionings? If it has done none of these things, the reason of its being is not apparent.

But, some of Mr. Whitman's admirers say, it is written from a democratic stand-point. If this is the case, the people ought to be able to understand it; but the ordinary man would regard *Leaves of Grass* as the production of a maniac. Only the "gifted few" can discover any sense in *Leaves of Grass;* and what particular message they get from it is past the comprehension of one of the ungifted many. The work, of course, is defective in its literary form. Even its author admits that. Moreover, it has the faults of bad grammar, incomplete sentences, misuse of words, and incoherence of ideas. There is about as much consecutiveness in the *Song of Myself as* there is in a dream originating in too much shrimp salad for supper. A transcript of the dream would be as valuable as the *Song of Myself.*

Mr. Whitman says that "the volumes were intended to be most decided, serious, *bona fide* expressions of an identical individual personality—egotism if you choose, for I shall not quarrel about the word." In this connection, Mr. Whitman quotes a saying of Carlyle's, that "there is no grand poem in the world but is at bottom a biography—the life of a man." It is noticeable here that Carlyle does not say an autobiography. Mr. Whitman is mistaken. The "ego" is usually voted a nuisance in fiction and works of imagination. And it is just as well for us to continue setting down as a vain and disagreeable fellow the man who speaks always of himself as if he were the universe. Egotism hardly does justice to Mr. Whitman's condition. It should be termed the delirium of self-conceit.

The *Song of Myself* is probably a fair sample of Walt Whitman's style and purposes, and there is no injustice in judging him by it. If the critic or the laborious reader were to devote himself to this "poem," what would he find in it? I will attempt a partial summary of it. He begins by saying "I celebrate myself and sing myself." After celebrating and singing himself, he continues: "I loafe, and invite my soul." We may define him then to be a sort of loafer-poet. Having shown that he is not too much of a loafer to be a poet, and *vice versa*, he continues: "I harbor for good or bad. I permit to speak at every hazard nature without check, with original energy." In other words, he erases the words restraint, modesty, and shame from his vocabulary, and drops the distinction between decency and indecency. He would confound all our previous conceptions of good and evil; and, if his theory were carried out, where would be maidenly modesty and youthful delicacy? He might as well contend that everybody should forswear clothes and strut about *in puris naturalibus.* The poet begins his pilgrimage in houses full of fragrance; then he goes out in the air to the bank by the wood and becomes undisguised and naked. "I am mad," he says, "for the air to come in contact with me." This is the language of the lunatic asylum rather than that of poetry. Then follows an enumeration of abstract and concrete things, about which he predicates nothing. It reminds one of the negro's story of the storm that blew down the house but left the roof standing. The poet fails to provide an adequate support for his words, but leaves them suspended in mid-air. After he has made mincemeat of these barbaric phrases, he says: "Stop this day and night with me, and you shall possess the origin of all poems." In the phantasmagoria that follows, if the reader can discover the origin of anything, he is entitled to it. Whitman continues:

There was never any more inception than there is now,
Nor any more youth or age than there is now;

And will never be any more perfection than there is now,
Nor any more heaven or hell than there is now.

This is the climax of nonsense, and carries one back to the alleged philosophers who claimed that motion was an impossibility, and pain a myth. What becomes of evolution, progress, civilization? There could be no more depressing belief than this, for it means nothing but universal death. Fortunately, it is disproved by science, by history, and by religion. After winging his way through another space of inky obscurity, the poet says: "The unseen is proved by the seen, till that becomes unseen and receives proof in its turn." Now what does this mean? He starts out with the seen, which needs no proof, and establishes from it the unseen. So far, it is clear; but now the seen becomes unseen, and receives proof in turn. Proof of what? That it is unseen. The necessity for proving the unseen is not apparent. If the poet intends to convey the idea that there is an invisible order of things, an unseen universe, why does he not say so? And if he did, it is not a matter of proof or demonstration, but of hope and conjecture. His dictum is mere verbal jugglery.

The poet then exalts his body, and this physical delirium runs all through the song at intervals; but there is no new and divine message here. The doctors tell us that the body is not vile, nor any of its parts; and when a genuine poet called it the temple of God, he said all that was necessary to say concerning it. Whitman "believes in the flesh and the appetites," meaning libidinous desire. In this respect he is not unlike the libertine. Indeed, this *Song of Myself* is the chant of the *roue*. Resuming, he enumerates the people around him, the events happening about him, the battles, the feelings, anything and everything that chances to run in his mind, and concerning them all he says:

These come to me days and nights, and go from me again,
But they are not the Me myself.

Has this passage any meaning? Whitman says he is not a battle, or a fever, or a dress, or a dinner, or a compliment. Neither is he a pancake, a turnip, or a sardine. If he means that his soul stands apart from and uncontrolled by matter, why does he not say so? If he means the contrary, why not say so? If he means that he is a mere isolated spectator of human events, is it not easy enough for him to make his meaning clear to the average intellect?

Then he announces to his soul that he believes in it, and goes on to chant: "Loafe with me on the grass, loose the stop from your throat," etc.

Naturally, one would infer that he was still addressing his soul. If so, he becomes ridiculous; for he gives the soul a throat and a voice. When we read farther we find he is addressing someone else, but whom we cannot divine. He says:

I mind how once we lay, such a transparent summer morning, etc.

The matter that follows is too vulgar for quotation. The passage is simply nauseating and devoid of sense.

The next incident is a child's bringing him a handful of grass, and asking him what it is. Of course, he does not know, but he proceeds to make up a wild "yawp" about it, nevertheless; and he drifts next to the subject of death, and says it is as lucky to die as to be born, and he knows it. For one, I don't believe he knows anything of the kind. He says:

I am not an earth, nor an adjunct of an earth;
I am the mate and companion of people, all just as
Immortal and fathomless as myself;
(They do not know how immortal, but I know).

Nor is he a comet, a meteor, or a ring of Saturn. "They do not know how immortal they are, but I know," is evidently regarded by him as a valuable bit of confidence. The plebeian mind, however, will wonder how there can be degrees of immortality. We could just as well ask how long a man would live if he lived forever.

Now follows another jungle of people and things, which he says are for him; but he omits to say why they are "for him," and what he intends doing with them. Let us catalogue them in regular order: Male and female, boys, those that love women, the proud man, the sweetheart, the old maid, mothers, mothers of mothers, lips, eyes, children, the baby, the youngster, the red-faced girl, the suicide, the corpse, the blab of the pave, tires of carts, sluff of boot-soles, talk of promenaders, omnibus, driver, sleighs, clank of horses, jokes, snowballs, hurrahs, the mob's fury, flap of litter, a sick man, meeting of enemies, oaths, blows, a fall, crowd, policeman, stones, groans, exclamations, speech, arrests, slights, assignations, rejections, etc. The writer gives us here a bare enumeration of living beings, inanimate objects, abstractions, that have no bearing on each other, obey no sequence, and teach no lesson. An inroad into Mitchell's geography would be far more significant and useful. As a description of a street scene it is lame, hueless, and unnatural.

The bard's next transition is to the country; but he fails to give us any connecting links to show whence he went, why he went, or whither he went, though he does not fail to tell us what he did when he got there. He did exactly what one would expect him to do, after one has read the *Song of Myself up* to this point. Instead of acting as a rational man, he "jumps from the cross-beams of the wagon, seizes the clover and timothy, and rolls head over heels and tangles his hair full of wisps." This kind of individual would jump out of a third-story window, instead of contenting himself with viewing the prospect through it. He is next hunting out in the wilds; then he is at sea; then at a clambake; then at the marriage of a trapper and an Indian girl. A runaway slave comes to his house and sits next to him at his table. This episode fixes his attention for a moment, and his mind wanders again, and he sees twenty-eight young men bathing by the shore—

> Twenty-eight young men, and all so friendly:
> Twenty-eight years of womanly life, and all so lonesome.

In the next paragraph the poet says:

> She owns the fine house by the rise of the bank;
> She hides, handsome and richly drest, aft the blinds of the window.
> Which of the young men does she like the best?
> Ah, the homeliest of them is beautiful to her.
> Where are you off to, lady? for I see you;
> You splash in the water there, yet stay stock still in your room.
> Dancing and laughing along the beach came the twenty-ninth bather;
> The rest did not see her, but she saw them and loved them.
> The beards of the young men glistened with wet, it ran from their long hair:
> Little streams pass'd all over their bodies.
> An unseen hand also pass'd over their bodies;
> It descended tremblingly from their temples and ribs.

Who they are, what they have to do with the poem, how they could lead twenty-eight years of "womanly" life, what difference it makes whether they were so friendly and so lonesome or not, how they could be so lonesome if there were twenty-eight of them, and how they could be so friendly if they were all lonesome, are a few of the riddles suggesting themselves to the mind of the unbeliever in reading this passage. It has been suggested to me that the paragraph is intended as a picture of twenty-eight women who are lonesome because deprived of the society of twenty-eight men who are accustomed to associate together to the neglect of the women; but the phrase "twenty-eight years of womanly life" is hardly synonymous with "twenty-eight women." And who is this mysterious "she," and what is she doing? Is she engaged in the unmaidenly act of watching the men bathe? If there is any suggestiveness here except the suggestiveness of an unclean mind, it is not apparent.

By this time the reader is in a positive whirl; but the poet continues to exhibit his wax-works, and introduces the butcherboy, the blacksmith, and possibly the baker and the candlestick maker. He next sees a negro driving a dray, and from him he goes by the usual degrees to the wild gander leading his flock. A little further on, "the pure contralto sings in the organ loft," and "the carpenter dresses his plank." Another convulsion seizes the writer at this juncture, and he gives us a catalogue of all sorts of people and professions. He jumps from a steam-boat to a ball, from one of the seasons to one of the States. At one time he is in Missouri, and at another in a street-car. There is no telling where he will alight next.

It would not be profitable to carry the analysis further. It is evident that the *Song of Myself* leads nowhither, and that it is the unsystematic, unpruned expression of a very peculiar mind. A few more quotations may be pardoned, as showing to what extremes language can go. For instance, this abrupt paragraph:

> Who goes there? hankering, gross, mystical, nude;
> How is it I extract strength from the beef I eat?

It is, of course, impossible for the reader to say who goes there. Possibly he doesn't care. As for the second question, that may be respectfully referred to the physiologist, who can answer it to any man's satisfaction. One fails to see what the bard is hankering after, and why he is nude. The connection between his being mystical and his eating beef is also a mystery, from which he has not lifted the veil. Again he says:

> I do not snivel that snivel the world over,
> That months are vacuums, and the ground but wallow and filth.

In one place he says, "I know that I am deathless," and in another declares himself a materialist. He speaks of the sea as the "howler and scooper of storms." He finds the scent of the armpits "aroma finer than prayer." These quotations might be strung out endlessly, but they would afford merely cumulative proof of the rankest kind of rebellion against common sense. It is not to be denied that at times the reader detects the gleam of the diamond in this mass of rubbish. The poet has evidently thought and read of many things, but his comments convey a hint of indigestion. When one finishes reading the *Song of Myself,* it is impossible for him to give a rational review of what it is, and what it is intended to teach. It is a failure, because the writer has neglected that very art which he professes to despise. The word "art," which is as wide in its significance as the heavens, has often been degraded by careless thinkers into a synonym of form, when it is in reality the execution of truth. Thought is never valuable unless it is clear and comprehensible. An obscure thought is hueless, tasteless, and devoid of nourishment. If Mr. Whitman's thinking is obscure, it is not worth the preserving. On the other hand, his thoughts may be true and clear, but he may lack fitting expression, just as a man may have a perfect conception of harmony and have no voice for song. It is in giving adequate, tangible expression to clean, valuable thinking, that the writer or poet justifies himself. He should have something to tell, and he should tell it. Unless he can do so, he has no business posing as a poet. Shakespeare found the English language and the established modes of composition spacious enough for his transcendent genius. Cicero, Virgil, and Horace were not trammeled by the polished completeness of Latin. Dante could express all his thoughts in artistic Italian, while Goethe and Schiller never thought of rebelling against the rules of German grammar and the accepted modes of composition. The man who has a story to build will never fail for want of verbal tools; if he falters, it will be because he knows not how to use them. If he has a message to deliver, wings are convenient; but he must know how to fly with them. We have a right to insist that a definite subject or story shall be selected, and that it shall be developed artistically, and in such a way as to be grasped. When Wagner, the musical revolutionist, set about the consummation of his theories, every musician understood perfectly what his theories *were,* though many angrily doubted and denied that music could respond to the call he made upon it. In all his labor there were system, consecutiveness, and art; otherwise, he would have failed. Has Mr. Whitman enunciated an intelligible theory? He speaks vaguely about poetry being written under the influence of our democratic institutions. Well and good. Now, Dame Columbia may insist on free thought and free speech; but she is not maudlin, nor incoherent. Her head is clear, her mien self-reliant, her actions brisk and animated, her perception acute, and her imagination warm and glowing. There is nothing confused or aimless about her. A literature in accord with democracy would partake of these attributes. If Mr. Whitman desires an original American literature, his plea is praiseworthy. The material for a literature that will do honor to the English tongue is to be found in this country, and the mine is now being worked. I feel no hesitation in saying that the spirit of Mr. Whitman's poetry is the contrary of the democratic spirit, because it is deficient in clearness, in consistency, in art, and in common sense. At first blush there may seem to be a kinship of liberty; but the liberty of democracy is the highest evolutionary step in the struggle for the rights of man, while the liberty of Walt Whitman's poetry is license of thought and anarchy of expression. Most people take pride in conquering the thoughts which he takes a riotous glee in giving vent to.

The thinking man of to-day finds himself beset with incrowding problems, and the mission of literature should be to relieve him from the depressing sense of the infinities. In no way can cheer be flashed into his darkened, perplexed mind except by preserving as a holy thing his faith in the unseen and spiritual, by keeping a line perpetually drawn between the just and the unjust, by placing what is good aloft in conspicuous splendor and sending evil to the gloomy shadows below; by preserving the ideals of purity and "sweetness and light"; by fixing virtue on a lasting pedestal and dethroning vice from its seat in the hearts of men. The man who obscures these valuable results of moral teaching, who leaves a doubt in the mind as to whether good is preferable to evil, who exalts the flesh—that incubus upon the loftiest dreams of purity—and calls the soul the body, can hardly be considered as bringing with him a message that we are bound either to receive or to respect.

—Walker Kennedy, "Walt Whitman,"
North American Review, June 1884, pp. 593–601

LESLIE FIEDLER (1960)

Scholar Leslie Fiedler argues that "Song of Myself" should be read as a love poem, not from Whitman to a specific person, but from a universalized Self to a universalized Other. Yet for Whitman, the Other can never be understood as fully as the Self; as a result, the existence of the Other can never be absolutely confirmed. Fiedler writes that "Song of Myself" also expresses the profound loneliness and alienation of an era of waning religious belief. Students writing on Whitman's concepts of the self, the other, and of love, will find Fiedler's discussion essential, and students writing about the role religion plays in Whitman's poetry will find that Fiedler's reflections on "the death of God" not only offer a new understanding of Whitman's spirituality, but also help connect him with his friend, the British poet Alfred, Lord Tennyson, who wrote extensively of the modern era's waning faith in *In Memoriam*, and with the German philosopher Friedrich Nietzsche, whose major philosophical work *Thus Spoke Zarathustra* Fiedler appears to reference.

'Song of Myself', though it stands at the center of Whitman's epic attempt
and can be read as a heroic poem intended to define the ethos of a nation,
is also a love poem: simultaneously a love song, a love affair (the poet's
only successful one) and a love child (the only real offspring of his passion,
for surely the five illegitimate children of whom he liked to boast were
fantasies). But who is the poet's beloved, the Beatrice he could never leave
off wooing, the Penelope to whom he could never return? As the hero
of his poem is called 'I', so the loved one is called 'you'; and their vague
pronominal romance is the thematic center of 'Song of Myself'. It is an odd
subject for the Great American Poem: the celebration (half-heroic, half-
ironic) of the mating between an 'I' whose reality is constantly questioned
and an even more elusive 'you'. The latter pronoun in Whitman's verse
almost always is followed by the phrase 'whoever you are'. 'You whoever you
are'—this must be surely the most compulsively repeated four-word phrase
in 'Leaves of Grass', for it embodies a riddle which torments the poet even
more than that of the Self: the riddle of the Other.

Is there an Other to whom one can speak: a real beloved, a real audience,
a real God? Unless such a 'you' really exists, there is no point, no possibility
of converting private 'vision' into public 'song'. It is because Whitman's
personal concern on this score coincides with a more general problem that
he touches us so deeply. His loneliness becomes a symbol for the alienation
of the modern artist and of modern man in a godless universe. He lived,
after all, at a moment when some thinkers were declaring the death of God,
and wrote at a time when poets grew increasingly unsure of whom they
were addressing.

—Leslie Fiedler, "Walt Whitman: Portrait of the
Artist as a Middle-aged Hero," 1960

Chronology

‒‒‒∿∿‒ ‒‒∿∿‒ ‒‒∿∿‒

1819   Birth of Walter Whitman, on May 31 near Huntington, New York, to Louisa Van Velsor and Walter Whitman, a carpenter and builder of houses, each descended from the earliest settlers on Long Island, and each a follower of the radical Quaker circuit rider Elias Hicks. The poet was the second born of eight Whitman children who lived beyond infancy, at least four of whom were disturbed or psychotic.

1823   Movement of Whitman family to Brooklyn, where the boy attends public school unti 1830.

1830–31   Office boy to lawyers and to a doctor.

1831–35   Apprenticed as printer's devil on the Democratic newspaper *Patriot* and then the *Star.*

1835–36   Works as a printer in New York City.

1836–38   Schoolteaching in various Long Island towns.

1838–39   Publishes and edits a new weekly, *Long-Islander,* from Huntington, then works on Jamaica *Democrat.* Early poems and sketches.

1840–41   Active in campaign of Martin Van Buren, and then returns to schoolteaching.

1841   From May on, he lives in New York City, working as a compositor for *New World,* and is active in the Democratic Party.

1842–45   Works in New York City for several newspapers, and publishes stories and sketches, as well as the "temperance novel" *Franklin Evans.*

1845–48   Works in Brooklyn again for *Star,* and then the Daily *Eagle.*

1848   Brief sojourn to New Orleans as a newspaper editor.

1848–49   Edits *Brooklyn Freeman,* as part of the Free Soil movement.

1849–54   The crucial years of return to his family; the notebooks of 1853–54 are the embryo of *Leaves of Grass.*

1855   Self-publication of the first edition of *Leaves of Grass* in early July, followed by death of his father on July 11. On July 21 Ralph Waldo Emerson mails the magnificent letter hailing *Leaves of Grass* and its author. The twelve untitled poems include what later will be titled "Song of Myself" and "The Sleepers."

1856   Second edition of *Leaves of Grass,* the new poems including what will come to be titled "Crossing Brooklyn Ferry." The volume includes Emerson's letter, and Whitman's extraordinary reply to it. Thoreau and A. Bronson Alcott visit Whitman in Brooklyn.

1857–59   Edits Brooklyn *Times.* Undergoes desolate period in late 1858 lasting well into 1859, presumably centering on the end of a homoerotic relationship.

1860   Publication of the third edition of *Leaves of Grass* in Boston by Thayer and Eldridge. In Boston to read proof, Whitman visits Emerson. Third edition includes "Calamus" poems and what will later be titled "Out of the Cradle Endlessly Rocking" and "As I Ebb'd with the Ocean of Life."

1861–62   Returns to journalism, while visiting the sick and war wounded at New York Hospital. Departs for Virginia battlefront in December 1862 to seek out his wounded brother George.

1863–64   The "Wound-Dresser" years in Washington, D.C., visiting wounded soldiers in the military hospitals.

1865   Dismissed from a clerkship at the Department of the Interior, perhaps due to the scandal caused by the third edition of *Leaves of Grass.* Composes "When Lilacs Last in the Dooryard Bloom'd" during the summer, in reaction to the assassination of Abraham Lincoln. The elegy is published in October, in *Drum-Taps and Sequel.* First meeting with Peter Doyle, then aged eighteen.

1867   Fourth edition of *Leaves of Grass.*

1870   Fifth edition of *Leaves of Grass; Democratic Vistas.*

1873   Paralytic stroke in January; death of mother in May; moves to brother George's house in Camden, New Jersey, in June.

1879   Travels in the American West.

1880   Travels in Canada.

1881 Final meeting with Emerson, in Concord, Massachusetts.

1882 Is visited by Oscar Wilde in Camden. *Leaves of Grass* is banned in Boston, but is reprinted in Philadelphia, where *Specimen Days and Collect* is published.

1884 Moves to own house in Camden.

1888 Severe paralytic stroke.

1891 Publishes *Good-Bye My Fancy* and final edition of *Leaves of Grass*.

1892 Dies on March 26 in Camden.

Index